Globalisation contested

MANCHESTER
UNIVERSITY PRESS

Globalisation contested

An international political economy of work

LOUISE AMOORE

Manchester University Press

Manchester and New York

Distributed exclusively in the USA by Palgrave

Published by Manchester University Press
Oxford Road, Manchester M13 9NR, UK
and Room 400, 175 Fifth Avenue, New York, NY 10010, USA
http://www.manchesteruniversitypress.co.uk

Distributed exclusively in the USA by
Palgrave, 175 Fifth Avenue, New York, NY 10010, USA

Distributed exclusively in Canada by
UBC Press, University of British Columbia, 2029 West Mall,
Vancouver, BC, Canada V6T 1Z2

British Library Cataloguing-in-Publication Data
A catalogue record for this book is available from the British Library

Library of Congress Cataloging-in-Publication Data applied for

ISBN 0 7190 6096 6 *hardback*

First published 2002

10   09   08   07   06   05   04   03   02   10 9 8 7 6 5 4 3 2 1

Typeset in Minion and Minion Display
by Koinonia, Manchester
Printed in Great Britain
by Biddles Ltd, Guildford and King's Lynn

Dedicated to Mary Elizabeth Amoore
and John Arthur Gregory,
in memory and with much love.

Contents

List of figures and tables   *page* viii

Acknowledgements   ix

List of abbreviations   xi

Introduction   1

1 Globalisation, restructuring and the flexibility discourse   14

2 International political economy and global social change   38

3 Producing hyperflexibility: the restructuring of work in Britain   67

4 Producing flexi-corporatism: the restructuring of work in Germany   93

5 The 'contested' firm: the restructuring of work and production
   in the international political economy   115

6 Globalisation at work: unheard voices and invisible agency   137

Conclusion: an international political economy of work   158

Bibliography   166

Index   188

List of figures and tables

Figure

2.1 Susan Strange's 'determinants of choice'   *page* 48

Tables

1.1 The OECD's 'Jobs Strategy' recommendations   30
3.1 Key legislative reforms of industrial relations in Britain, 1980–99   84–5
3.2 Workers involved in strikes and lockouts   89
4.1 Average hourly labour costs in manufacturing industry, 1999   107
4.2 Standardised rates of unemployment (as % of civilian labour force) 110

~

Acknowledgements

~

During the course of the research and writing of this book I have discovered that matters 'global' are truly close to people's everyday lives. Barely a day has passed when someone somewhere has not challenged my thinking. The influences and signposts along the route have been numerous – not only scholars, but also corporate managers, workers and trade unionists – I hope to recall at least some of them here. The book reached its first draft stage as a Ph.D thesis, researched and written between 1995 and 1998, and submitted in the Department of Politics, University of Newcastle upon Tyne. Particular thanks go to Phil Daniels, Ronen Palan, Randy Germain and Andrew Gamble for their inspirational comments and challenges. During this period the Newcastle Working Group on Globalisation provided an important source of intellectual challenge, debate and criticism. Particular thanks to Barry Gills, Richard Dodgson, Don Marshall, Iain Watson and Paul Langley. For providing inspiration and support during fieldwork travels, I am grateful to the staff and students at the Center for German and European Studies, Georgetown, and to all at the Max Planck Institute, Cologne, especially to Wolfgang Streeck. The research for this book would not have been possible without the assistance and enthusiasm of managers and workers in firms across three countries. I can only hope that I have done some justice to their extraordinary insights into the 'globalness' of their everyday lives. Their number is too great to thank them all by name here, but their contributions have been invaluable. That said, my profound thanks to Bob Reid, Peter Rostock and Richard Gibbs for their support of the project.

During the later stages of research I have had invaluable inspiration and critique from ongoing debates and discussion with scholars and friends. Special thanks to Jeff Harrod (for warning me of the hazards of studying work and labour!), Robert O'Brien, Dimitris Stevis, Roger Tooze, Matt Davies, Chris May, Tony Payne, Magnus Ryner, Rebecca Harding, Gigi Herbert, Kim Hutchings and Mark Boyer, and to the anonymous reviewers of the articles from which some of the material is drawn. My former colleagues at the University of Northumbria supported this project in many ways: thanks to Phil Garrahan, Lynn Dobbs, Rosie Cunningham, Doug Miller, John Fenwick and Keith Shaw. My colleagues in the Department of Politics, University of Newcastle have provided much encouragement in the final stages of the work. Thanks to Peter Jones, Tony Zito and Ella Ritchie for support and encouragement. The discussions taking place in two reading groups have provided intellectual stimulus and respite, provoking thought and revision: thanks to Tim Kelsall, David Campbell, Erna Rijsdijk and Ralph. A special thank you to Marieke deGoede, a challenging scholar and good neighbour.

Finally, thanks to my family, John, Jenny and Jonathan, for their support and good humour. It is difficult to express a debt of gratitude that is as great as that owed to Paul Langley. He has tirelessly read and commented on drafts of chapters and the final manuscript, and has permitted me to develop ideas that were first presented in a co-authored paper, in the second chapter. I have had the luxury of being able to discuss IPE in the car, the kitchen, on holiday and in our everyday lives. Yet, Paul also represents all that is not about work and writing, and for this happy balance I am eternally grateful.

On a more formal note, I wish to thank the ESRC for financial support (award R00429534005), and the Department of Politics for supporting travel in the later stages. The staff at Manchester University Press have enthusiastically supported and guided the project throughout. I also express thanks to the editors and publishers of the following journals for permission to reprint revised passages from papers first published in their series. Parts of chapter 1 first appeared in *Global Society* (1998), 12: 1, pp. 49–74. Parts of chapter 5 first appeared in *New Political Economy* (2000), 5: 2, pp. 183–204.

List of abbreviations

AICs	advanced industrialised countries
BBC	British Broadcasting Corporation
CEC	Commission of the European Communities
ECJ	European Court of Justice
EDRC	Economic and Development Review Committee
EI	employee involvement
EIRO	European Industrial Relations Observatory
EIRR	European Industrial Relations Review
EPZs	export processing zones
FDI	foreign direct investment
G7	Group of Seven: Canada, France, Germany, Italy, Japan, UK, US
GPE	global political economy
HRM	human resource management
ICTs	information and communication technologies
IDW	Institut der Deutschen Wirtschaft (Institute of the German Economy)
IILS	International Institute for Labour Studies
ILO	International Labour Organisation
IMF	International Monetary Fund
IPE	international political economy
IR	international relations
JIT	just-in-time
LDCs	less developed countries
LIEO	liberal international economic order
MNC	multinational corporation
NAFTA	North American Free Trade Agreement
NGO	non-governmental organisation
OECD	Organisation for Economic Cooperation and Development
SMEs	small/medium size enterprises
TQM	total quality management
TUC	Trades Union Congress
UNDP	United Nations Development Programme
WIRS	Workplace Industrial Relations Survey
WTO	World Trade Organisation

Introduction

The mood is shifting in the contemporary globalisation debate. Only a few years ago, talk of the contested and politicised nature of globalisation would have met with scepticism from those who emphasise the sheer economic power of globalising forces. The orthodox popular and academic representations of globalisation have for several decades sustained the image of a powerful economic and technological bulldozer that effortlessly shovels up states and societies. The very discourse of the 'competition state' (Cerny, 1990) effectively sanitised the globalisation process, removing the messiness of politics and leaving only the 'right and necessary' policy measures. As the millennium turned, the picture began to change so that we now begin to see partial glimpses of the push and shove of a social and political contestation that was, in truth, always present. Now we see the news media popularising debates about the power of multinational corporations (MNCs), the plight of the global economy's 'new slaves' and the 'anti-globalisation' protests (Klein, 2000; Bales, 1999; British Broadcasting Corporation (BBC), *Panorama*, 2000; Channel 4, 2000). The effect is to bring less comfortable and optimistic images of globalisation to our armchairs. At the same time, scholars within international political economy (IPE), international relations (IR) and sociology have called for the essence of politics to be restored to our understandings of globalisation and restructuring (Marchand and Runyan, 2000; Hay and Marsh, 1999; Bauman, 1998; Beck, 2000a).

This book acknowledges and develops the emergent challenge to the economic and technologically determinist representations of globalisation. It is critical of the 'globalist' representations of transformation as an imperative-driven and inexorable process. For people in their everyday lives, there is perhaps no sphere of social life so consistently bombarded with globalist accounts as that of production and work. For states, such a reading reinforces the imperative of a policy agenda that creates a competitive and capital-friendly environment for MNCs. Firms are cast as the primary agents of global change as they restructure towards the ultimately 'lean' and 'flexible' organisation. The combined restructuring activity of states and firms is presented as a fait accompli that demands prescribed responses from individuals and social groups. Competition states, lean production systems and flexible workers become the dominant mantra in the grip of an unstoppable globalising process.

Though broadly supportive of the critical turn that has been taken to counter the globalist dominance, this book also marks a departure from the central thrust of these contributions. Those who have sought to counter the economism and determinism of orthodox accounts have tended to focus on restoring agency to explanations of globalisation. Globalisation is represented as a project that is driven by the conscious political actions of identifiable individual and collective agents. In contrast to the globalist emphasis on technological and economic process, here we have globalisation as either promoted or resisted by governments within distinctive national capitalisms (Hirst and Thompson, 1996; Weiss, 1998), by a transnational class with common interests in a neo-liberal global order (Gill, 1995a, Van der Pijl, 1984), or by new social movements engaged in an anti-globalisation struggle (Falk, 1999). While such diverse perspectives have restored political agency to the globalisation debate, I argue that there remains too little attention paid to the contested and contradictory dynamics of social change.

This book develops a perspective that views globalisation as, in significant part, contested through and contingent upon structured social practices. Globalisation is imbued with a contingency that rests upon the diverse concrete experiences, interpretations and meanings that are intertwined with the dynamics of transformation. From this perspective, it is highly problematic to assume that state-societies will simply absorb and adapt to global imperatives, or that firms adopt convergent global strategies in different historical contexts, or that workers attribute common meanings to the discourses of flexibility that confront them. Globalisation, cast in this light, is not a single, universal and homogenising process, nor is it a clearly identifiable strategic project. Rather, it is uniquely understood and experienced by people in the context of their known and familiar social practices. To this end, the chapters that follow integrate theoretical discussion of the concept of globalisation with the study of the debates, contests and compromises that are taking place in the restructuring of production and work.

Perspectives on globalisation

In much of the literature on globalisation the primary focus has been on outlining the various aspects or dimensions of transformation in, for example, finance, production, culture, the state and technology, that combine to constitute an identifiable process of change (Amin *et al.*, 1994; Waters, 1995; Jones, 1995). In identifying these aspects, the first order question has been 'what is globalisation?'. That is to say, the central guiding objective has been to evaluate the evidence of the extent and nature of globalisation in each of the spheres. This has served a useful function in that it has revealed the unevenness of globalisation as it cuts across the multiple layers of social life.

However, the 'what is it' question does limit inquiry when we consider that the aspects or layers of globalisation are selected, defined and explained in divergent ways so that both the theory and the practice of globalisation could now be said to be contested (Scholte, 2000: 12; Amoore, 2000: 200; O'Brien *et al.*, 2000: 2–6). With this caveat in mind, perhaps the only answer to the pressing contemporary question 'what is globalisation?' can be 'it depends on how you look at it'. Framed in this way, the first order question becomes 'how has the problem been approached, interpreted and understood?'. The singularity and universality that so often surrounds ideas about globalisation is replaced by the possibility of multiple and multi-layered conceptions, each with a distinctive epistemological and ontological commitment.

It is only in the most recent phase of the globalisation debate that scholars have begun to seriously address the question of divergent conceptions of globalisation. This has tended to take the form of the development of typologies or categorisations of perspectives on globalisation. Held *et al.* (1999: 2–10) have developed a threefold typology of perspectives – the 'hyperglobalists', 'sceptics' and 'transformationalists'. The typology is based upon the divergences that exist between accounts of the *extent* of globalisation and, in particular, the implications for nation-states. Thus, for the hypergloblists, economic and political power becomes 'denationalised' and 'borderless' in the face of extensive global forces (1999: 3). By contrast, the sceptics share the view that globalisation is an overstated and convenient myth that facilitates the implementation of unpopular policies, effectively extending state power (1999: 6). For the transformationalists, the extent of globalisation is uneven and multi-layered as national governments reconstitute and restructure their power in response. Within this typology, the focus on the intensity and extensity of globalisation does result in some rather incongruous groupings. For example, Stephen Gill (highly critical of neo-liberal policies) is referenced alongside Kenichi Ohmae (supportive of neo-liberal policies) on the grounds that they share a hyperglobalist account of the emergence of a global economy (1999: 4). They do, of course, have very different conceptions of how we produce knowledge about the global economy (GPE), or indeed whether it is the global economy or the global political economy that is the object of analysis. The Held *et al.* typology does, to an extent, limit the analysis of epistemological and ontological divergence in the globalisation debate.

A second influential typology of perspectives has been that advanced by Jan Aart Scholte (2000). This typology categorises the perspectives according to their view of the *nature* of the globalisation process – globalisation as internationalisation, liberalisation, universalisation, westernisation or deterritorialisation. It is argued that the first four perspectives cannot adequately capture the nature of contemporary globalisation because they reduce it to pre-existing processes. Scholte favours 'deterritorialisation' as an account of globalisation that emphasises 'far-reaching change in the nature of social space' (2000: 46). His rejection of the first four perspectives reinforces his own perspective on globalisation as the transformation of social relations and social space. Scholte's important contribution has been to bring consideration of globalisation out of the realms of 'economic forces' and into the realm of society and social relations. However, his typology of perspectives does not bring us any closer to considering why globalisation is represented in certain ways in particular settings, and at specific historical moments. Though he argues that the first four perspectives 'cover most academic, official, corporate and popular discussion of things "global"' (2000: 46), he does not ask why this might be so. Why is globalisation most commonly defined as a process of universalisation or liberalisation, for example? Why do opposing perspectives seek to 'put globalisation back in its box' by defining it as nothing more than internationalisation? What are the implications of the framing of the globalisation debate for our understanding of the contemporary global problematic?

In order to address such questions we would need a typology that helps us to think about the relationship between conceptions of globalisation and particular sets of interests in the framing of restructuring discourse. We would need to consider the different perspectives on globalisation as distinctive constructions of knowledge that have significant implications for what we see – and importantly what we do not see – in contemporary processes of restructuring. Below I advance a threefold typology of perspectives on globalisation, each of which has particular implications both for the study of global change and for the restructuring discourse that emerges in production and work. I do not suggest that these perspectives are either internally coherent and cohesive, or entirely discrete and separate entities. They are simply constructions that aid thought about the relationship between particular modes of knowledge about global change, and the 'common sense' that emerges to deal with that change via a programme of restructuring.

Process

Under the predominant process perspective, globalisation is a master concept that is used to capture material and institutional transformations across contemporary economy, politics and society. In broad terms it encapsulates the orthodox representation of globalisation, one that can be found in the statements of national governments, international organisations and media commentators.[1] Globalisation is cast in teleological terms as the inevitable outcome of the expansionary ambitions of a global market economy and the transnationalisation of technologies (Amoore *et al.*, 1997). In this vision, states, societies and firms have no alternative but to conform and compete amidst processes of change that occur above and beyond them. The social costs of globalisation are commonly presented either as the temporary problems of transition, or as the inevitable short-term losses in a process that will yield benefits in the longer term.

The process perspective on globalisation has done much to inform dominant common sense understandings of transformation in the everyday practices of work. The discursive representation of globalisation as an inexorable process enables particular neo-liberal deregulatory interventions to be made and legitimated. So, for the Organisation for Economic Cooperation and Development (OECD) 'the globalisation process requires economies to be more adaptable and workers more willing to change' (1996: 13). For the World Bank: 'Governments and workers are adjusting to a changing world. The legacy of the past can make change difficult or frightening. Yet realization of a new world of work … is fundamentally a question of sound choices in the international and the domestic realm' (1995: 11).

A similar vocabulary of globalisation and the imperative of transformation in the form and nature of work can be found in Group of Seven (G7) government policy documents, International Monetary Fund (IMF) structural adjustment programs, management journals and corporate strategy documentation. Here the message is that in order to respond effectively to globalisation it is necessary for production costs to be reduced through the removal of barriers to the free market in factors of production – predominantly in labour. Globalisation is cast as an indomitable process, equated with a shift to new forms of work organisation in line with lean production, just-in-time (JIT), teamwork and kaizen. Workers are assumed to move towards more flexible working practices and 'atypical' forms of employment such as part-time, temporary, zero-hours and fixed contracts, outsourcing and home-working.[2] This reading treats labour as a commodity that must be restructured in line with global logics. The concrete transformation of social practices is not problematised and the whole process is sanitised of politics. Indeed, it is those societies and workers who fail to adapt to the new realities who are perceived to incur the 'costs of inaction' (OECD, 1996: 21). All distinctive social practices are subsumed by a single global 'best practice' of flexibility. Hence, any discussion of politics is confined to an instrumental role in implementing prescribed reforms. The globalisation process is taken as given, and what Robert Cox refers to as a 'problem-solving' mode of knowledge is generated to 'deal effectively with sources of trouble' (1996: 88).

Project

When broadly represented as a form of 'project', globalisation is tightly interwoven with the liberal ideological and neo-classical economic doctrines in whose name powerful actors seek to restructure the material and institutional bases of the contemporary world order.[3] Globalisation is given concrete expression in and through the various restructuring projects that are carried out under the neo-liberal banner. From the field of IPE it is possible to distinguish a number of schools of thought that contribute to the impression of an identifiable project of global transformation. First, what might be termed the 'transnational school' identify transnational interests that consciously act to produce and reproduce a globalised economy. Such interests may take the form of a global elite or ruling class whose conscious actions become a 'directive, strategic element within globalising capitalism' (Gill, 1994: 179). In a similar representation, the project of globalisation may be viewed as driven by the expansionary ambitions of MNCs (Stopford and Strange, 1991; Sklair, 1998). Transformations in production and work are thus viewed as central to a strategy of global capitalism pursued by corporate actors, a range of international institutions such as the World Trade Organisation (WTO), IMF and Trilateral Commission (Gill, 1990; Overbeek, 1990), together with government interests, that may constitute some form of class alliance (Van der Pijl, 1984; Sklair, 2001).

Second, a broad 'national capitalisms school' represents globalisation as overstated, mythical and rooted in the institutions and actions of national authorities. The world economy is held to be essentially international or regional rather than global and thus can be shaped or directed by the policymakers and institutions of competing nation-states and regions (Zysman, 1996; Weiss, 1998; Albert, 1993; Hirst and Thompson, 1996). In terms of the restructuring of production and work this implies that embedded systems of production and industrial relations give distinctive character to divergent national restructuring pathways (Crouch and Streeck, 1997; Ruigrok and van Tulder, 1995).

There are, of course, fundamental differences between the approaches taken by the above scholars. If we take Held *et al.*'s (1999: 3-5) schema, for example, we would identify both Stephen Gill and Susan Strange with a 'hyperglobalist' position, while Linda Weiss and Graeme Thompson would stand at the opposed 'sceptical' pole. However, in terms of ontology, Susan Strange's work on production has more in common with Winfried Ruigrok's work than with Kenichi Ohmae's work (a fellow globalist). Identified as theorists united by their attention to an emergent global project, this perspective demonstrates that globalisation can and should be analysed in terms of the restructuring done in its name. Furthermore, adherents to the project perspective tend to normatively oppose neo-liberal programmes of restructuring and to seek out the political space for alternatives amidst structural constraints. However, the politics of globalisation is presented as coherently designed and directed by rational collective agents. These agents, whether MNCs, classes or states, are imbued with a unitary identity that is defined by the shared project itself. The tensions, contests and conflicts that surround the form of the project are seriously underestimated. The project perspective can tell us much about the elite actors who contribute to a discourse of global restructuring, but little about the everyday forms of thought and action that characterise the nature of that restructuring.

Practice

The central terrain of the globalisation debate has been occupied by the disputes between those who claim that globalisation is essentially inexorable (the process perspective) and those who claim that globalisation is driven by the purposeful actions of individual and collective agents (the project perspective). The difficulty is that globalisation may well take on both these dynamics simultaneously, and to a differentiated degree in the experiences and practices of people in specific historical contexts and social spaces. So, how might it be possible to capture the contested and highly contingent nature of contemporary global transformation? The argument to be made in this book is that a third perspective – what I term a 'practice' perspective, can illuminate the tensions, contradictions and politics of globalisation that are left in shadow by many existing frameworks of analysis. A number of scholars have begun to map out a perspective that represents globalisation in terms of emergent patterns of globalised social relations and the structured social practices that make these possible (see Langley, 2002). For Jones, the contemporary world is characterised by a 'multiplicity of purposes' that expose the controversial, incomplete and potentially reversible nature of globalisation (2000: 245). In the same volume Germain posits that 'globalization is as inherently contested as a "reality" as it is as a concept or representation of that reality' (2000: xiii). The common thread here is that what we call globalisation is best understood as representative of sets of complex and often contradictory globalising social practices.

It is, however, difficult to find among the various IPE perspectives on global social practices, a genuine effort to explore the normal, commonplace or everyday social practices that make up peoples' experiences of life in a proclaimed global era. Existing avenues into globalisation as social practice have tended to focus almost exclusively on the social practices of elite groups whose actions produce direct effects in the GPE – for example, bankers, corporate managers, politicians and media actors, among others. An understanding of the role of such practices is undoubtedly crucial in the mapping of the contours of global social change. However, the argument to be made here is that globalisation is experienced, given meaning, reinforced and/or challenged in the everyday social practices of individuals and groups at multiple levels, from state-societies and MNCs through to the routine practices of the workplace.

The development of a practice perspective on globalisation, I will argue, follows a 'new' or 'heterodox' approach to IPE in its challenge to the dichotomies of state/market, domestic/international, public/private and local/global (see Murphy and Tooze, 1991; Amin *et al.*, 1994). Social practices by their nature intersect and cut across these dichotomies. This may occur through direct means such as the use of transborder communications in the organisation of global production, or via indirect means such as the emergence of a 'global consciousness' that connects discrete social practices through global frameworks of thought (Scholte, 2000: 54). James Rosenau has, for example, argued for the consideration of the 'micro-macro' dynamics of contemporary transformation (1997: 59). Tim Sinclair has called for the theorisation of the relationships between ordinary everyday lives and wider structural change, to reveal the 'international political economy of the commonplace' (1999: 165). Matt Davies and Michael Niemann have explored the means by which globalised social relations are produced in the 'daily practices of workers, families or consumers' (2000: 6). Feminist scholars have encouraged reflection on concrete everyday experiences in order to make sense of the 'abstract structure known as the international political economy' (Enloe, 1989: 4; see also Marchand and Runyan, 2000).

Considered through the lens of a practice perspective, globalisation is characterised by contests over the reality and representation of social change. Such contestation can and does take the strategic and organised forms of promotion and resistance highlighted by the project perspective. However, the oppositions and tensions of global restructuring are also present in everyday life. It is helpful to consider the everyday nature of globalisation in terms of contradictory relationships between 'near' and 'far'. For Bauman, the 'near' is characterised as '... primarily that which is usual, familiar and known to the point of obviousness; something seen, met, dealt or interacted with daily, intertwined with habitual routine and day-to-day activities' (1998: 13).

This image of nearness and familiarity can be contrasted with the 'far' as something that is unusual, unfamiliar and unknown to the point of being obscure and extraordinary. By the very nature of globalisation as a 'real or perceived intensification of global interconnectedness' (Held *et al.*, 1999: 2), it is the confrontation and assimilation of near and far that mark the restructuring of government policies, corporate strategies and the everyday practices of the workplace.

Viewed from the perspective of the practices of everyday life, transformations in production and work bring the globalisation debate into commonplace experience. Productive and working practices lie at the heart of capitalist social relations and have provided the focus for debates surrounding the need for adaptation and change. There are indications that the manifestations of global change in the workplace are beginning to be considered more closely by scholars from across disciplinary divides (see Panitch, 2001; Leisink, 1999; Beck, 2000b). It is my view that the restructuring of work is a critical terrain on which the current and future shape of globalisation will be contested. While IPE has appeared comfortable with the theoretical and empirical study of the firm, it has been much less comfortable with the study of labour and work. Meanwhile, MNCs increasingly have become fractured entities, 'outsourcing' their production so that work takes place in sites that have become invisible to IPE inquiry. Where labour and work have been acknowledged in the globalisation debate this has tended to be confined to the study of trade unions and their potential as new social movements. This book proposes that production and work be considered within and across multiple interrelated layers of restructuring – state-societies, firms and workers. Within each of these layers the restructuring of productive and working practices is experienced in diverse ways, varying in its meaning, interpretation and implications.

This book develops a practice-centred view of globalisation in order to make visible two central interrelated features of the contemporary global restructuring of production and work. First, globalisation does not exist independently of the meanings that are imputed to it by policymakers, corporate strategists, workers, unions, social groups and citizens. This is not to say that there are no structural features of globalisation, but that even the identifiable forces of global financial markets, transborder technologies and global production have vastly differential effects and elicit distinctive patterns of accommodation and resistance. I explore the social and political-economic contests that characterise the distinctive British 'hyperflexible' and German 'flexi-corporatist' approaches to the restructuring of production and work. Robert Cox identifies the tensions within and between the German and British political economies as a 'proving ground' for future world order (1993: 286). The historical context that is reflected in state-societal institutions, norms and practices is not ruptured by globalisation. Rather, it provides one of many frames of reference within which questions are raised, responses are negotiated, and social groups find themselves included or excluded. In doing this, I suggest an alternative value for so-called 'models of capitalism'. Conventionally conceived, national models of capitalism have been variously used to refute globalist claims, to bolster claims to a 'nicer', 'friendlier' social-democratic mode of capitalism, or to offer best-practice examples to be emulated and transposed. In my analysis, state-societal contexts are identified merely as 'ideal types' (Cox, 1987: 4-5) of the patterns of compromise, tension and conflict that define a programme of global restructuring. Despite the apparent intractability and dominance of the neo-liberal model of restructuring, it is important to challenge the notion that there is normative unanimity on the model within and across state-societies.

The second key feature of global restructuring that is revealed by a practice perspective is the disruption and contestation that suffuses a restructuring programme as it enters the everyday lives of workers. While IPE studies of the globalisation of production have focused almost exclusively on the MNC, industrial relations scholars have revealed the concrete manifestations of flexibility in the workplace, directly connecting workplace to world order (Harrod, 1997a; Leisink, 1999). A focus on the workplace reveals the tensions that permeate the juxtaposition of near and far as established working practices confront demands for change based on some distant and unfamiliar 'best practice'. Such tensions are exacerbated as the restructuring of working practices create new patterns of inclusion and exclusion, reinforcing or challenging prevailing social power relations. The strategic projects of restructuring may be undermined via 'silent resistance' (Cheru, 1997: 153) and tacit opposition (Scott, 1990), 'blunting the action' in a Polanyian 'double movement' (1957: 76). Capturing the vacillations of global restructuring serves to challenge economistic and teleological accounts, restoring the human and political essence of globalisation.

Structure of the book

Chapter 1 explores the conceptions of globalisation and restructuring on which the discourse of labour flexibility is based. Of course, entire books have been devoted to the subject matter of globalisation alone. However, this chapter explores the particular representation of globalisation as an indomitable process that demands specific restructuring responses. The analysis is focused on five defining aspects of the process-centred view of globalisation: exogenous transformative forces, disciplinary imperatives, historical convergence, social prescription and the death of conflict. I argue that these guiding assumptions about the nature and form of contemporary social change have much in common with the modernisation thesis of the industrial society school. Rather than constituting a fundamental break with past practices, the global process model of social change has recast a set of ideas that are deployed to legitimate a programme of labour flexibilisation. The contemporary fixation with flexibility in work and labour is effectively legitimated and perpetuated via a discursive attachment to representations of a natural, automatic and imperative process of globalisation. Such representations have enabled the restructuring of work to be undertaken in a depoliticised atmosphere of 'essential' management strategies. The chapter, therefore, presents the case for a renewed emphasis on the social power relations and social contests that condition and shape the restructuring of work.

Chapter 2 investigates the contribution that the field of IPE can make to raising the visibility of alternative politicised understandings of social change. In many senses the field has defined itself in terms of its capacity to shed light on the dynamics of contemporary global social transformation, strenuously arguing that it captures change in a way that 'static' IR cannot grasp (see Strange, 1994). I sketch out the parameters of the claims made by so-called 'new IPE' scholars, and analyse their departure from 'orthodox' IPE perspectives. Though I use some of the insights of the 'new IPE' in the chapters that follow, I do so with criticism and caveats. There are further steps to be taken in prising open some of the doors that have been closed by dominant IPE ontologies, and I outline one of them here: an IPE of social practice. I propose that such a perspective can reveal the politics and contingency of globalisation as it is characterised by contests over the reality and representation of social change. First, a sensitivity to the historicity and contingency of global social change serves to uncover the diverse interpretations and experiences of restructuring within and across state-societies, firms and worker groups. Second, attention to the webs of power that surround and suffuse a programme of global restructuring challenges the notion that a prescribed 'best practice' such as labour flexibility is merely a matter for apolitical technical adaptation. Finally, an emphasis on the 'everydayness' of the restructuring of work brings the rarefied world of global finance, production and technology into a domain where it can be opened up to debate and contest. The IPE of social practice perspective is further developed in the chapters that follow, focusing on the restructuring debates within state-societies, firms and the daily lives of workers.

Taken together, chapters 3 and 4 explore the distinctive meanings of globalisation that are constructed through the restructuring programmes of different state-societies. I argue that state-societies debate and represent the problematic of globalisation in ways that are historically specific, and that interventions are made on the basis of these representations. Chapter 3 discusses the representation of globalisation underpinning British programmes of 'hyperflexibility' in the restructuring of work. The chapter addresses the 'national capitalisms' debate, exploring the making of a distinctively British capitalism, and discussing the contemporary discursive remaking of a 'global Britain'. I am particularly concerned here to use the IPE of social practice to reveal the tensions and contradictions of British hyperflexibility.

Chapter 4 moves to consider the restructuring debate taking place in German state-society. In popular and academic discourse Germany is often presented either as a proving ground for globalisation (the assumption being that the state-society may be forced to abandon its distinctive social market model in the face of global forces), or as a rebuttal to globalisation (the assumption being that the institutions and practices actively resist neo-liberal restructuring). In this chapter I argue that perceptions of the German relationship to globalisation, both inside and outside the state-society, are contradictory and contested. I explore the historical institutions and practices of state, capital and labour that have made possible particular programmes of restructuring in Germany. The contemporary restructuring of working practices is discussed, revealing the dominant negotiated programme of 'flexi-corporatism'.

In the context of the globalisation of production, MNCs have been most commonly depicted as the key vehicles of global transformation. They have, however, tended to be considered as unitary 'non-state' actors, that is to say defined in terms of identifiable agency that is significant because of its 'bargaining power' with states (see Stopford and Strange, 1991; Strange, 1996). Chapter 5 opens up the presumed unity of the MNC to explore the social power relationships that constitute this 'global actor'. Defined in terms of the relationships between corporate managers, financiers, shareholders, suppliers and a diverse range of worker groups, the firm represents a site of contest in the ascription of meanings and realities of globalisation. Chapter 6 extends the inquiry into the contested nature of restructuring in production and work by exploring the concrete everyday experiences of workers. In line with an IPE of social practice approach, the chapter explores the everyday practices of work that variously enable, contest or confound the emerging social relations of globalisation. How do workers, broadly defined, engage with processes of global restructuring? What are the patterns of tension and co-ordination between different worker groups? As firms intensify their efforts to outsource production functions, what are the implications for unprotected workers? Overall, this chapter takes the analysis of the restructuring of work beyond a discussion of the politics of states and firms, toward an increased visibility for the concrete experiences of workers who are differentially positioned in the IPE of work.

In essence, the argument presented in this book seeks to extend the politicisation of globalisation beyond the image of direct street demonstrations and protests. The 'Seattle effect' is an undeniably significant feature of the contemporary contests surrounding globalisation. However, it is but one element of a much broader acknowledgement that globalisation is political by its very nature, not least as a result of its intertwining with the thoughts and actions of our everyday lives. Multiple modes of contestation can be revealed that open up both the concept and the experience of globalisation to political inquiry – for instance the politics of the making of particular policies of restructuring, the politics of accommodation and compromise that enable particular forms of restructuring, and the politics of tension and resistance that confound and transform a restructuring agenda.

Notes

1 At the closure of the Fujitsu Corporation's semi-conductor plant in north-east England, the British Prime Minister, Tony Blair, announced during a television interview that 'regrettably there is little a government can do about the twists and turns of world markets in a global economy'. Under the heading of 'globalisation', a recent IMF paper noted that 'The last decade of the 20th century has been marked by immense changes in the world economy. The new phase of the technological revolution and the far-reaching internationalisation of capital have changed the patterns of economic performance ... Hence, on the eve of the new century, there are not only mounting structural problems, but several new issues that must be addressed properly' (2000b: 6). A similarly process-centred statement is made by Jonathan Freedland, for whom '... the economy has moved ahead of politics... vast global corporations influence every aspect of our day-to-day lives. Our only weapon is national governments – and these have proved themselves all but powerless' (*The Guardian*, 1 December 1999: 21).

2 A focus on broad shifts in industrial and workplace relations in ideal-type neo-liberal and neo-corporatist political economies would indicate that globalisation has indeed been accompanied by transformation in forms and modes of work. The 1998 British Workplace Employee Relations Survey reports that 47 per cent of firms located in Britain had no union members, a figure that has increased from 36 per cent in the 1990 survey (Cully *et al.*, 1998). The number of part-time workers grew by 5.4 per cent over 1999 to total 24.9 per cent of total employment (European Industrial Relations Observatory (EIRO), 1999). Ninety per cent of British firms use subcontracting, 44 per cent use fixed-term contracts and 28 per cent use agency workers (EIRO, 1999). Figures for Germany show that trade unions lost 30 per cent of their membership between 1991 and 1998 (Institut der Deutschen Wirtschaft (IDW), 1999). Part-time working accounted for 18.3 per cent of total employment in Germany for 1999, while temporary work accounted for 10.8 per cent (EIRO, 1999). Eurostat figures suggest that the use of non-standard (temporary, part-time, fixed contract) employment has

increased in all EU member states over the last decade, though this has been accompanied by varying degrees of legislative protection in different states (information sourced from personal enquiry to Eurostat, June 2000).

3 While the key elements of a project perspective have been discernible for some time, there are now analyses that explicitly refer to a globalisation project (see Rupert, 2000, ch. 3; McMichael, 2000; Sklair, 2001: 1).

1

~

Globalisation, restructuring
and the flexibility discourse

~

Industrialisation characteristically redesigns and reshapes its human raw materials, whatever the source ... The development of an industrial workforce necessarily involves the destruction of old ways of life and work and the acceptance of the new imperatives of the industrial work place and work community. (Kerr *et al.*, 1962: 193)

Industries and firms almost everywhere are said to be leaving behind the old, tired, boring, inefficient, staid past and entering into the new, highly efficient, diverse, exciting, and flexible future; and if they are not, they should be. (Curry, 1993: 99)

Throughout much of the twentieth century the social sciences have invoked 'master concepts' (Giddens, 1982) in the explanation and shaping of patterns of social change. The use of the action-process verb form[1] – in modernisation, industrialisation, globalisation – imbues the concepts with a sense of movement, logic and direction. Simultaneously, they operate as nouns that name and describe a historical condition, thus offering an elusive promise of a destination that can never quite be reached (Ashley, 2000). For a group of sociologists writing in the 1960s, the master concept of industrialisation captured the dynamics of transformation in a form that effectively enabled social change to be ordered and mastered. Industrial capitalism, with its inherent contradictions, was viewed as a temporary and transitory form of industrial society. The processes of industrialisation and technological advance defined all economic and social organisation, ultimately leading all societies passively to a convergent system of 'pluralistic industrialism' (Kerr *et al.*, 1962: 266). The concept of industrialisation itself acquired an imperative logic that named and defined the parameters of new forms of production, work and social life. It offered the enticing prospect of a defined destination, coupled with an explanation of the transformations that should be expected along the way.

In contemporary times the new master concept of globalisation has become the explanatory tool that is applied to all areas of economy, polity and society. The concept has become a kind of horse for every course, infinitely malleable and amorphous, 'vague in referent' and 'ambiguous in usage' (Jones,

1995: 1). Indeed, some have concluded that the term should be abandoned to prevent its reification in political, academic and corporate debates. However, it is precisely the amorphous and empty nature of the concept that gives it the capacity to exercise power. It can be filled with multiple meanings and used to legitimate a range of restructuring programmes, from labour market flexibility and mobility, to privatisation. Of course, the contemporary period of globalisation is commonly defined as a break from the logics of industrialisation, taking the form of, for example, the 'post-industrial society' (Castells, 1989) or 'post-Fordism' (Lipietz, 1987; Piore and Sabel, 1984). However, the representations of industrialisation and globalisation make common appeals to notions of technological externality, epochal newness and novelty and convergence in economic and social organisation. As devices employed to explain the human and social world, the concepts of industrialisation and globalisation as 'processes' represent highly simplified understandings of social change. They embody 'problem-solving' approaches to knowledge (Cox, 1981: 128), reflecting a preference for generalisable and codifiable modes of thought, and informing the terms of a policy discourse.

In the attempt to highlight the contested nature of globalisation in production and work, a first step is to question its role in underpinning and legitimating the all-pervasive discourse of flexibility. In this chapter the common discursive dynamics of the industrialisation and globalisation theses are explored. The analysis focuses on five common aspects that reveal a central dominant representation of social change: the identification of exogenous transformative forces, disciplinary imperatives, historical convergence, social prescription and the death of conflict. I argue that it is these assumptions about social change that underpin and perpetuate the contemporary discourse of imperative labour flexibility. Flexibility itself has an amorphous quality that allows it to be applied 'flexibly' to describe the many facets of the contemporary restructuring agenda. In line with globalisation, flexibility comes simultaneously to mean all things and yet nothing precise at all. The discourse on flexibility pervades the policy agenda of the competition state (Cerny, 1990; Porter, 1990), the restructuring strategies of firms (Ruigrok and van Tulder, 1995) and the everyday experiences of workers (Pollert, 1991; Beck, 2000b). The conception of globalisation as a process reinforces the assumption that the state is compelled to 'retreat' or adopt new policy instruments (Strange, 1996), the flexible firm in a 'global web' is the essential corporate strategy for a global era (Atkinson, 1985; Reich, 1991) and that workers must accept greater risk and insecurity as they 'make the leap' to new practices.

Transformative forces

The proponents of the industrial society thesis identified exogenous factors as the central driving forces of industrialisation. A society is driven into adaptation by the challenges that exist 'on the outside' or 'by the exigencies of the situation

external to it' (Parsons, 1960: 138). Viewed in this way, the principal characteristic of all industrial societies is that progress is dependent upon the
absorption of exogenous technological advances and the adaptation of social
practices to their dictates. The assumption is that the 'more modern' is always
the 'more superior' (Kerr *et al.*, 1962: 279) so that the diversity of the pre-
industrial world is gradually homogenised through the advancement of
technology: 'Technology is a unifying force. At one moment in time there may
be several best economic combinations or social arrangements, but only one
best technology' (Kerr *et al.*, 1962: 284). Technology is presented as a universal
force that imposes common challenges on all advanced states and societies.
The progress of science, technology and production methods essentially
determine the actions to be taken by state actors, industrialists and workers. In
a sense technology becomes both structure and agent as it simultaneously acts
to initiate change and defines the structures within which change takes place.
Transformations in social relations, practices and values are held to emerge
out of technological change and this unilinear logic is never reversed.

The predominant image in the orthodox accounts of globalisation is of
similarly exogenous forces that act upon states and societies. Conventional
logic would have it that a series of conjunctural events in the 1970s effectively
freed the globalisation 'genie' from his lamp and marked the emergence of a
distinctive global era. The collapse of the Bretton Woods System, the oil
shocks, the claims to US decline and the subsequent emergence of globalised
financial and productive systems, all are offered as explanations of a transformed world order. However, it is not the events themselves that have
informed the predominant explanations of global change. Rather, it is the
technological and market forces held to lie behind them that are most
commonly perceived as 'creating globalisation'. Susan Strange argues that
'technology has got ahead of regulation' (1997a: 54) with the effect that technological change has become the 'prime cause of the shift in the state-market
balance of power' (1996: 7). Others assert that 'at the heart of the flexibiliza-
tion of both production processes and firms themselves has been the explosive
development of information technology' (Cerny, 1995: 615). Variants of post-
Fordist analysis position technology as the driving force of change, arguing
that the productivity gains central to the Fordist system become eroded by
maturing technologies. The system of production itself then transforms from
Fordist mass production and consumption with its associated technologies, to
post-Fordist 'flexible specialisation' (Freeman and Perez, 1988). There is an
overwhelming sense of inevitability in these accounts of the 'domino effect' of
technology acting on states and societies that, in turn, act to restructure
production and work. Strange writes: '*Accelerating technological change* …
explains the rapid internationalization of production in the world market
economy, a *process* which, *inevitably*, relaxes the authority of the state over the
enterprises based and directed from inside their territorial borders' (Strange,
1995: 59, emphasis added).

Globalisation is thus presented in terms of the opposing forces of, on the one hand, technology acting from without and, on the other, politics and society simply responding from within. The 'deterritorialised' forces of finance (Wriston, 1988; Cerny, 1996; McKenzie and Lee, 1991), production and trade (Porter, 1990; Reich, 1991) and culture (Fukuyama, 1992) are cast in opposition to the presumed territorial realities of state and society. States and societies are consistently positioned as passive receivers of technological transformation. We are left with the impression that global restructuring is nothing more than an effect of the 'global process' of technological interpenetration. As Marchand and Runyan argue, a mythical image is created in which globalisation becomes 'a process generated outside our own (immediate) environment' (2000: 7). When conceived as 'outside' our immediate experiences, the technologically-driven globalisation process becomes conveniently and safely insulated from the politics of negotiation, contestation and resistance.

Disciplinary imperatives

To represent globalisation and industrialisation as the products of exogenous forces is to assume that transformation is to some degree an inevitable response to irresistible pressures. It is but a short step from this inevitabilism to the assertion that there is no alternative for states and societies but to adapt and restructure their policies, structures and practices. For the scholars writing at the peak of post-war growth, the most significant transition was considered to be that from traditional to industrial society. This shift represented the underlying movement in all state-societies as they responded to external pressures. Talcott Parsons' systems-centred social theory sought to understand the adaptation of social systems in line with pressures from 'outside': 'In the present situation, for the "diffusion" of this organizational type *[industrialism]* from the Western world to other areas, it seems clear that the most favourable conditions will center on the *right type* of political initiative' (1960: 128, emphasis added).

There is an in-built disciplinary imperative here – it becomes incumbent on states and societies to respond with the 'right' strategies. The imperative of industrialisation is expressed in terms of political responses that are 'essential', 'rational' and 'right'. A reading of Daniel Bell reveals a belief in a generally held consensus on the 'right' forms of political organisation: 'the acceptance of a welfare state; the desirability of decentralised power; a system of mixed economy and of political pluralism' (1961: 402). Viewed in this way there can be no impediment to, or contingency in, the processes of restructuring and transformation. Social relations, institutions and practices are at once structurally determined, yet rendered inherently malleable and adaptable: 'Even the most economically advanced countries today are to some degree and in some respects underdeveloped. They contain features derived from earlier stages of development which obscure the pure logic of the industrialization process'

(Kerr *et al.*, 1962: 33). Social change is characterised in periods or epochs of social arrangements that prevail until external conditions dictate that they undergo further transformation. The disciplinary dynamic of the process is reinforced by a presumed desire for modernisation that ultimately drives out difference and distinctiveness, leaving one clear route. Societies are assumed to absorb the imperatives of transformation such that they sustain them with their own thoughts, actions and desires.

The notion of an epochal shift and essential political and social adaptation is inherent within diverse accounts of globalisation. In common with the industrial society theories, the external forces of the global economy are viewed as creating imperatives for the restructuring of state and society. In contrast with these theories, however, the norms that are established are for the 'retreat of the state' (Strange, 1996), the 'hollowing out of the state' (Cerny, 1996: 91) and the rise of the 'competition state' (Cerny, 1990). The transformations from a perceived old to a new epoch are characterised in terms of shifts: from 'comparative' to 'competitive' advantage (Porter, 1990); from the 'decommodifying' to the 'commodifying' state (Cerny, 1990); and from 'industrial' to 'post-industrial' society (Hepworth, 1989; Block, 1990). While commentators do not agree on the normative aspects of such transformations (some celebrate the process, while others condemn it), both liberal and neo-Marxist theorists share common ground on the extent of global change. Among the more extreme formulations we read that: 'The nation-state has become an unnatural, even dysfunctional, unit for organizing human activity and managing economic endeavour in a borderless world' (Ohmae, 1990: 93). The dissolution of state authority and the rise of marketised frameworks of authority are presented as imperative transformations in a globalisation process. Fundamental breaks with the past are staked out and labelled in diverse ways, though with remarkably similar effects. Among the diverse perspectives on post-Fordism, common notions of epochal shifts are communicated, whether through 'regimes of accumulation' (Aglietta, 1979; Lipietz, 1987; Boyer, 1986), 'techno-economic paradigms' of the neo-Schumpeterians (Freeman and Perez, 1988) or 'industrial divides' (Piore and Sabel, 1984).

In process-centred accounts of globalisation there is a certain predilection for claims to novelty, the staking out of a capitalist 'crossroads' and the establishment of a qualitative break with the past. As Rob Walker observes '... it is undoubtedly tempting to exaggerate the novelty of novelty' (1993: 2). With the ethereal lure of industrialism or globalism on the horizon, it becomes possible to legitimate particular policy decisions on the basis of 'no alternative'. The very idea of an imperative process of change creates a sense of urgency that dictates a particular response from society. While acknowledging the competing normative views within the 'globalisation as process' perspective, there is an identifiable common emphasis on discontinuity. It is possible to either celebrate or condemn the process but still to agree that it is essentially inexorable. A sense of 'no alternative' prevails and politics becomes confined to instrumental discussions of the 'right' and 'competitive' way to respond and harness the opportunities of the new stage. In effect, the 'no alternative' logic reinforces the sense of disciplinary imperatives. The hypermobility of foreign direct investment (FDI capital, for example, can be constructed and reinforced through the 'talked up' threat of exit (Watson and Hay, 1998). The state and public policy become disciplined by the need to prove their credibility and consistency and secure the confidence of their investors (Gill, 1999). In this way, sometimes wholly inadvertently, the 'disciplinary forces of neoliberalism' (Gill, 1995a) can be perpetuated and reinforced by the straightjacket effect of dominant modes of thought.

Historical convergence

The assumption that technological advances force change, and that this change is part of an inexorable and inevitable process, has tended to lead to the perceived logic of convergence. From divergent historical and cultural viewpoints, diverse institutional arrangements and distinctive social power relations, societies are believed to become increasingly alike in their basic structures. As John Goldthorpe argues:

> This is the general model of society most consistent with the functional imperatives that a rationally operating technology and economy impose: and *it is in fact the pressure of these imperatives which must be seen as forcing the development of industrial societies on to convergent lines,* whatever the distinctive features of their historical formation or of their pre-industrial cultural traditions. (1984: 316, emphasis in original)

Industrial society was said to take precedence over capitalist society because all technologically advanced countries displayed similar structures, whether capitalist or not (Aron, 1967). In this sense capitalist industrialisation was but a moment in a longer historical drive to industrialism. Much of this argument was based on the analysis of the ideologically divergent US and Soviet Union, arguing that they were following a convergent path of industrialisation, as in Talcott Parsons' work: 'Virtually the whole world has, within our time, come to assign to economic productivity a very high value indeed. The essential differences between American and Soviet orientations, which some feel is the deepest difference in the world, is not primarily a difference over the valuation of productivity' (Parsons, 1960: 100).

The suggestion is that despite divergence in ideologies, institutions and practices, the overriding trend is towards a convergence around basic organising principles. Societies may be 'travelling at different speeds on different roads' (Kerr *et al.*, 1962: 2), but the consensus is that the direction and destination are the same. The 'uniformity of texture' and similarities in 'patterns of behaviour' are considered to be the significant features of social transformation (Shonfield, 1965: 65). The focus lies firmly on the commonalties between societies and these are then 'aggregated up' to form a systemic theory of social change.

The tendency to presuppose a process of historical convergence is characteristic also of many contemporary accounts of the globalisation process. It is striking that Susan Strange associates IPE with the study of the structural dynamics of the world economy as a whole: 'As an international political economist, I am more interested in the pace and direction of change in the whole world market economy than in the pace and direction of change in particular parts of it contained within the rather arbitrary territorial borders of states' (Strange, 1997b: 182). With a particular focus on the future of distinctive national 'versions' of capitalism, Strange argues that the 'common logics' of world markets would lead all states and societies on to a convergent pattern of change (1997b: 182). Of course, Strange does this to emphasise the extent of transnational sources of power and authority. However, it would seem problematic to represent globalisation as a singular process of political and social convergence and, in doing so, to ignore the many different interpretations of globalisation. Social change becomes a matter of common pressures promoting convergent solutions. Where difference is acknowledged this tends to be framed in terms of a 'pathway' that may temporarily diverge from the dominant route.

Within the convergence accounts there are specific policy instruments suggested as the common ground for states and societies. In the 1960s the convergent trends were identified as the extension of public power in a modern capitalist system, the preoccupation with social welfare and the acceptance of a steady growth in incomes and wages (Shonfield, 1965: 65). As discussion of globalisation took hold in the 1990s, convergent trends were mapped out that represented the complete reversal of these ideals. We see the extension of private power in the global system, the shift from welfare state to competition state (Cerny, 1990), and the acceptance of labour flexibility and wage restraint as policy doxa (World Bank, 1995). The global competition imperative is overwhelmingly adopted as a business mantra, provoking debates regarding the 'right path' for the twenty-first-century organisation of the production and labour processes (see Peck and Tickell, 1994; Peters and Waterman, 1995), and for nations to follow in their response to globalisation (Reich, 1991; Department for International Development, 2000). The overwhelming image is one of a convergence of state policy, firm behaviour, and societal response around a single 'best' solution. Much of this analysis subordinates the politics of restructuring to the economic imperative of particular policy responses. Distinctive social institutions, understandings and practices are neglected in the process of identifying converging agendas.

Policy prescription

The defining of social change in 'process' terms – as industrialisation or globalisation – tends to avoid engagement with the inherent 'messiness' of social and political life. This problem-solving mode of knowledge simplifies and codifies social change into a series of identifiable (and predictable) shifts. In a pure form, this approach seeks to emulate the natural science model of observation, rule-generation and application. The post-war behavioural revolution in social science embodied a search for reliable causal theory that could explain social and political activity. The ambition was to simplify the complexity of social and political processes into a generally applicable theory. As Easton has it: 'Industrialism need not force us into what we consider to be the evils of urban life. Knowing what the effects of undirected industrial development are, we can use relevant generalizations to help construct a new pattern of life' (1965: 30).

The idea that if we can identify and know the process then we can learn how to respond to it is never far from view. There is a close relationship between process-centred models of social change and the desire to discipline or manage a political response. I am not suggesting that contemporary accounts of globalisation adopt a behavioural approach to social science, but the instrumental rationality of behaviouralism is echoed in many of the dominant academic, media and corporate claims about globalisation:

> People who construct knowledge in secular, anthropocentric, techno-scientific, instrumental terms have generally exercised the greatest power in global spaces. Rationalist epistemology has reigned supreme in global enterprises, global governance agencies and the more influential parts of global civil society like think tanks and professional NGOs. (Scholte, 2000: 187)

It is at this point that we begin to see the power that is exercised within and through dominant representations of globalisation. As Palan has it 'state or transnational firms are assumed to be rational, calculating actors, with clear … preferences and goals' (2000: 15). Where complex and contingent dynamics of change are presented in instrumental and rational terms *descriptively*, it becomes possible to use these generalisations *prescriptively*. The nuances and contradictions of contemporary global restructuring become obscured by a burgeoning literature prescribing 'best practice' policy models. Following from the identification of exogenous forces that demand imperative responses, there is a space opened up for the prescription of best practice models. As Winfried Ruigrok and Rob van Tulder have argued: 'there is a grateful market for those who translate the "new complexity" into simple formulae and unambiguous recommendations' (1995: 1). Those analysts, consultants and auditors who make it their business to offer global solutions become the key players in both state and corporate strategy. Their pre-eminence is difficult to challenge from within a perspective that positions them as the problem solvers in the process. Academic analysis cuts across business management and political strategy and we see the rise of gurus who occupy central space in academic, political and corporate arenas (see Ohmae, 1990; Drucker, 1995; Toffler, 1980; Giddens, 1998). Borrowing from the generalisations of the industrial society school, everything becomes 'manageable', society becomes a 'social system', politics a 'political system' and global social relations part of a 'global system'. The emphasis has been predominantly placed on the mapping of the contours of global change so that a 'route guide' can be produced to ensure successful navigation.

The death of conflict

It is commonplace in social science to find claims to the 'end' of particular struggles at particular historical moments. In particular, there seems to be a temptation to claim that a consensus around basic core values and ideas in a society brings the end of a period of social conflict or contestation. Thus, for example, the industrial society was conceived as a pluralist system of peaceful political competition and industrial negotiation (see Dahrendorf, 1959: 67). Daniel Bell's 'End of Ideology' thesis, proclaimed that the consolidation of a Keynesian compromise had effectively erased the grounds for disruptive class conflict, offering in its place a more manageable kind of conflict (see Bell, 1961; Lipset, 1960; Waxman, 1968). In these formulations the politics of negotiation, contestation and compromise represent the struggles of transition. They are ultimately by-products of social change and can only temporarily disrupt the process. The dynamic behind social transformation is argued to lie, not in the contradictions and tensions of capitalism, but in the rational progress of technology. The rationality, achievement, mobility and plurality of the adaptive industrial society signals the 'supercedence of capitalism' (Dahrendorf, 1959: 67). Kerr *et al.* similarly argue that analysis should move beyond a focus on conflict to an examination of the 'universal phenomena affecting all workers' (1962: 7). Ultimately, this view of social change envisages a role for contest and conflict only in an unstable transitional phase that will be followed by a new and stable order with the reconciliation of social groups.[2]

The contemporary globalisation debate operationalises similar ideas about the dissolution of sources of social and political conflict. Among IR scholars there is debate as to the extent of the 'triumph' of liberalism (Brown, 1999). Fukuyama's (1992) *End of History* thesis represents perhaps the strongest statement that disagreement over the form and nature of politico-economic and social organisation is now of marginal concern. In terms of party politics, there is the suggestion that advanced industrialised countries have witnessed the death of socialism and the convergence of left and right (Giddens, 1998). In terms of industrial conflict, it is argued that this is confined to an adjustment phase in which the corporatist arrangements of a

Fordist era are replaced by a 'yeoman democracy' of informal networks of trust (Piore, 1990; Sabel, 1992). The emergence of the 'network society' (Castells, 1996) has been heralded by some as the harbinger of individual autonomy and freedom in the workplace (Negroponte, 1995). In these representations, political thought, action, conflict and contestation are institutionalised phenomena; they are contained by ideological positions, party politics and formalised industrial relations. As a result, it is held that once the embedded norms of the perceived past era have been totally displaced by 'new' and individualised arrangements, conflict becomes a thing of the past. A wholly benign image of global restructuring is created, within which the conflicts and struggles that characterise and condition processes of social change are invisible.

The restructuring of work and the flexibility discourse

Within the mode of knowledge that frames globalisation as an essential and inexorable process, there has been a central proposed solution to the conundrum of what to do. The answer that has come back from public and private managers is to 'flexibilise', to introduce flexibility into all spheres of social life. The emergence of a political, corporate, societal and academic discourse of flexibility has become a highly visible everyday face of the globalisation debate. Flexibility, as featured in the statements of international economic institutions, national governments and corporations (see, for example World Bank, 1995; OECD, 1996; Beatson, 1995; Department for International Development, 2000), has become a multifarious concept and a universal panacea. It is presented as synonymous with deregulatory government, lean production and the flexible firm, the decollectivisation of industrial relations and the overall dissolution of work and employment into a fluid and transient form. In its broadest usage, flexibility has come to define the properties of a society that has embraced the imperatives of immediacy and risk within globalisation and has accepted the required adaptations. At its most specific and precise, flexibility defines the techniques and practices of JIT production, kaizen (continuous improvement), teamworking and 'total quality management' (TQM). In its many guises, flexibility in production and work means that entire countries, individual firms and workers can respond without delay to shifts in global demand for a good or service, and to global market shocks.

In this section I will explore the close relationship between the ascendant 'common sense' representations of globalisation as process, and the contemporary preoccupation with all things flexible. The previous section outlined the key features of such a globalist mode of knowledge: transformative forces, disciplinary imperatives, historical convergence, policy prescription and the death of conflict. The section that follows will map out the terrain of the flexibility discourse through these features. In common with some other scholars, I propose that the study of global restructuring can reveal the power, agency and contingency that is absent from much contemporary discussion of the 'G word' (Ruigrok and van Tulder, 1995: 130; Marchand and Runyan, 2000: 7). The formulae of flexibility present in global restructuring discourse offers a particularly powerful example of the reification of a particular representation of global social change.

Technology, markets and the restructuring of work

It has become commonplace to locate the intensification of global com-petition and the onset of neo-liberal restructuring in a particular historical period, and in relation to apparently exogenous technological and market forces. For many commentators on the transformation of work, the 1970s represent a turning point in the regulation of the international system and a benchmark for contemporary globalisation. Despite fierce disagreement over the causes and implications of the unravelling of the Bretton Woods System, the oil crises and the rejection of Keynesian demand management and welfarism, there is general agreement that the nature of regulation, product-ion and work underwent fundamental change in response. The competitive challenge of Japan and Germany, the consolidated power of the MNCs, the crisis of Fordism and the ascendancy of 'offshore' production and finance have all become emblematic of a new world order in which the buffers between production and global markets have been eroded. Furthermore, they have become central to explanations of the 'necessary' transformations in the policies and practices of states, firms and workers in response.

The question is not whether technological and market transformations have been significant in the restructuring of production and work; of course they have played a fundamental role. Rather, the central question raised here is how these transformations have been represented as external events that are somehow decoupled from the realms of politics and social life. The claims that nation-states have, by necessity, become 'marketised', that firms adopt 'lean' strategies (Womack *et al.*, 1990), and that labour must become more flexible (Oliver and Wilkinson, 1988), are established in the context of a linear and opposed relationship between technology/markets and society/politics. The globalisation of markets in goods, services and finance is presented as a reality that is imposed 'from without' and must be seized 'from within': 'International flows of goods, services, capital, and people bring new opportunities for most ... Some workers will indeed be hurt if they are stuck in declining activities and lack the flexibility to change' (World Bank, 1995: 4). In the World Bank's statement the 'flows' are presented as external forces that may 'bring' oppor-tunities or threats into the lives of workers. States, industries and workers that fail to recognise the shifts in their external environment will be 'left behind' in the competitive race. Flexibility is itself defined as an attribute of rapid and adaptive responsiveness to 'outside' pressures. There is a strong emphasis on the embracing of new and superior technologies and the adoption of new and flexibilised productive and working practices in line with their dictates (see Womack *et al.*, 1990; Hirst and Zeitlin, 1989). Fordist mass production is presented as technologically outmoded as new information and communication technologies (ICTs) increase the possibilities for flexibilisation and the geographical and temporal dispersal of production. The 'flexible firm' becomes the fêted site for global production, bringing with it new demands for the reorganisation of work (Atkinson, 1985). The combination of technological advances, intensely competitive markets and new models of production is discursively tied to 'new opportunities' for the organisation of work:

> Three factors – human resources, markets and technology – have a fundamental impact on the way workplaces are organised ... The new flexible firm is a demanding form of organisation of work ... In the new decentralised and network-oriented organisations, workers perform a range of tasks, rather than pass the job on from one to another ... As workers develop a wider range of skills and become more adaptable, the new organisation of work will further facilitate geographical mobility. This in turn will enable workers to exploit their potential more fully and exercise their rights in this respect. (Commission of European Communities (CEC), 1997: 7)

The European Commission positions the restructuring of work as a direct response to exogenous technological and market forces. Indeed, the flexibilisation of work is represented in terms of the opportunities and rewards of 'up-skilling', training and greater labour market mobility. The discourse that has emerged and made flexibility 'common sense' for the global era has firmly positioned technological change on the outside, and states, firms and workers on the inside in a responsive mode. There is no acknowledgement that market competition and technological development may themselves be constituted in part by the social forces engendered by the production process in specific places and at specific historical moments (Cox, 1987). For example, the relationships between states, firms and financial institutions in a particular context may place limits on the development of particular technologies. To take this further we may want to question the alliance that is presented between high-tech/high-skill work and workers performing 'flexible' roles and tasks in the GPE. In many instances flexibility is associated with repetitive, low-skill and intensive working practices (Pollert, 1991; Anderson, 2000; Moody, 1997), and with sectors that are not internationally traded. Viewed in this way, the linear and deterministic relationship between techno-economic globalisation and the restructuring of work is tenuous. A consideration of the social relations that intimately bind 'workplaces' into the dynamics of 'world order'[3] reveals that the inside/outside dichotomy of the flexibility discourse is a convenient illusion that masks the political power and social contest that surrounds the restructuring of work.

Flexibility as disciplinary imperative

In recent times there has been a subtle change in the discourse surrounding policy responses to globalisation. That change involves a greater willingness to acknowledge the inequities and unevenness of globalisation. The British Government acknowledges that 'the impact of globalisation on poor people varies widely' (Department for International Development, 2000: 18), the United Nations equates a globalising world with 'new threats to human security – sudden and hurtful disruptions in the pattern of daily life' (United Nations Development Programme (UNDP), cited in Held and McGrew, 2000) and the World Bank states that 'widening global disparities have increased the sense of deprivation and injustice for many' (2001: vi). In every case, however, the acknowledgement of inequity is qualified by judgements on which state-societies have most successfully 'harnessed globalisation', thereby avoiding the negative effects. Put simply, the message is that globalisation simultaneously presents opportunities and threats, and that individual governments, industries and people take responsibility for ensuring that they avoid the threats and embrace the opportunities. Thus, the World Bank refers to 'harnessing global forces for poor people' (2001: 179), the British Government seeks to 'make globalisation work for the poor' (Department for International Development, 2000), the British Prime Minister states that 'the global market is a good thing for us' (Held, 1998: 26), and *The Economist* puts the 'case for globalisation' (23 September 2000: 19).

The problems that are associated with globalisation are viewed as inherently 'treatable' in the sense that effective policy responses can be formulated. The 'golden solution' to 'make globalisation work' has been flexibility – providing both a disciplinary ethos and a concrete set of strategies through which to 'harness' globalisation. The central question on the global agenda becomes 'what reforms would improve the capacity of the labour markets to accommodate structural changes smoothly and rapidly?' (OECD, 1994: 12-15). The flexibility discourse thus has a strong disciplinary effect and becomes a 'no alternative' policy imperative. A failure to create flexible labour markets and flexible workers is presented as a failure to grasp the opportunities of globalisation and, in all likelihood, will 'incur the costs of inaction' (OECD, 1996: 21).

The dominant thesis in policy and corporate literature is that labour flexibility is the solution to the challenge of mobile global capital or, to put it another way, that firms will locate where labour is malleable and deregulated. What globalisation means, according to those who reproduce the flexibility imperative, is that 'old' systems of production, labour and regulation become rigid constraints in otherwise free markets. For the World Bank, for example, the countries that have achieved the greatest gains for their workers are those that decided early on to take advantage of international opportunities, and to rely increasingly on market forces rather than the state in allocating resources' (1995: 10). The neo-classical view, that the operation of the global market stands in tension with the rigidities of an interventist or regulatory state, lies at the heart of the flexibility discourse. The major OECD governments become wrapped up in a constraining neo-liberal mantra that says 'make space for capital' and this is projected to less developed countries in similar terms. As the European Commission has it: '… firms must achieve global competitiveness on open and competitive markets. It is the responsibility of the national and Community authorities to provide industry with a favourable environment' (CEC, 1993: 57). A central feature of this 'favourable environment' is assumed to be a flexible and adaptable workforce. Part of the 'responsibility' of political authorities, then, becomes the task of removing regulatory impediments to a flexible labour market (Baglioni and Crouch, 1990). For policymakers and corporate managers this has signalled moves towards explicit (formalised and institutionalised) and implicit (informal and tacit) forms of flexibilisation in labour and work. Within the flexibility discourse it is possible to identify a number of interrelated conceptions of the nature and implications of flexibility.

Functional flexibility implies that working tasks and practices can adapt to changes in demand on the production process (Pinch, 1994). The focus here is on internal or firm-centred flexibility. The assumption is that traditional job demarcations and hierarchies create rigidities that should be eroded or 'flattened' to be replaced by multi-functional 'teams' or production 'cells'. In this model the firm becomes the locus for determining the necessary skills, and training is likely to be 'in-house' and task specific. In essence skills are owned and defined by the firm and are not carried by the worker in the wider labour market.

Numerical flexibility is a labour market 'textbook' term for the capacity of an employer to expand or contract the workforce in line with demand. This is said to be achieved through a variety of mechanisms such as working time flexibility, casual and part-time working, subcontracting and outsourcing and the use of temporary contracts or agency staff. The underlying imperative is that traditional employment relations must be dissolved via, for instance, the relaxation of dismissal, redundancy and benefits regulations. A parallel and related shift has occurred in the composition of the workforce, with an increase in women's participation in the workforce, the use of early retirement policies (Rubery, 1999), and the employment of unprotected migrant workers attributed with '… an uncommon willingness to work hard at unappealing jobs' (*The Economist*, 6 May 2000: 19). There is an underlying assumption that welfare and active labour market policies must be limited in order that there may be no disincentives to take on 'flexible' work: 'To ensure that most participants are poor and to maintain incentives for workers to move on to regular work when it becomes available, programs should pay no more than the average wage for unskilled labor' (World Bank, 2001: 156). This example, drawn from the World Bank's 'principles of successful workfare programmes', demonstrates the market-centred logic of the flexibility discourse. Taken to its conclusion, so-called numerical flexibility has led to the use of child and sweatshop labour. Indeed, where this has arisen the response has been to appeal to 'corporate social responsibility' and the implementation of labour codes of conduct (Department for International Development, 2000: 156). It is difficult to see how this can be effective when numerical flexibility is designed precisely to limit the number of workers for whom the firm has direct responsibility.

The final major strand of the contemporary fixation with flexibility has been *pay flexibility* (read cost flexibility). The imperative of decentralised and deregulated pay bargaining structures has been constructed through the representation of embedded and unionised industrial relations as punitive and rigid (Treu, 1992). Ultimately, individualised employment contracts and performance-related or target-focused pay structures have become the model of pay flexibility. State-societies that sustain high wage and non-wage labour costs are presented as uncompetitive and inflexible. The overall effect of this multi-layered flexibility discourse is to create a disciplinary imperative that celebrates the dissolution of collective and stable employment relations and the rise of the self-responsible, risk-bearing individual worker (see Beck, 2000b; Bauman, 1998).

The central problem of the representation of flexibility as an automatic disciplinary feature of globalisation is that this closes down the possibility for alternative strategies and tactics. The message that flexibility is the best way to 'harness' globalisation, and that a failure to flexibilise will bring out the claws of globalisation, is a frightening and powerful one. Indeed, it serves to constrain political and social debate about the restructuring of work as people feel themselves to be faced with no alternative. The disciplinary character of flexibility warns that a failure to expose oneself further to the forces of global markets (through flexibilisation) will result in greater exclusion from the potential rewards on offer. The portrayal of flexibility as a way of dealing with the globalisation process has fundamentally oversimplified and depoliticised the problem. The definition, interpretation and experience of so-called flexibility is multiple, contingent and diverse. In particular, we do not find the archetypal blueprint of a 'flexible', 'multi-skilled', yet 'empowered' worker in all places (if, indeed, we find him or her at all). The disciplinary effects of flexibility are highly contradictory, not least because they are inseparable from the proclaimed 'rigidities'. Flexibility, when viewed in concrete practices, rests upon its antithesis – rigidity. For example, government policies that emphasise flexible labour markets require tightly defined welfare policies where there is little or no room for political manoeuvre, whether to raise taxes or to use active labour market policies. Similarly, firms that seek flexibility via the hiring of agency or temporary workers, accept greater constraints on skills, training and employee 'trust' (Rubery, 1999: 125). Workers that provide optimally flexible labour in paid work find simultaneously rigid constraints in their household and family life. Far from being an overarching solution to the challenges of globalisation, flexibility comes at a high price that is paid across the realms of social and political life.

Competition and convergence

The flexibility discourse that has emerged in pursuit of solutions to globalisation has cut across corporate, academic and policy literature. Flexibility has thus become an 'icon or incantation' (Curry, 1993: 99), strengthened by its discursive attachment to dominant representations of globalisation. According to the advocates of labour flexibility, the imperatives of globalisation make flexibilisation a necessity that is common to all societies. As a result it is assumed that the political and corporate agendas of different state-societies will be essentially convergent in their post-restructuring institutions and practices: 'The debate about reforms is not over a choice between reforms or no reforms ... Rather, the debate is on how reforms to build markets can be designed and implemented in a way that is measured and tailored to the economic, social, and political circumstances of a country' (World Bank, 2001: 62). While it is acknowledged, then, that deregulatory reforms take place in specific social and historical contexts, there is apparently no space for dispute over the need for restructuring – the diagnosis is the same and the 'medicine' can simply be adapted to suit. The policy priorities of the Washington consensus shape a convergence of government programmes around the provision of the optimal location for global capital. A central emphasis is on the removal of restrictions on the flexible organisation of work in order that FDI decisions might favour a particular location. As the World Bank has it 'the most important reforms involve lifting constraints on labor mobility and wage flexibility, as well as breaking the ties between social services and labor contracts' (World Bank, 1995: 109).

The neo-liberal deregulatory restructuring characteristic of the US and UK becomes the model around which it is assumed that all social change will conform and converge. The blueprint offered calls for a diminution in levels of regulation on labour relations, but also seeks to exert downward pressure on welfare and social benefits that are presumed to 'inhibit' the incentive to work. The OECD's *Jobs Strategy* typifies the policy recommendations that accompany claims to a flexibilised and competitive labour force (see Table 1.1).

Intensified global competition, according to those advocating neo-liberal flexibilisation, means that all state-societies must restructure along the lines of this model. Indeed, in a report that compares the relative success of member countries in implementing the Jobs Strategy recommendations, the OECD identifies the US, UK, Canada, Australia, New Zealand and Ireland as having made 'significant policy developments' in the flexibilisation of labour (1997: 8). The Economic and Development Review Committee (EDRC) applaud the UK for its 'reform of industrial relations', New Zealand for its 'reduced government intervention', Ireland for the lowering of the 'generosity of unemployment

Table 1.1 The OECD's 'Jobs Strategy' recommendations

---

1 Set macroeconomic policy such that it will both encourage growth and, in conjunction with good structural policies, make it sustainable, i.e. non-inflationary.

2 Enhance the creation and diffusion of technological know-how by improving frameworks for its development.

3 Increase flexibility of working-time (both short-term and lifetime) voluntarily sought by workers and employers.

4 Nurture an entrepreneurial climate by eliminating impediments to, and restrictions on, the creation and expansion of enterprises.

5 Make wage and labour costs more flexible by removing restrictions that prevent wages from reflecting local conditions and individual skill levels, in particular of younger workers.

6 Reform employment security provisions that inhibit the expansion of employment in the private sector.

7 Strengthen the emphasis on active labour market policies and reinforce their effectiveness.

8 Improve labour force skills and competences through wide-ranging changes in education and training systems.

9 Reform unemployment and related benefit systems – and their interaction with the tax system – such that societies' fundamental equity goals are achieved in ways that impinge far less on the efficient functioning of labour markets.

Source: OECD, 1996.

benefits' and the US for its policies 'consistent with flexible labour' (1997: 7-8). These countries are directly identified as converging around the OECD Jobs Strategy blueprint for labour flexibility. By contrast, Germany, France, Belgium, Denmark and Sweden, among others, are criticised for their structural impediments to wage flexibility, their high levels of social transfers, and their use of active labour market policies: 'It remains an open question whether a policy approach that sees public intervention in post-compulsory education, training and active labour market policies as a substitute for relative wage flexibility is effective, let alone cost-effective, particularly in a world of rapid structural change' (OECD, 1997: 12). The message is that a failure to converge around the policy requirements for labour flexibility will result in a failure to attract inward investment, persistently high levels of structural unemployment and an overall loss of competitiveness. A failure to adapt along neo-liberal lines is interpreted as a failure to change at all, as a kind of institutional stasis amid a changing world.

The convergence assumption is closely allied to teleological and depoliticised readings of globalisation (Amoore *et al.*, 1997). An 'inevitabilism' surrounds the construction of a flexible and deregulated reality, and the social and political-economic dynamics that frame this reality are never brought into question. The suggestion that restructuring can, or should, conform to a menu of deregulatory reforms follows a highly simplified understanding of social change. The achievement of an 'attractive location' for business, or a 'flexible workforce', though presented as a convergent process by key public and private agencies, is a highly contested and contingent possibility. By way of example, governments may negotiate their policy agenda through established and embedded relationships with business, labour groups and employers' organisations.[4] Flexibility, for one society, social group or individual, may represent inflexibility, insecurity and intensified risk for another. Within the EDRC's analysis of the implementation of the OECD Jobs Strategy, the divergent emphases of member countries' policy agendas are presented as problems rooted in the failure to adopt the recommended strategies. However, there is an implicit acknowledgement that fundamental social and political questions may be interpreted differently in given contexts: '... representatives from some English-speaking countries saw low unemployment as an essential condition for, or element of, horizontal equity. And those from some continental European countries saw equity as a more fundamental goal than low unemployment' (OECD, 1997: 12).

While for the OECD such divergence represents a problem to be resolved, a different reading of the findings reveals that the identified aims of 'flexibility', 'mobility', 'equity' and even 'competitiveness' are interpreted, contested and given meaning in specific contexts. Space is opened up within the global restructuring debate that reveals a contingent and contradictory set of practices. So, on the one hand we see governments pursuing policies that do not conform to neo-liberal dictates, but that have grabbed the attention of the business press, as in the case of France: 'The 35-hour week may be a hassle, but at least many employers have managed to extract valuable concessions from employees on more flexible working practices in return' (*The Economist*, 1 April 2000: 13). This is a long way from a critique of neo-liberal defined flexibility and, indeed, the article later goes on to speculate: 'If the French economy can power ahead despite the tight grip of the state, just imagine what it could do if the state let go'. However, there is a tacit recognition here that the restructuring of work is negotiated and contested in the context of social power relations, that bargains may be needed and accommodation may be necessary, that politics may not quite be redundant.

On the other hand, and to reinforce the point, we see the archetypal neo-liberal competition states experiencing problems that are not anticipated by the flexibility rhetoric. The decision by US telecommunications corporation Motorola to close the Bathgate plant in Scotland with 3000 redundancies appears to defy the logic that the flexibility thesis proclaims. The decision, taken in April 2001, effectively closed a profitable plant of 'flexible' workers in favour of a lossmaking plant of 'high cost' workers in Flensburg, Germany. Roger Lyons, General Secretary of the Manufacturing Science and Finance Union, when interviewed by *The Guardian*, said that it was 'easier and cheaper to sack workers in the UK than elsewhere in Europe' (24 April 2001). This example of the 'flight' of productive capital from an archetypal 'flexible' competition state clearly does not fit the picture of an inevitable competitive advantage through reduced labour costs. Such contradictory and contested dynamics of the restructuring of work cannot be understood by recourse to simplistic notions of a convergence around flexibility. They can only be revealed by an exploration of the social power relations that condition specific, contingent and divergent 'solutions'.

Prescription and human resource management

Alongside the state-centred discourse of flexibility as a policy imperative, there has emerged a corporate management language that shrouds the restructuring of work in imagery that appeals to science. Human resource management (HRM), TQM and employee involvement (EI), among many other strategic instruments, have been prescribed in the reordering of the employer-employee relationship.[5] These management labels for the restructuring of work are presented as 'logical' and 'evolutionary' responses to the competitive pressures of the global economy (Williams, 1994: 5). Globalisation is offered as the context within which 'strategic' and 'rational' instruments are required to achieve changes in the production process (see Womack, Jones and Roos, 1990; Wickens, 1987). The HRM prescriptions recast the employment relation so that it is individualised, permitting optimal flexibility. Workers are not perceived as a collective group, or indeed as conscious people capable of apprehending the shape of change in the workplace: 'A management language has emerged which redefines workers as employees, individuals and teams, but not as organised collectivities with some interests separate from management' (Ackers *et al.*, 1996: 5).

In positioning workers as essentially malleable, adaptable and flexible commodities, the HRM literature offers itself as a scientific approach to the management of restructuring. In effect, it reaffirms the notion that objective knowledge can be acquired and applied in pursuit of global competitiveness. The ascendancy of management consultancies whose role it is to 'legitimate change in corporate practices' (Strange, 1996: 138), lends a strategic and calculable air to the restructuring of work. These agencies explicitly offer to simplify the complexity of global competition, as one human resources consultancy put it: 'to capture the upside of uncertainty', to make globalisation manageable and translatable into simple formulae. Corporate decisions can then be said to be based on the rational judgements of an objective expert who can prescribe optimal solutions to the problems of intensified global competition. Where once the large accountancy firms were seen to be concerned with 'sound' financial management, they now offer an auditory and advisory role in all aspects of corporate restructuring. Indeed, their roles have been constituted within the problem-solving mode of knowledge represented by 'globalisation as process'. The management consultancies market themselves as 'business process reengineers' capable of fundamentally restructuring 'old' practices in line with 'new' imperatives.[6] As Charlotte Hooper has argued, a kind of 'frontier masculinity' emerges which offers an inseparable mix of business and science 'to solve all our problems' (2000: 67). In this way restructuring is represented as a global challenge that can be tackled with the expertise of consultants armed with an arsenal of HRM strategies.

The HRM mantra of restructuring offers a menu of prescribed 'rational' solutions to the perceived process of globalisation. However, this presupposes that restructuring and social change will simply roll out as prescribed. Indeed, it implies that social relations can themselves be treated as factors in an equation. When the restructuring of working practices is viewed in concrete terms, the quasi-science of HRM is revealed as a construct that ignores the complex historical and social relations that underlie restructuring. Strategic and scientific management prescriptions for the reorganisation of work are decoupled from the prevailing practices of a particular workplace and, indeed, it is this abstractness that is deemed to lend objectivity to the strategic analysis. They are cast as though they represent pure and logical responses to the exigencies of globalisation:

> The sources of management preferences do not come from some auto-matic and innate character to the task of producing and marketing a good or service, laying down the exact steps to reach corporate goals ... Instead, preferences regarding strategies derive from general practices in the industry, from technological and managerial knowledge, and from the society of which the firm and its managers are part. (Haufler, 1999: 201)

We are thus reminded that every apparent 'strategy' emerges from the context of social power relations, within which knowledge and power are inseparable (Foucault, 1980b). To reproduce HRM, and other strategic manage-ment tools, as automatic responses to the competitive pressures of globalisa-tion is to obscure the power that suffuses such dominant modes of knowledge. So, on the one hand, HRM is not simply 'exercised' or 'implemented'. The softness of the language employed in notions of 'involvement', 'human' and 'empowerment' is bound up with a subtle power that brings workers into the monitoring of their own practices. As Garrahan and Stewart observed at Nissan 'success depends upon a tight nexus of subordination that can be read as control, exploitation and surveillance – the other side of quality, flexibility and teamwork' (1992: 59).

However, it is insufficient simply to seek to expose the power relations that are masked by the technical and scientific discourse of flexibility, for this may lead us to conclude that their dominance crushes all dissent in its path. Thus, on the other hand we find contestation surrounding the reorganisation of work around strategic management principles. A number of studies demonstrate that within a discourse of the flexibilisation of working practices,

spaces open up for the contestation and disruption of restructuring programmes (see McCabe, 1996; Waddington, 1999; Milkman, 1998). The scientific
calculations of strategic human resource managers are confounded by the
contingency of actual concrete working practices.

Industrial relations and the death of conflict

The restructuring of work around the concept of flexibility has become almost
synonymous with the breaking open of embedded systems of industrial relations. The process of deunionisation across advanced industrialised countries
has been legitimated 'in the name of globalisation' (du Gay, 1999). The
contemporary period of intensified global competition is widely understood
to require competitive and open labour markets, a central element of which is
a deregulated industrial relations arena. The shifts in employment from high
trade union density manufacturing to low density service industries, coupled
with a restructured core labour force and the rise of contingent labour, have
contributed to a decline in union membership, density and, arguably, power
and influence. The individualisation of employment contracts has been accompanied by a shift in union activity towards the representation of individual
clients (Hyman, 1997). For the advocates of restructured employee representation, collective forms of representation are 'outmoded' and irreconcilable
with workplace realities. Trade unions are cast as unrepresentative, rigid and
inflexible, prone to 'monopolistic behaviour' and 'opposition to reform'
(World Bank, 1995: 80). Resistance to flexibilisation strategies is held to be a
phenomenon of organised labour and, by implication, can be eradicated
through deunionisation and worker individualisation. Regulated and centralised forms of industrial relations become part of the 'burden' that must be
shed in order that globalisation can be effectively 'harnessed'. Governments
must create space for firms to flexibly manage their own individual workers
through, for example, the use of 'no-union' agreements and decentralised pay
bargaining (OECD, 1991).

Not only is conflict and contestation effaced by the flexibility discourse, but
this is presented as an opportunity for workers to experience the 'empowerment' of individual self-management (Hyman, 1999a: 108). The advent of the
digital age has been particularly strongly equated with emancipated labour
and rewarding work (Negroponte, 1995). Similarly, adversarial industrial
relations are held to obstruct the possibilities for workers to reconcile their
interests with the corporate mission. Conflict in the workplace is represented
as a transitory by-product of the process of work reorganisation. The collective and institutionalised politics of the trade unions is understood to be the
only source of political activity in the workplace. Thus, deunionisation is equated
with a depoliticisation of the workplace and, in effect, the death of conflict.

The discourse of labour flexibility draws upon a narrow conception of
politics in its process-centred understanding of social change. The 'mechan-

ical solidarities' (Hyman, 1999a) of organised labour certainly represent one form of the expression of the politics of labour and work. However, it is not the case that the squeeze on traditional industrial relations has brought about the death of conflict, though of course this is a myth that is useful in driving restructuring. Removing union representation, though undeniably circumscribing workers' political expression, does not remove the social power relations of the workplace. Nor does the information economy inevitably lead to an empowered workforce (May, forthcoming), or reduce the contestation that surrounds challenges to working practices. First, the threats to institutionalised and organised labour have been resisted, both through the defensive strategies of labour groups in the social market economies (Scharpf, 1998), and by the informal and everyday tactics of workers (Elger and Fairbrother, 1992; Waddington, 1999). In a lean production system which lacks the buffers of inventory stock, the everyday practices and tactics of workers may have significant effects. In this sense, the formation of fluid 'organic solidarities' (Hyman, 1999a) may offer alternative sites of political struggle based on common (if fleeting) experiences and immediate controversies. Indeed, the politics of the workplace may lie less in the unitary actions of defined organisation, and more in the 'contradictions, contingencies and unintended consequences' (Walker, 1994: 672) that characterise everyday working lives.

Yet, and this brings me to my second point, there are also scholars who are observing a greater fluidity and mutability of the organised trade unions themselves. This 'global social movement unionism' (Lambert, 1999; Lambert and Chan, 1999) suggests a decoupling of trade unions from their roots in nation-states and a desire for a transnational representativeness. The technologies assumed to reduce the need for workplace representation and organised labour may be used precisely to reconstitute communication between labour groups (Hyman, 1999b; ILO, 2001). Viewed in this way the politics of the restructuring of work is not separable from the struggles of a 'globally conscious' civil society (Scholte, 2000) that transcends received boundaries. Finally, while not wishing to underplay the very real challenges that face organised and unprotected workers in the GPE, it is also important to avoid reinforcing the 'no alternative' logic that prevails in the flexibility discourse. Political agency and social contest are denied in the face of something that is 'larger than us' and thus 'cannot be resisted because the outcome has already been determined' (Marchand and Runyan, 2000: 7). While it is clear that conventional spaces of workplace politics are being closed down, we must question conceptions of politics that do not enable us to see the opening up of alternative political spaces.

Conclusion

The dominant representations of globalisation and industrialisation as processes offer the alluring prospect of a name for our contemporary condition, along with an explanation of how it should be managed. They make common appeals to economic and technological externalities that create imperatives for global restructuring. The understanding of social change is purely linear. It reads that globalisation exerts pressure on states and firms to ratchet-up their competitiveness through a downward pressure on social welfare, taxation and labour market regulation. The social practices of everyday life are assumed to be fundamentally and necessarily restructured and reshaped as a result. In this way, human and social relations are understood only in a responsive mode, and politics is conceived only in instrumental 'management' terms. The impetus of social change is represented as dwelling 'outside' of social and political life, thereby securing and insulating global restructuring from the politics of negotiation, contestation and resistance (represented as dwelling 'inside'). Indeed, the disciplinary imperatives of globalisation are assumed to squeeze political agency, social contestation and historical contingency to the point that they no longer matter.

The conception of globalisation as techno-economic process has done much to transform perceptions of the ways in which working practices should function in a global era. Whether or not we consider globalisation to be an 'ambiguous' and 'fuzzy' concept (Waters, 1995), its amorphous character gives it the power to legitimate much that is done in its name. It is this global restructuring conducted 'in the name of' globalisation that is in need of critical interrogation in our research. The contemporary fixation with flexibility is legitimated and perpetuated by its discursive attachment to dominant representations of a natural, automatic and irrevocable process of globalisation. There is an explicit assumption that globalisation can be 'harnessed', and that a central means to this end is flexibility in labour and work. If states, firms and workers adopt policies and practices of flexibilisation, argue the proponents of labour flexibility, they will reap the rewards of the global economy. The overall effect of the flexibility discourse has been to create a disciplinary imperative that celebrates the dissolution of collective and stable employment relations and the rise of the individualised and 'risk accepting' worker.

The disciplinary effect of the threat that the 'failure to flexibilise' will unleash the full fury of global forces constrains political and social discussion and contestation. The contestation that takes place within and through the restructuring of work is effaced by deterministic and teleological accounts of social change. The idea that state-societies, firms and workers may be differentially placed in global restructuring is anathema to this discourse. The unevenness, inequality and power that suffuse the experiences of flexibilisation in the workplace have been afforded insufficient attention. It is precisely the aim of this book to contribute to a conception of global restructuring that is open to contestation and contingency. In the chapter that follows I explore the contribution that the field of IPE can make to raising the visibility of the social power relations that condition and shape global restructuring.

Notes

1 Ian R. Douglas raised the significance of 'global[i]zation' as action-process verb in a paper presented to the International Studies Association, San Diego, 1996.

2 The diminution of conflict between social groups is argued to arise from the equality of opportunity envisaged to result from increased mobility within society and the labour market. See, for example, Durkheim (1964) for the origins of the idea that inequalities may be eliminated via mobility and the reordering of status according to skills and talents.

3 The interrelationships between workplace and world order are explored in Cox (1987) and Harrod (1987). See chapter 2 of this volume for further discussion.

4 The significance of established social relations and practices is evident from European case studies which illustrate that the historical evolution of trade unions remains a salient factor in contemporary policy-making. See, for example, Baglioni and Crouch (1990) or Nolan and O'Donnell, (1991).

5 These concepts function as labels for a diverse set of management practices. HRM can be traced to the use of individualised employment relationships in the USA from the 1960s. It became common currency in the 1980s, when it became associated with the strategic management of what had previously been known as 'industrial relations'. TQM is a concept that refers to the breaking up of quality monitoring and assurance functions into stages. These functions are then devolved through the workforce to the level of individual workers, implying that quality assurance becomes a task that is performed by all workers. EI seeks to connect workers (as individuals) to the needs of the firm. This includes, for example, problem-solving teams, performance-related pay and the use of video and pictorial illustrations of new practices.

6 Insights from interview with British-based international management consultants, June 2000.

2

~

International political economy
and global social change

~

> Political economy is concerned with the historically constituted frame-
> works or structures within which political and economic activity takes
> place. It stands back from the apparent fixity of the present to ask how
> the existing structures came into being and how they may be changing,
> or how they may be induced to change. In this sense, political economy is
> critical theory. (Cox, 1995: 32)

The field of IPE is inextricably bound up with understandings of global
social transformation. Indeed, for many, the revival of IPE in the 1970s
precisely coincided with the inability of conventional IR frameworks to 'fully
comprehend structural change' (Gill, 1997: 7). IPE, by contrast, claims to offer
a distinctive ontology, one that is attuned to social forces and social relations
on a global scale, and also a distinctive epistemology that is 'open' to diverse
insights on social transformation (Strange, 1984; 1994).[1] Hence, as Robert
Cox has it, IPE embodies inherent critical potential, an ability to 'stand back'
from the apparent order of things and to consider 'the ways reality is defined
for different peoples in different eras' (Cox, 1995: 35). A significant part of this
critical bent is held to lie in the interdisciplinarity that is embraced by
'heterodox' IPE (Amin et al., 1994). The willingness to consider the insights of
a range of scholars; the acceptance of a range of subject matter and issues; and
the raising of voices previously unheard in IR, combine to present IPE as an
effective vantage point from which to view social change. Indeed, the IPE
perspectives on globalisation could be said to bring together the analytical
insights necessary to look critically at global transformation (Germain, 2000).
There is perhaps even a suggestion that IPE has become 'globalisation studies'
(Payne, 2000) and that global forces will 'dominate IPE for the foreseeable
future' (Tooze, 1997: 213).

Despite a potential 'hijacking' of IPE by concerns with globalisation, in
recent years there has emerged a critical agenda that directly seeks to challenge
the prevailing globalisation discourse. Scholars have directly called for the
'political' to be central to analysis of globalisation (Amoore et al., 1997; Hay
and Marsh, 1999); and for IPE to 'historicise' its studies (Amin and Palan,
1996; Amoore et al., 2000). This chapter focuses on the ways in which the field

of IPE has grappled with the problematic of global social change. Taking Murphy and Tooze's (1991) categories of 'orthodox' and 'new' IPE as analytical tools, I explore the different ontological and epistemological positions, and the implications for understandings of social change. The 'orthodox' origins of IPE may be aligned with a problem-solving mode of knowledge that seeks to 'manage' change in the GPE. 'New IPE' purports to offer a critical perspective in that it begins from a position of problematising the making and transformation of the GPE, thereby restoring reflexive political agency to global social change. Concurring with the broad spirit of the 'new IPE', this chapter nonetheless raises questions surrounding the extent of heterodoxy and openness that IPE has achieved. I suggest that, in part, IPE has reproduced old dichotomies and hierarchies of issues and subjects. In particular, it continues to represent power as something that is wielded by elite global actors, thus rendering the 'ordinary' realms of work and labour secondary concerns to finance and production. I identify the central elements of an IPE of social practice which, I propose, makes everyday practices such as work visible and amenable to inquiry.

Orthodox perspectives in IPE

IPE as a field of inquiry, a set of questions and a range of assumptions, is a highly contested discipline (Tooze, 1984). Indeed, it is perhaps misleading to consider IPE to be a discipline at all, given that it is characterised by diverse ontological, epistemological and methodological commitments. As a branch of social science IPE has most commonly been labelled a 'sub-field' of IR. Despite its origins in the apparent inability of IR to deal with a globalising world, IPE has been an inheritor of certain legacies of the IR tradition. In this way it perhaps paradoxically comes to represent both a 'break' with IR conventions and an upholding of embedded IR principles. In the context of post-war American social science, IPE takes on a particular orthodoxy that derives from the IR 'science at the service of big-power management' (Cox, 1996: 57). It is in this historical context, of US scholarship in the early 1970s, that IPE was defined in a particular way, reflecting dominant modes of thought and embodying a particular world view. Thus, Stephen Krasner has it that 'the achievements of international political economy have been generated by an epistemology that conforms with the Western Rationalistic Tradition' (1996: 122). We may consider early 'orthodox' IPE to follow the conventions of rationality and positivist inquiry that were outlined in chapter 1.

Despite IPE's diverse roots in classical political economy, sociology and economic history (these are acknowledged more freely by the so-called 'new' IPE scholars), its relationship to IR is an important one to explore. The IPE orthodoxy reproduces significant elements of the realist/liberal IR synthesis, and in so doing establishes a particular understanding of the dynamics of transformation. Emerging at a time of change in world politics, nonetheless much of the emphasis was placed on how this change should be managed, and the prevailing order maintained. Though the emphasis on system mainten- ance has now been critiqued by a proclaimed 'new' IPE, the orthodoxy continues to exert significant influence on the production of knowledge.

If IPE perspectives were to have a unifying feature, a prime candidate would be the analysis of the interrelationships between the 'political', the 'economic', the 'domestic' and the 'international' realms of social life. However, the fundamental cleavages between IPE schools of thought exist around the matter of how we should conceive of these realms. IPE is thus 'defined more by agreement among scholars about what to study than by agreement about how to study it' (Murphy and Tooze, 1991: 1). So-called orthodox scholars answer the question of the relationship between the economic and political realms in a particular way. Researching at the time of the 1971 collapse of the Bretton Woods System and the 1973 oil crises, scholars were struck by the potential for what they considered to be economic issues to impact upon the fundamental relations between nation-states. In this formulation the 'economic' is con- ceived as the realm of market interactions characteristic of world trade, held to be separate from the 'political' as the realm of state interactions characteristic of IR. IPE becomes a field of study 'concerned with the political determinants of international economic relations' (Krasner, 1996: 108). The separate and unitary realms of politics and economics are conceived as in a linear relation- ship of tension: 'The tension between these two fundamentally different ways of ordering human relationships has profoundly shaped the course of modern history and constitutes the crucial problem in the study of political economy' (Gilpin, 1987: 11).

Indeed, as Murphy and Tooze argue, the separation and opposition of the realms of politics and economics was an important part of the raison d'être of orthodox IPE: 'What spurred much of the initial IPE research in the early 1970s was a search for new technical rules and norms that could preserve the division between the political and the economic' (1991: 4). The decline of US hegemony and the challenges that were posed to the liberal international economic order (LIEO) were thus understood to have come about as a result of the interpenetration of the political and the economic. Thus, the decline of US hegemony is variously held to have disrupted the operation of the LIEO (Gilpin, 1987), or to necessitate the construction of political regimes and institutions to take on this role (Keohane, 1984; Krasner, 1983). The emphasis is on the problematic of maintaining the LIEO in the absence of a hegemon, or put another way, on the management of change in the world economy.

Out of the overriding concern to theorise and preserve the dichotomy between politics and economics emerged a focus that has conventionally provided the key terrain of debate in IPE – the relationships between states and markets. Gilpin has it that 'the interaction of the state and the market' represent the 'embodiment of politics and economics in the modern world' and that this 'creates political economy' (1987: 9–11). It is clear that states are viewed as the central units of political activity, while markets constitute an opposed economic realm. In effect, the sphere of the market is simply added as a 'variable' to the interactions of states dominant in neo-realist IR theory. These spheres are treated theoretically and normatively as discrete entities – the task of political economy being to analyse their 'impacts' on one another. The opposition of state to market is mirrored in the identification of domestic and international realms as separately defined spheres. Hence, the focus of study becomes 'the causes and effects of the world market economy … and the significance of the world economy for domestic economies' (Gilpin, 1987: 14). We cannot simply assume that this conception of states and markets, and domestic from international, reflects a particular historical moment in the study of IPE. Gilpin entrenches the state-market dichotomy still further fifteen years on:

> In this book I define global political economy as the interaction of the market and such powerful actors as states, multinational firms, and international organizations, a more comprehensive definition than in my 1987 book The Political Economy of International Relations, although both take a state-centric approach to the subject. (2001: 17)

It is striking that Gilpin here explicitly opposes 'the market' (conceived as a structure), and the actions of states, and in particular multinational firms (conceived as agents). To what extent is it possible or even desirable to conceive of the market as somehow distinct from multinational firms or international organisations? What are markets without the production structures of MNCs and the frameworks of the WTO and IMF? So, not only does Gilpin separate state from market, but also MNCs and international organisations from markets.

The ontological privileging of states-markets relationships has predisposed the IPE orthodoxy to particular methodological concerns. In identifying the 'agency' and power fundamentally with states, and 'structure' with world markets, the orthodoxy can only conceive of social change as state-led. The study of state actions is considered to be at the heart of IPE, just as it was in traditional IR. Global social change, conceived this way, can only be an 'outcome' of changes in 'relational power' such as the demise of a hegemon (Strange, 1988: 24). The preservation of some notion of stability and order, I would argue, is thus given prominence over the struggles and contests that mark the potential for change and transformation. Gilpin's consideration of the question of globalisation leads him to conclude that states remain the central 'power wielders' in the GPE: 'Economic globalisation is much more limited than many realise, and consequently, its overall impact on the economic role of the state is similarly limited' (2001: 363). This clearly demonstrates that the preservation of discrete realms for politics and economics – with 'economic' globalisation and 'economic' roles – allows IPE scholars to avoid contemplation of the political dynamics of global social change. The discussion of transformative energies in civil society is effectively closed off, or even considered to be 'outside' the discipline, residing in sociology. For the orthodox writers 'plus ça change, plus c'est la même chose', the more world politics appears to change, the more it remains static. While they can conceive of the structural economic environment for the state as transforming, this can only be a function of state power.

In the orthodox framework the purpose of IPE knowledge is to explain the maintenance and loss of order in an international system of states. The expertise of the scholar, so the orthodoxy has it, must be employed objectively in the study of states and markets as unitary entities. There is an overarching impression that the scholars in the orthodox IPE school position themselves as passive observers of the states and markets that they study. It is this claim to objectivity and rationality that has been central to the objections of scholars who consider themselves to be 'doing' 'new' IPE.

New perspectives in IPE

The so-called 'new IPE' does not represent a cohesive body of scholarship, or even a clearly defined research agenda. The loose grouping of scholars do, however, share a common dissatisfaction with the ability of early 'orthodox' IPE to critically address the dynamics of global social transformation. Thus, Andrew Gamble noted that 'changes in the ideological, political and economic parameters of the world system have created the possibility of a new political economy' (1995: 516). For Palan, 'critical international or global political economy changes the order of the question; it asks how order and change came about' (2000: 17). While the new IPE scholars take different issues and subjects to be the focus of their research, employing a range of theories and methods, they concur that traditional IR and orthodox IPE are epistemo-logically and ontologically ill-equipped to deal with contemporary global social change. From this standpoint the essence of a 'new IPE' lies in a reaction against the positivist epistemology and ontological separation of the 'political' and 'economic' that is characteristic of the orthodox IPE paradigms.

There have been a number of statements of the 'essence' of the new IPE agenda (Murphy and Tooze, 1991; Amin *et al.*, 1994), and certainly no reading of this terrain would be complete without consideration of Murphy and Tooze's thought provoking 'four steps beyond the orthodoxy' (1991: 26). However, for our purposes it is useful to summarise the central claims of the new IPE scholars.

First, the new IPE seeks to challenge the ontological centrality of the state and interstate relationships that has dominated much of IR and IPE inquiry. This challenge is brought through an ontological commitment to the study of society and social relations. Thus, for Strange IPE: 'Concerns the social, political and economic arrangements affecting the global systems of produc-tion, exchange and distribution and the mix of values reflected therein' (1988:

18). The focus of IPE inquiry becomes 'the basic values which human beings seek to provide through social organisation' (1988). In this way the duality of states-markets and politics-economics is challenged through an understanding of these categories as ways of organising human society or, indeed, ways of thinking about social organisation. The claims to objectivity and rationality made by orthodox scholars are also challenged by a belief in the 'inter-subjective making of reality' (Cox, 1995: 34), thus rendering it neither possible nor desirable that we separate the categories that bring to IPE inquiry from the experiences we have of living in the GPE. This brings me to the second central claim made by the new IPE scholars – that knowledge is historically 'made' in the context of social power relations.

For orthodox IPE scholars, as I have argued, it is important that IPE generates reliable and scientific knowledge that is 'testable against external evidence' (Krasner, 1996: 108). The new IPE rejects this positivist epistemology in favour of a historicism that embodies 'a willingness to investigate and try to explain the contingent historical social construction of agents or actors, which, at other times, may be treated as axiomatic in explanations in terms of rational choice' (Murphy and Tooze, 1991: 28). The focus of IPE questions thus shifts from the explanation of the rise and demise of particular states, to a historically sensitive understanding of why particular agents and structures may be represented as such. Robert Cox's oft-cited 'theory is always *for* someone and *for* some purpose' (1996: 87), and Susan Strange's compelling call that we ask 'Cui bono?, Who benefits?' (1988: 117), lead us to consider that orthodox IPE has tended to produce knowledge for certain purposes and for the benefit of particular groups. The new IPE, by contrast, claims to reflect critically on the production of knowledge about the world and on their role in that production. In a world described as globalising, new and critical IPE scholars would need also, then, to reflect on their own relationships to, and experiences of globalisation (see MacLean, 2000).

The third broad claim made by the new IPE scholars is that their IPE is a more inclusive and 'open' field of inquiry. Founded upon a rejection of the privileging of issues of trade and security by the orthodoxy, the claim is that a new IPE is better equipped to explore issues of, for example, technology, finance, production, knowledge, and geography (Amin *et al.*, 1994). Though it is clear that the new IPE agenda of study has not wholly rejected conventional issue hierarchies (Denemark and O'Brien, 1997), there is at least an overt awareness that issues of poverty, struggle and inequality are relatively invisible and need attention (Tooze and Murphy, 1996). Related to this third claim concerning the issue agenda of IPE study, is a fourth claim that raises the question of the theoretical and conceptual 'toolbox' of IPE. Across the various contributions to a proclaimed new IPE there is a unifying thread of 'openness' – or, at least, a professed openness to diverse understandings and competing explanations:

> One small corner of social science is still open and unenclosed ...
> International political economy is still unfenced, still open to all comers.
> It ought, we believe, to remain so' (Strange, 1984: ix)

> Those who practice a new IPE share a culture of openness to different
> theories and empirical referents. (Murphy and Tooze, 1991: 30)

In each instance the unifying theme is 'openness' and the idea that IPE should
provide a vantage point for an interdisciplinary and heterodox set of understandings. Out of a problematising of the orthodox tendency to dichotomise
realms of social life for study, emerges the acknowledgement of the contested
nature of IPE knowledge and an 'open' attitude to the structures and agents of
social change.

The final claim identifiable in the new IPE literature is precisely its
potential to place social change at the heart of inquiry. Against the backdrop of
an IPE orthodoxy that explains change in the actions of sovereign states in the
context of international economic relations, the new IPE holds that social
change is perennial, contingent and dialectical in nature. While for orthodox
IPE scholars the purpose of IPE is to bring stability and maintain order, for the
scholars of a new IPE the task is to reveal and explore the contradictions,
conflicts and tensions that bring about social transformation (Cox, 1995; Gill,
1997; Scholte, 2000). Viewed in this way social change potentially becomes
characterised by contestation among agents, and understandings of such
contests may open up spaces for alternative structures and practices.

Of course, to identify the claims of the new IPE scholars is not to say that
the potential represented by each claim has been fulfilled. Is the new IPE
successful in breaking open the linear relationship between politics and
economics conceived in orthodox IPE? How 'open' is the new IPE to diverse
issue areas and heterodox voices? Does it simply replace 'old' orthodoxies with
a new hierarchy of issues and questions? And what light do the different
strands of the new IPE shed upon the dynamics of contemporary global social
change? Having distilled the essence of a new IPE to its key elements, I will
now go on to explore three specific contributions to what we might term new
IPE scholarship: the work of Susan Strange, the use of Karl Polanyi's 'double
movement' by IPE scholars and the use of Antonio Gramsci's insights in IPE.
There are two caveats to be made here. First, these contributions do not in any
sense represent the full gamut of contributions to the new IPE; they are chosen
simply because they have become central to the contemporary study of
globalisation and because they have considerable bearing on the subject
matter of this book. Second, the three contributions identified are in many
senses interrelated and provide a common pool from which scholars draw.

Strange paths to IPE[2]

Susan Strange's unique brand of IPE has unquestionably shaped the concerns and outlook of the field, and will continue to do so. Strange's work does, however, serve to demonstrate that there is not such a clear and stark divide between the orthodox and new ways of 'doing IPE'. In many ways Strange's vast and rich body of work constitutes a 'bridge' between the intentions and assumptions of scholars such as Robert Keohane and Robert Gilpin, and the agenda of the new IPE that she so clearly embraced in the first volume of the *Review of International Political Economy* (1994). This bridge was shifting and contradictory but persisted throughout her work. On the one hand, Strange was direct in her criticisms of orthodox scholars, as in her plea to 'Wake up, Krasner, the world has changed':

> I would plead with my old friend to re-examine his realist assumptions about the units of analysis and the central problematic of international political economy. It becomes much more interesting to teach, to research and to write about when you drop the idea that states are the units of analysis and that war is the main problematic of the international system. (Strange, 1994: 218)

Here, as in many other places in her work, Strange distances herself from a mainstream IR and IPE that 'assume the maintenance of order to be the prime if not the only problématique of the study' (1988: 14). On the other hand, however, appreciative critics have, nonetheless, suggested that Strange is 'prevented from realising the full potential of her radical ontology' (Tooze, 2000a: 287), that she wastes the opportunity to 'challenge international relations theory at its very core' (Palan, 1999: 128) and that she 'closes the Pandora's box that she has opened' (May, 1996: 184). Indeed, there is even the suggestion that she herself invoked multiple forms of 'realism' so that her 'work is torn by internal tensions' (Guzzini, 2000: 217). Strange's path to IPE is highly ambiguous, then. She must be credited with much of the impetus for the new IPE, and yet she closes off some of the avenues and approaches that are central to a genuinely critical ontology and epistemology.

Perhaps Strange's first order contribution to a new IPE is her challenge to the politics-economics dichotomy, achieved through the development of her ontology of structural power. Indeed, for Strange questions of power represent the very essence of IPE: 'it is impossible to study international political economy without giving close attention to the role of power in economic life' (1988: 23). IPE and power form a mutually constitutive relationship for Strange, it is not possible to study one without reference to the other. This is a considerable departure from the orthodox representation of power as the expression of state interests, a conception referred to by Strange as 'relational power' and criticised for its 'distinction between economic power and political power' (1988: 24-25). The opposition and distinction between political and economic power is apparently not a tenable one for Strange. The concept of structural power is her tool for breaking up the distinction: 'Structural power is the power to shape and determine the structures of the global political economy within which other states, their political institutions, their economic enterprises and (not least) their scientists and other professional people have to operate' (1988: 25).

So, for Strange, power in the global political economy does not rest with single unitary states, but is exercised by a number of public and private authorities through the structures of finance, security, production and knowledge.[3] Strange opens up a number of possibilities with her identified dimensions of structural power. She makes it possible for sources of agency to be made more visible in IPE inquiry, and for this agency to be 'non-state' in nature, exemplified by her probing of the role of MNCs in the production structure (Stopford and Strange, 1991). She opens up the possibility for markets to be politicised in the sense of their 'making' by states and societies, for example her work on global financial markets (1997a; 1998a). Simultaneously, she raises the question of states becoming 'marketised', as in her work on the declining authority of the state (1995; 1996). It is clear that for Strange IPE is not a rational, unemotional or objective field of inquiry, and that her subject matter is intrinsically human and social.

In identifying the dimensions of structural power beyond the conventional confines of security and trade (for Strange trade is a 'secondary power structure'), Strange also opens the door on a more heterodox IPE. In terms of issue areas, though she does not fully explore these in her own work, Strange extends our conventional notions of the realm of the 'political' in IPE with discussion of the activities of the mafia, consultants and accountants (1996), the roles of telecommunications and technology policy (1988) and environment and the biosphere (1994). In line with this apparent openness to issues in IPE, Strange consistently invoked the need for IPE scholars to open up to the insights of business scholars, economic historians, geographers and sociologists (1996: xv; 1994: 218; 1988: 15). Her remonstrations that IPE scholars should 'theorise from what they know' led her to argue that they should engage with those who 'know about' other realms of global social change. For Strange knowledge is essentially 'information', a commodity or resource that is possessed and used (May, 1996), leading her to invoke heterodoxy but to pursue this in an empiricist fashion, as 'data gathering'.

Finally, Strange's work was influential in focusing IPE on the dynamics of global social change. Her analysis of the changing shape of the state-market dialectic led her to pose the question 'who or what is responsible for change?', and to answer 'technology, markets and politics' (1996: 185). There is a clear attempt to address the issue of how and why change takes place in the GPE, and to extend the agency of change beyond unitary nation-states. Nor does Strange shy away from the normative implications of global change. For her the risk and uncertainty of global transformation is unequally produced, distributed and mitigated (1983; 1998b).

Despite the groundbreaking nature of Strange's work, there are a number of constraints imposed by her approach that throw into question the promise of an open and 'unenclosed' field and place obstacles in the path of a new IPE as it is outlined by Craig Murphy and Roger Tooze, and as I conceive of it. The first problem concerns Strange's reinscription of the very dichotomy between politics and economics that she seeks to transcend. A number of passages illustrate this point:

> Economics is about the use of scarce resources for unlimited wants ... Politics, though, is about providing public order and public goods. (Strange, 1988: 14)

> The impersonal forces of world markets ... are now more powerful than the states to whom ultimate political authority over society and economy is supposed to belong. (Strange, 1996: 4)

The orthodox distinction between politics and economics is redrawn here. Politics is conceived in narrow terms as authority exercised in the provision of order and stability, and economics as the allocation of resources by private authorities. We begin to see how Strange might be categorised as 'hyperglobalist' (Held *et al.*, 1999) or as holding a 'process-centred' view of globalisation. Her later work strongly asserts the triumph of liberal economics over state authority (politics as she sees it) and, fundamentally fails to 'reintegrate politics and economics' (Tooze, 2000b: 176).

Strange's conception of the nature of the political falls short of allowing us to conceive of everyday practices as political acts in the global political economy. Her work, in a sense 'adds agents' to IPE inquiry but without reflecting upon how we arrive at these agents or 'whom' they represent. We are urged, for example, to consider markets and technologies alongside states as agents of change (see Figure 2.1). In this 'flow diagram' representation of global social change technology is depicted separately and alongside states and markets, begging the question of how technology can be conceived as a realm that is separate and comparable to these realms. The model of social change represented by the flow diagram in Strange's (1991) analysis identifies agents acting through structures to produce 'outcomes'. The representation of social change is unilinear and deterministic, with contingency only arising out of different combinations of actors and structures that may affect the outcomes. The people, workers, firms and social groups inside the markets, states and technologies are simply invisible in this representation.

Of the four structures that are central to Strange's conception of global social change, it is the knowledge structure that has been most widely critiqued (Tooze, 2000a, 2000b; Palan, 1999; May, 1996; Cox, 1992a). Strange's conception of knowledge, as a resource of information that can be wielded or exercised, allows her to position the knowledge structure alongside the structures of production, security and finance. Knowledge, in this sense is an instrument in the global political economy just as a particular production

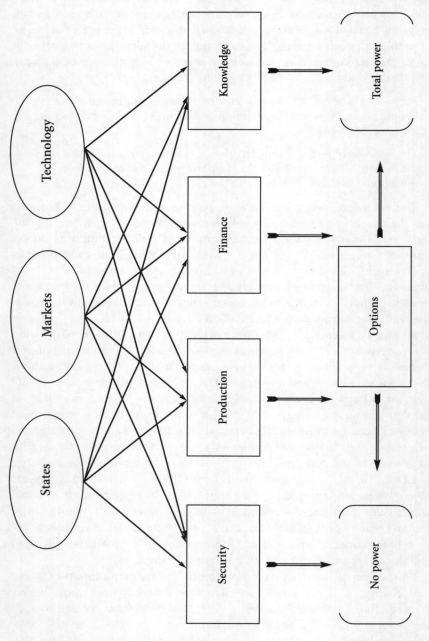

Figure 2.1 Susan Strange's 'determinants of choice' (Source: Strange, 1991).

structure may be an instrument, for example of US hegemony (Rupert, 1995). If Strange had embraced the full implications of a new IPE ontology then the knowledge structure would have to surround and suffuse the agents and structures she depicts. If knowledge is also to imply 'intersubjective meanings' and frameworks of thought, then surely the states, markets, technology and structures identified by Strange would have, to some extent, to be produced and reproduced by our frameworks of thought. So, for example, dominant ideas about how society should be organised at a given historical conjuncture will both inform and reflect the interactions of structures and agents. Agents are reflexive; they have the capacity to reflect upon, challenge or reproduce the structures that they confront. Tooze finds it 'ironic that it is precisely her view of knowledge and ideology' that precludes Strange from achieving a reflectivist mode of thought in IPE (2000a: 176). If there is a principal missing element in the Strange path to IPE it is the failure to adequately explore the relationship between power and knowledge, two concepts that she para-doxically inscribed deeply in the collective IPE common sense.

Polanyian insights and the new IPE

As the new IPE has sought to bring critical insights to the study of global social change, a number of scholars have drawn upon the work of economic histor-ian Karl Polanyi.[4] The dominance of linear and deterministic understandings of the relationship between politics and economics has led some scholars to search for a society-centred theory from which to develop their critique:

> The inclusion of civil society together with a strong historical dimension constitute important contributions by Polanyi to IPE. In spite of its ambition to integrate the "political" and the "economic", current IPE gives only a partial view of societal change. We can perhaps define a New International Political Economy as attempts to go beyond the state-market contradiction. (Hettne, 1995: 5)

We can read the appropriation of Polanyi's writings by the new IPE as a reopening of the 'Pandora's box' that is closed by Strange. Polanyi's work appears to offer a route into an understanding of the historical and political contingency of market expansion and social transformation. From Polanyi's rich and diverse writings, contemporary IPE has drawn out two central themes which it finds useful in the study of contemporary global social change: the embeddedness of economy in society and the 'counter movement'. If we are to use Polanyi's insights to move us closer to the contestation of global social change, then it is important to consider the context and problematics of IPE's retrieval of his thought.

The central question of Polanyi's *The Great Transformation* was to explore the historical transformation of nineteenth-century capitalism, and to explain the social effects of an imposed 'self-regulating' market economy:

> Man's economy, as a rule, is submerged in his social relationships ...
> Neither the process of production nor that of distribution is linked to
> specific economic interests attached to the possession of goods; but every
> single step in that process is geared to a number of social interests which
> eventually ensure that the required step be taken. These interests will be
> very different in a small hunting or fishing community from those in a
> vast despotic society, but in either case the economic system will be run
> on noneconomic motives. (1957: 46)

The primacy of society and social relationships in Polanyi's analysis is
evident here. The market forces of the economy cannot, in Polanyian terms, be
understood separately from the society in which they are situated, so that 'the
economic order is merely a function of the social, in which it is contained'
(1957: 71). Thus, for Polanyi a market is a politically and socially constituted
entity, made in particular ways in defined historical places and times. He
presents a powerful critique of the economic determinism that says that
societies are shaped by the actions of rational economic man, branding this an
'economistic fallacy' (1957: 111–129). A laissez-faire market order is 'nothing
natural' and requires a constant process of reproduction and reinforcement,
not least by the actions of the state (1957: 139). Viewed in this way politics and
economics become mutually constitutive within a context of social relations.
The creation of markets in land, labour and capital, for example, are held to
represent 'fictitious commodities' (1957: 68) that cannot be traded without
agitating and disrupting the human and social fabric. The commodification of
labour represents for Polanyi the central contradiction of market society, both
the 'core' and the 'core weakness' of its organisation (Block and Somers, 1984:
57). As Polanyi has it:

> To argue that social legislation, factory laws, unemployment insurance,
> and, above all, trade unions have not interfered with the mobility of
> labour and the flexibility of wages, as is sometimes done, is to imply that
> those institutions have entirely failed in their purpose, which was exactly
> that of interfering with the laws of supply and demand in respect to
> human labor, and removing it from the orbit of the market. (Polanyi,
> 1957: 177)

Markets for labour do not occur as natural or self-regulating realities.
Their uneasy relationship with the human needs and practices of daily life is
mitigated through sets of social institutions that must be constantly produced
and reproduced if the contradictions are to be masked. Polanyi is not, however, advocating the taming of capitalism through the protective layer of social
institutions or, as Hannes Lacher puts it he should not be regarded as a
'prophet of interventionist welfare capitalism' (1999: 314). At the heart of
Polanyi's reading of industrialisation is the identification of an intractable
contradiction between the social and human activities of 'life itself' (1957: 72),
and the dictates of the market:

The idea of a self-adjusting market implied a stark utopia. Such an institution could not exist for any length of time without annihilating the human and natural substance of society; it would have physically destroyed man and transformed his surroundings into a wilderness. Inevitably, society took measures to protect itself, but whatever measures it took impaired the self-regulation of the market, disorganized industrial life, and thus endangered society in yet another way. (1957: 3)

Polanyi does not offer the oft-cited 'counter-movement' as a solution or 'source of resistance' to the ravages of the market economy. Rather, he indicates that the inherent tensions and agitations of market society demand continuous action and intervention to run interference between economy and society. Yet, this interference in itself is unsustainable since it disrupts the assumptions on which a market is based. The logics of industrial capitalism and human life cannot be reconciled in this reading; they are inherently provocative and contested. This conception of contradiction, provocation and ambiguity, as Lacher (1999) points out, has been rendered invisible and obscure by most appeals to the 'counter-movement' in the new IPE texts.

New IPE scholars have appropriated the concepts of 'embeddedness' and the 'counter-movement' in a number of ways. What we might broadly consider to be an institutionalist strand of thought has drawn on the concept of embeddedness to counter the economic determinism of the globalisation thesis. In this reading global economic forces are re-embedded in nation-states (see Hollingsworth and Boyer, 1997; Hollingsworth, 1998) and MNCs are embedded in national systems of production (see Grabher, 1993; Sally, 1994; Zysman, 1996). The relationship between Polanyian political economy, historical sociology and comparative institutionalism is, thus, an intimate one.[5] The new IPE has embraced this appropriation of Polanyian analysis on the grounds that it contextualises global social change, apparently politicising through attention to the social institutions that may 'redirect' global forces. However, the neo-Polanyian use of embeddedness has imposed a stasis that is not evident in Polanyi's work. His sense of agitation and tensions within the economy-society relation is absent from much of the neo-institutionalist strand of the new IPE. In its place we get the image of the forces of globalisation being filtered through the distinctive social institutions of nation-states. As Block and Somers have it, 'global opportunity structures shape what is possible for particular governments', while a 'national opportunity structure' shapes 'what is possible' for societies (1984: 74). The dichotomies of economics/politics, exogenous-global/endogenous-national, are thus reinscribed and globalisation is presented as a 'project' directed through national institutions.

It is Polanyi's concept of a 'counter movement' that has captured the attention of a large swathe of new IPE scholars. In a supposed era of globalisation there is considerable interest in a theory that potentially says 'societies will seek to protect themselves' from the 'disembedding' of economics from the social realm (Bernard, 1997: 79). The idea that there may be space and opportunity for resistance to globalisation or the possibility to shape global futures is a seductive one, and has led scholars to identify Polanyi as a conceptual kindred spirit (Mittelman, 2000: 8; Rice and Prince, 2000: 171). Polanyi's society-centred political economy does undoubtedly open up the possibility for IPE theorists to discuss the responses of civil society groups and new social movements to the vacillations of globalisation. However, it is important to recognise that this is not the 'counter-movement' envisaged by Polanyi, who leaves the question of social order wide open. Polanyi's work does not conceive of an emancipatory space for the contestation of liberal logics and the negotiation of alternative futures (though, of course, this does not preclude others from reading him this way). What should not be forgotten is that Polanyi demands that we direct our attention to the 'continuing contradictions between society and the market' (Lacher, 1999: 323).

The appropriation of Polanyi's notion of a 'counter-movement' is not sufficient in itself to further a new and critical IPE that can account for contingency in global social change. Indeed, it is not a 'solution' or 'strategy' that is implied by Polanyi, but rather presents IPE with an opportunity to further politicise and historicise its knowledge. In the terms of this book, Polanyi's work is a constant reminder that markets for labour are created and reproduced over time, that they are contradictory and in tension with the lives of the people that they embody and that social change is made and contested in ways that are contradictory and contingent. A critical and historicist[6] reading of Polanyi demands that we disrupt the simple notion that global forces have disembedding effects on societies, to reveal the tensions that pervade the economy-society relation and the multiple interpretations and experiences that individuals and social groups may have of the perceived disembedding.

Gramscian insights and the new IPE

> For Gramsci, it is the ensemble of social relations configured by social
> structures which is the basic unit of analysis, rather than individual agents,
> be they consumers, firms, states or interest groups. (Gill, 1993: 25)

For those IR and IPE scholars who have interpreted Gramsci's work for con-temporary problematics,[7] the first order questions are concerned with society and social transformation. In the Gramscian ontology, social relations and social structures are the primary elements to be considered, for they alone constitute the limits of the potential space for change to take place. Of course, while for Gramsci the central terrain of social organisation was the national social formation, for his IPE interpreters the terrain may be transnational or global (Germain and Kenny, 1998). Gramsci's work has been viewed by new IPE scholars as offering the potential to critique linear and determinstic accounts of social change via a critical focus on the capacity of political agents to communicate with, mobilise and induce change in society. Social change thus derives its shape and meaning as it is played out by agents acting within and through social structures. In this way 'reality' becomes a 'product of the application of human will to the society of things' (Gramsci, 1971: 171). The intersubjective realms of ideas, knowledge, theory and social institutions thus become central to processes of social transformation (Gill, 1993: 23), and may engender or constrain social contestation, conflict and dissent (Femia, 1981: 35; Rupert, 1995: 13).

For the neo-Gramscian scholars, the study of change in IPE has tended to focus on the reciprocal relationships between forms of state, social forces and world orders (Cox, 1981). Drawing on Gramsci's notion of a historical bloc (blocco storico), social transformation is viewed as complex, contradictory and multi-faceted. Murphy (1994) interprets Gramsci's historical bloc as an apparently unified social order that may be compared, using an architectural metaphor, to a block of flats and shops that represent an underlying order. When a historical bloc is stable and hegemony is built on coercion and consent, life goes on 'as it should' (Murphy, 1994: 20). But when the bloc is in crisis and one of its facades begins to crumble there is space for the structures to be 'rebuilt or reclaimed' (1994: 29). Murphy's interpretation of Gramsci serves to problematise representations of social institutions as given or static entities. The 'project' of global restructuring thus becomes part of a wider fabric of social power relations that may be cut or hewn in new forms, but not without tension or contest:

> The active politician is a creator, an initiator; but he neither creates from nothing nor does he move in the turbid void of his own desires and dreams … What 'ought to be' is therefore concrete; indeed it is the only realistic and historicist interpretation of reality, it alone is history in the making and philosophy in the making, it alone is politics. (Gramsci, 1971: 172)

The contests and bargains over what 'ought to be', in the sense of the shape of a historical bloc or how society should be organised or reorganised are, thus, for Gramsci and his IPE interpreters, the essence of politics. For a study such as this, seeking to reveal the contests and struggles that surround and suffuse the restructuring of work, the Gramsci-derived insights open up the possibility of a conception of contestation in social change. In our terms of reference the social forces that intersect workplace, state-society and world order become key sources of contingency in social transformation (Cox, 1987; Harrod, 1987). Production and work are conceived in a broad sense, with production representing 'life, for the dispensation of energy (work) which results in life (product)' (Harrod, 1997a: 109). IPE studies have drawn upon Cox's and Harrod's theses of power and production to demonstrate the production and reproduction of webs of social power relations over time. As Rupert has it, attention is directed to the 'processes through which power has been produced' and the 'conflicting social power relations which at once underlie and make possible that production, and which also problematise its long-term reproduction' (1995: 1). Gill's account of the elite that constitutes a disciplinary set of neo-liberal social forces, similarly emphasises the web of power relations binding international capital, accountants, consultants, large firms and workers in supply chains (1995: 400). There would seem to be potential here to explore the ongoing social contests that paradoxically underpin a particular historical bloc, yet also raise the contradictions that are likely to call it into question.

As with all strands of IPE inquiry, the neo-Gramscian 'school' cannot be uncritically applied to studies of global social change. While they open up critical avenues of inquiry and seek to 'politicise' accounts of globalisation, they do this in a particular way that leaves other avenues opaque and uncharted. A central problem with the uncritical adoption of Gramscian insights is the sustained separation of an apparently coherent 'global elite' from potential, and apparently less coherent 'local resistors': 'The writings of open Marxism present political power as a thing formed outside social formations, in the rarefied atmosphere of the world economy ... imposing closure from the start on active politics in the world economy, relegating struggles to the sphere of national social formations' (Drainville, 1994: 120–121). The image is one of a transnationally 'hyperliberal thinking' organised elite directing a top-down project, that constrains nationally located social groups who may 'resist'. The 'global' is thus reinscribed as a realm of expertise, technical knowledge and strategy, while the 'local' is a peripheral space of everyday social relationships. Given that I seek to disrupt the reflex of representing societies as 'responding to' the imperatives of globalisation, I suggest that it is just a short step from 'responding' to 'resisting'. In both formulations, societies and social groups are separated from, and opposed to, some ethereal process or project of globalisation. Power is 'wielded' in both instances, either by the promoters of the project, or by the resistors in their 'anti-globalisation' strategies.[8]

Just as social change is conceived by the neo-Gramscians in terms of social forces within a historical bloc, so it is also presented in 'periods' of transition, from one set of structures to the crisis, and then to the rebuilding. The dichotomies of the IPE orthodoxy are replaced by a series of new dichotomies that characterise social change in terms of 'order/disorder', 'Westphalian/post-Westphalian',[9] 'hegemony/post-hegemony'[10] and 'starting-point/end point'.[11] The assumption that restructuring and social change takes place in a crisis-ridden interstice between two stable orders raises significant questions. Are we to distinguish strategic formal restructuring programmes from the more general and continuous rhythms of social change? The breaking up of social change into defined periods serves to further marginalise certain issues in IPE inquiry. The realms of finance, production and technology are privileged above 'everyday' realms of work and social practice since the latter can only change at the margins or in the gaps in the historic bloc.

The neo-Gramscian frameworks offer one route into the problematising of transformations in workplace, state-society and world order. However, some of the doors that have been closed by these scholars can be pushed further ajar. There is a particular need to identify ways to break open the opposition of 'perpetrators' and 'resistors' of globalisation. I am reminded of a report from the Seattle protests that asked 'Did the protester who was filmed kicking lumps off the Nike sign while wearing Nike shoes see the irony?' (Elliott, 1999). In this allegory the neo-liberal elite and the actions of the protester are closely interwoven. In our everyday practices we rarely consciously adopt a reinforcing or challenging role in relation to the shape of social change. Further, and in order to challenge the periodisation of global social change, we need to be able to contemplate how programmes of restructuring communicated by international organisations, governments or corporate actors intersect with individual and collective social understandings and practices. Such a focus can begin to challenge the notion that power is wielded in the global realm and 'received' or resisted in the local.

An international political economy of social practice

It is clear from the above analysis that the new IPE has sought to expose and transcend the bounded terrain of orthodox IR and IPE, exploring alternative political terrain through firms, institutions, financial centres, technology, and to a lesser extent labour and work. Susan Strange's questions of the nature and sources of power, the neo-Polanyian highlighting of the contradictions of market society and the neo-Gramscian emphasis on social forces within and across states and world orders – taken together they lead us to reflect upon global social change in particular ways. Global social change potentially becomes a contested, contingent and politicised process that is expressed, first and foremost, through everyday social practices. However, the boundaries of IPE knowledge that have been agitated by the new IPE do leave us short of what Sinclair has termed an 'IPE of the commonplace' (1999: 164). The new IPE has tended to focus predominantly on the politics 'at the top', residing in the actions and interests of global elite groups and organisations. Where everyday modes of political action and expression are discussed, these have been located in a 'local' or 'national' sphere. Yet, it is in the everyday aspects of people's lives that global social change is interpreted and experienced. It is in the realms of everyday thought and practice that competing interests confront one another, and where the contradictions and tensions of social transformation are expressed. Indeed, we might say that the 'everyday' realm is one where the boundaries of national/transnational, local/global, economics/politics and states/markets are both constituted and confounded.

In order to bring IPE close to the social practices that characterise our everyday lives, three further steps can be taken. The first is a response to the call for a 'historicised IPE' (Amin and Palan, 1996; Amoore *et al.*, 2000), that is to say a representation of social change, and all knowledge of social change, as *historically contingent*. The second is a challenge to the prevailing IPE conception of *power* as something that is 'held' or 'wielded' by particular elite agents in a global sphere. The final step proposed here is a conception of *everyday social practices* as a key terrain of politics and, in particular, as the central spaces in which global restructuring is played out and contested.

Historicity and contingency

I began this chapter by reference to Cox's claim that IPE *is* critical theory by virtue of its standing apart from structures in order to explore their historical constitution and transformation. What does it mean to consider social structures and their transformation to be 'historically constituted'? And is this a sufficient step towards a new IPE that is sensitive to historicity and contingency?[12] Certainly the new IPE has made claims to an epistemological self-awareness that infers that all IPE knowledge is historically constituted. Yet, the historical turn in IPE has been, in the main, rather limited. The work of the historical sociologists (see Hobson, 1997; Skocpol, 1984), and others who advocate a 'historicised IPE' (Amin and Palan, 1996), can be said to add history simply as an adjunct to the study of structure and agency. That is to say, they consider the historical context of the agency of human beings through a sensitivity to their role in the 'building' of institutions, and the constraining effect of these institutions on their lives. Their concern is thus with what Mills calls 'historical push and shove', and Amin and Palan term the 'fixity and flow of social evolution' (1996: 211).

Such invocations to 'consider history' fall some way short of allowing us to consider global social change as substantially constituted and contested through the consciousness, reflections and experiences of people. For this we require a historical mode of inquiry, an approach that views social structures and institutions as 'the historically apprehended knowledge of the particular circumstances of the human condition' (Amoore *et al.*, 2000: 56). Viewed from a historicist vantage point, Strange's knowledge structure is recast as a domain that suffuses all other structures, thought and action. The configurations of states-markets, economics-politics, domestic-international and structure-agency are understood through the dimension of human knowledge of these relationships:

> The real is not "out there" and thought within the quiet lecture theatre of our heads, "inside here". Thought and being inhabit a single space, which space is ourselves. Even as we think we also hunger and hate, we sicken or we love, and consciousness is intermixed with being; even as we contemplate the "real" we experience our own palpable reality. (Thompson, 1978: 211)

We are thus reminded of the nature of IPE as webs of interrelationships of which reflective human beings form the key constituent elements, and within which we (and the subjects of our research) act, interact, experience and understand. From an extensive body of work that we may broadly term 'critical history',[13] I draw out the themes that offer insights to the furthering of an IPE of social practice.

First, a historical mode of thought directs attention to the act of reflection that connects agents with frameworks of thought and action (Iggers, 1995: 131). Agents and structures do not simply push and pull one another through periods of social change, rather they are mutually constituted through acts of reflection, what Collingwood terms 'thinking about thinking' (1946: 307). Others, from sociological perspectives, have developed the concept of 'reflexive modernisation' to refer to the 'changing relationship between social structures and social agents' (Beck, 1992: 2; see also Giddens, 1990). Such readings of history share a view of human beings as participants in the making of social transformations. As Collingwood has it 'thought is not mere immediate experience but always reflection or self-knowledge, the knowledge of oneself as living in these activities' (1946: 297). The significant contribution that this mode of knowledge can make to the new IPE is that it grounds global social change in the reflective self-understandings that people have both of themselves and their circumstances and surroundings. Global social change does not simply 'happen to' people, it is experienced, interpreted and lived. The thoughts and actions of those living in the production structure, for example, become at least as central to the reproduction or undermining of that structure as the abstract entities of states, firms and technologies are currently assumed to be.

Second, a historical mode of thought can shed light upon the role of the historian, researcher or IPE scholar in the constitution of knowledge about 'our world'. Carr reminds us that the historian is also a participant in the process of change she or he observes and documents: 'The historian, then, is an individual human being. Like other individuals, he (*sic*) is also a social phenomenon, both the product and the conscious or unconscious spokesman of the society too which he belongs; it is in this capacity that he approaches the facts of the historical past' (Carr, 1961: 35). Carr thus reminds us that as we observe, write or teach about society, we also exist within, interpret and experience its dynamics. The interpretative choices of historians, influenced by their experiences, their 'history', will be reflected in the issues and subjects that are selected for documentation and theorisation. In an era that is persistently labelled 'global' it is particularly significant that we reflect on the experiences and perceptions that we bring to inquiry. It becomes possible to account for globalisation as one particular representation of global social change, and one that can be interpreted and expressed in numerous and contingent ways.

Finally, attention to the historicity of knowledge reveals the interpretative nature of all inquiry. History, for Collingwood is the 'science of res gestae, the attempt to answer questions about human actions done in the past' (1946: 9). Carr's (1961) retrieval of Collingwood's ideas captures the 'philosophy of history' as concerned with the interrelationships between the past and contemporary thought about the past. For him, history is given shape and meaning by 'seeing the past through the eyes of the present and in the light of its problems' (1961: 21). Human activity is made intelligible through acts of reflection that re-enact possible past social meanings on a stage that is lit by our contemporary experiences and understandings of social change. From this perspective, understandings, interpretations and experiences of global social change are as 'real' in concrete historical terms, as the technological and economic flows that so many IPE theorists seek to account for.

In terms of a wider conception of global social change, a historicised reading makes visible the open-ended and contingent nature of the restructuring of social practices. In the realm of work these insights are particularly significant. Following the historical mode of thought employed by E. P. Thompson (1978; 1980), we are led to view the material restructuring of the production process as intimately bound up with the everyday histories of the workplace and understandings of workplace realities. Of course, this does not mean that transformation is impeded (Femia, 1981). Rather, that any attempt to construct a 'project' of the flexibilisation of work does not simply confront the material factors of the production process, but also the understandings and shared frameworks of thought between the people that make this process. A project of restructuring is one expression of how change should be ordered, but it is not the only one and it makes sense only when played out through social practices, where it may mutate and take on a very different or unintended form. In this sense, what is often considered to be 'history from below' is not in any meaningful sense separate from a global imperative 'from above', since it is in daily histories that global imperatives become contested and reorganised so as to be understood.

Power and agency

IPE, as I have argued, has generally failed to recognise the agency of non-elite groupings of people in its understandings of global social change. It has had a particular blind spot with regard to workers and their relationship to the power relations that suffuse processes of change. Where labour and work do feature in the new IPE this has predominantly been in terms of their assumed 'powerlessness' in the face of a global restructuring 'project' that is executed by the 'powerful' neo-liberal elites. A key source of the invisibility of work and workers in IPE lies in the conception of power that dominates inquiry. Power is predominantly considered to be a commodity or resource that is exercised by particular agents over the lives of others. Thus, for much of the IR and IPE literature 'the capacity to wield power as a resource over other agents is an important proviso of agency' (Campbell, 1996: 11). Agency is in itself defined in terms of the ability to hold and apply power, and for those considered 'powerless' agency is denied and subjects are considered of peripheral importance to the field of study. Such conceptions of agency, found particularly in neo-Gramscian conceptions, are exacerbated by the identification of 'global' and 'local' levels of agency, where the global becomes the source of restructuring strategies, and the local has agency only insofar as it responds or resists through counter-strategies of its own. Technologies are, for example, represented as having agency in a global sphere that is simply 'received' 'on the ground'. Where IPE has sought to reflect on the agency of non-elite groups these are also assumed to be 'on the ground', such as in the responses of labour groups to the global strategies of firms.

An IPE of social practice must reinvigorate the 'openness' that is promised by the new IPE to reflect upon alternative conceptions of power expressed in philosophical and critical sociological writings. In the first instance power as an entity that is held, plotted or wielded is problematised. Where power in IPE is most commonly represented as structural capabilities that constrain and limit the actions of others, it becomes more fluid in the writings of Michel Foucault: 'Power is not an institution, and not a structure; neither is it a certain strength we are endowed with; it is the name that one attributes to a complex strategical relationship in a particular society' (1980a: 93).

Power thus becomes a network or matrix of forces that operates through society and social relationships. In this way power is not simply a static matter possessed by some individuals to limit others, but is practised in a more mobile, subtle and intricate way. Power moves, circulates and shifts (Bleiker, 2000: 134); it is 'elaborated, transformed, organised' (Foucault, 1982: 224). It is thus not possible simply to reduce power to a named group, individual, institutions or 'actor', as many of those seeking to identify the architects of globalisation would wish to do. Agents and institutions are undoubtedly central to the exercise of power, but they do not personify the source of power itself. Thus, states, firms and international corporations, for example, may through their actions define a field of possible future actions, but they do this as part of a wider web of power relations. In this sense 'one must analyse institutions from the standpoint of power relations, rather than vice versa' (Foucault, 1982: 222). Viewed in this way an apparent 'project' of the flexibilisation of work is not controlled or exerted in any simple linear sense. The firm, the policy agenda, the industrial relations institutions, become forums for webs of power-knowledge relations that actually extend the 'limits' of the institution.

The conception of power and knowledge in a correlative, and not a causal relationship (Dreyfus and Rabinow, 1982: 203), raises significant questions for Strange's (1988) distinction of the production and knowledge structures.[14] If we see power and knowledge as 'tangled up in the knot of a "not without"', (Keenan, 1997), then their separation as a resource (power) versus a means of power (production and knowledge) is problematised. In our terms, if we seek to explore the knowledge and techniques that have defined and managed the flexibility discourse, then we cannot observe these concretely without analysis of the webs of power relations that suffuse the restructuring of work (and vice versa). This brings us to the question of levels of analysis and 'how' and 'where' such power relations should be studied. A sustained separation of an 'outer world' of elite world politics from an 'inner world' of the localised politics of struggle obscures the 'transgression of these fine lines' (Walker, 1994: 700). A number of studies have identified 'transversal struggles'[15] or 'infrapolitics' as the immediate struggles that characterise 'globalised life' (Campbell, 1996: 24; Bleiker, 2000: 130; Scott, 1990: 183). Viewed in this way 'people criticise instances of power which are the closest to them ... They do not look for the chief enemy, but for the immediate enemy' (Foucault, 1982: 211). In our terms, whilst government policy statements, corporate strategies and indeed the 'anti-globalisation' groups, may communicate globalisation as the 'chief enemy', their actions within networks of power focus on their immediate environs, effectively demonstrating the illusory separateness of an exogenous global level.

A conception of power as a network or chain of relations thus takes the politics of global social change out of the sole domain of elite agents. Of course, the strategies and actions of bankers, policymakers and corporate managers are significant in global social change, but they cannot be adequately analysed in the absence of the social power relations of which they are part. In this sense 'contesting globalisation' is not primarily about the outlining of a 'counter-hegemonic' project to confront an identifiable neo-liberal restructuring agenda. Rather, it is about exploring the web of power relations that apparently under-pin the 'project', revealing the contradictions and tensions that are manifested through everyday social practices.

Social practice, social space and the 'everyday'

Amidst the clamour of voices seeking to understand globalisation, a small group of scholars has drawn attention to the emerging social relations of global-isation and the structured social practices that make these possible (Sklair, 1991; Germain, 2000; Jones, 2000). However, the existing work that comprises this embryonic perspective has focused almost exclusively upon the social practices of elite groups, thereby reinforcing the idea of a global project, albeit one that has become entangled with social relations. By contrast, the perspec-tive advanced here views global social change as experienced, given meaning, reinforced and/or challenged in the everyday structured social practices of individuals and groups, such that globalisation is marked by contestation over the reality and representation of social change. Such a perspective rests upon a conception of 'everydayness' and 'everyday life' that does not locate itself primarily in supposed 'ground level' activity or the 'local' dynamics of global change. Rather, the everyday is conceived as a 'common denominator of activities, locus and milieu of human functions ... the uniform aspect of the major sectors of social life: work, family, private life, leisure' (Lefebvre, 1987: 10, see also Lefebvre, 1991a). The everyday is thus a 'contested place' (Davies and Niemann, 2000: 3), a realm of tensions and contradictions, where the banale and routine meet the potential for social transformation:

> The quotidian is on the one hand the realm of routine, repetition, reiter-
> ation: the space/time where constraints and boredom are produced ...
> Even at its most degraded, however, the everyday harbors the possibility
> of its own transformation; it gives rise to desires which cannot be
> satisfied within a weekly cycle of production/consumption. The Political
> is hidden in the everyday, exactly where it is most obvious: in the
> contradictions of lived experience, in the most banal and repetitive
> gestures of everyday life – the commute, the errand, the appointment.
> (Kaplan and Ross, 1987: 3)

It is in the realm of the everyday that our understandings, experiences and meanings of globalisation are made. To locate the political, as many IPE scholars do, narrowly in the actions of states, firms, organisations or social movements, is to miss this 'commonplace world of everyday experience', where conflicts and contests take place, and 'change is most widely felt' (Sinclair, 1999: 158). Indeed, far from underestimating or denying the emergence of globalised ways of life, a focus on the everyday reveals 'the concrete produc-tion of internationalised social relations in the daily practices of workers, families or consumers' (Davies and Niemann, 2000: 6). The everyday sphere thus challenges the mode of thought that separates a 'global' sphere of legitimate IPE inquiry from a 'local' sphere of empirical evidence to support claims to globalisation, 'constructing global capitalism as a more abstract system than it really is' (Thrift, 1995: 21). The idea that globalisation is 'bigger than us' and, therefore that social change is always a result of external forces, is thrown into question. As Bruno Latour depicts it: 'A giant in a story is not a bigger character than a dwarf, it just does different things. The same two metre-square print may represent a battlefield or an apple; no one will say that the first is bigger and more encompassing than the second' (Latour, 1988: 30).

IPE's claims to be concerned with the spatial 'bigger picture' of the 'whole world' rather than 'particular parts of it' (Strange, 1997b: 182) are thus chal-lenged by the insights of Latour's actor-network theory.[16] Coupling these insights with those of Lefebvre, globalisation becomes one conceptual means of identifying and naming social change, but one that disguises the myriad of conflicting and contingent meanings and experiences that are translated in networks of everyday social life. If we conceive of 'social space as a social product' (Lefebvre, 1991b: 26), then there cannot exist a global space that is independent of the actions and contests of people engaged in social practices. The spaces of states, firms and organisations conceived by IPE cannot simply 'contain' social relations and practices, nor do they exist prior to these relations and practices. The restructuring of such spaces cannot, therefore, be predicted or linear in nature. Lefebvre reveals multiple layers of space via three dia-lectical 'moments of space' within and between which people may constantly move: *spatial practices*, the realm of *perceived* daily reality and the interaction with 'material and physical flows' (Agnew and Corbridge, 1995: 7); *represen-tations of space*, the realm of space as *conceived* by 'scientists, planners and social engineers'; and *representational spaces*, the realm of space as *lived* or imagined (Lefebvre, 1991b: 39).

Workplaces can be seen as embodying all of these spatial moments, of which the idea of an 'imperative' of flexibility captures only one particular representation of space. Drawing on Lefebvre's terms, the workplace as a conceived space may be reinforced, contradicted or undermined by perceptions and lived experiences. The restructuring of work does not simply confront a material reality contained within unitary states and firms, but a set of human and discursive representations (du Gay, 1997). As Kaplan and Ross have it: 'institutions, codes and paradigms are not abstract constructs confronting us in some official "out there". Nor do we come to institutions alone. We live them in historically specific ways … as collective or virtually collective subjects' (1987: 4). We can see that the spaces that IPE terms 'national political economies' or 'multinational corporations' or 'social movements' embody an array of social spaces and networks. We can never consider these spaces to be complete or static, since they are continually made and remade: 'All networks of social relations, whether we are talking about capitalism, or firms, or any other institutions are incomplete, tentative, and approximate' (Thrift, 1995: 33).

The workplace thus does not simply provide an institutional 'context' for social change. It does more than 'trace out the traces of spaces' (Bingham and Thrift, 2000: 299). It is shaped by the articulation of conflicts, tensions and compromises that are played out in social practices. An IPE of social practice challenges the unitary and abstract conception of states and markets interacting to produce global social change. The 'state' and the 'market' are opened up to reveal the webs of social relations that agitate their parameters. Work (and by implication the restructuring of work) is conceived as everyday structured social practice through which the emerging social relations of globalisation may be enabled, contested or confounded.

Conclusion

While the previous chapter explored the linear and imperative construction of social change that underlies the discourse of labour flexibility, the present chapter mapped out the terrain of social change as conceived in contemporary IPE. I have argued that the new IPE has positioned the understanding of global social change centrally in its inquiry, a crucial departure from the emphasis of orthodox IPE. The attempt to transcend state-centrism, to politicise and historicise the study of globalisation, and to create an 'open' field – all serve to disrupt teleological and deterministic representations of social change. Though I seek to take some of the new IPE insights forward into the chapters that follow, I do so critically and with caveats. Susan Strange's conceptualisation of structural power, and particularly the firm as a powerful agent, has raised the profile of production in IPE inquiry. Yet, her states and firms take on the status of 'power wielders', leaving the webs of power relations that surround and suffuse them less visible in analysis. To uncover the power-knowledge webs that run through the restructuring of work, as I have argued, requires further steps to be taken.

From Polanyian frameworks in the new IPE, this study embraces the assertion that labour is a 'fictitious commodity', that labour markets are politically and socially produced and reproduced over time, and are made and defined in particular ways in different places. However, I have argued that caution should be exercised in the use by IPE of the concept of the 'double movement'. To argue that societal dissent and organised resistance will flow automatically from the damaging forces of the market is, paradoxically, to remove the politics from understandings of restructuring. It is, by contrast, in the contradictions highlighted by Polanyi that we find the politicisation of social change. This book is concerned with revealing the contradictions and tensions that run between markets for labour and experiences of work in human and social life.

Similarly, from neo-Gramscian analysis, the social forces that intersect workplace, state-society and world order become key sources of contingency and contestation in social transformation. This study, however, rejects the notion that globalisation is a project driven by the interests of global elites, and resisted by the actions of local groups. Where aspects of global restructuring do become represented as 'project-like', as in the flexibility thesis, this project is not simply 'executed' and absorbed by societies. Rather, it is translated, given many different meanings and lived out in diverse ways. Again, these steps require some further conceptual doors to be nudged open. If the promise of openness and heterodoxy is to be fulfilled in IPE, then there is a need for some conscious reflection on wider discussions of social change, and the avenues they may open. In particular, this chapter has identified the need to challenge IPE's conceptions of power as 'wielded', and knowledge as a commodity or resource that is simply possessed and traded. I have argued that if we can transcend these conceptions we can challenge the hierarchy of issues in IPE that says finance, technology and production 'matter' because they are sources of power, whilst work and everyday life are only the 'effects' of wider transformations.

My central argument in this chapter has been that an IPE of social practice can reveal the politics and contingency of globalisation as it is characterised by contests over the reality and representation of social change. I have mapped the terrain of an IPE of social practice, as I see it, through the intertwining of three strands of thought on social change. Each has particular implications for the study of the restructuring of work in the chapters that follow:

1 *Historicity and contingency* – Following a historical mode of thought, we are uniquely placed to account for, and to understand global social change, as our everyday lives are bound up with its rhythms. It is not separate from us, nor is it greater than us or beyond apprehension by individuals and social groups. Viewed in this way, the apparent 'project' of the restructuring of work is simply one expression of how social change is

ordered, and it is not the only one. The transformation of work is historically contingent. Thus, globalisation and flexibility become imbued with
different meanings in different places. Such meanings, though often
having the appearance of coherence, are contested within and across their
boundaries. In the chapters that follow I explore the diverse interpretations and experiences of restructuring within and across state-societies,
often understood as 'national capitalisms'; within and across firms, often
considered as 'actors' rather than sites of struggle; and by individual and
groups of workers.

2. *Power and agency* – In the analysis of global social change it is insufficient
to locate power primarily in the hands of the 'architects' of globalisation.
As I have argued, if we see power as shifting and circulating in webs or
networks, the making of globalisation becomes more complex than the
elite design of a global architecture. Sites of global restructuring become
part of a web of social power relations that transcend and defy the boundaries of states, firms and organisations. An apparent project of labour
flexibilisation is not controlled in a linear manner by holders of power,
but is riven with contradictions and tensions. Groups that we may define
as significant in shaping the restructuring of work – for example, policy-
makers, corporate managers and workers – do not always do so in predictable and instrumental ways. It will be clear from the chapters that follow
that not all managers promote globalisation and flexibility, and nor do all
workers resist. Indeed we can say that some worker relationships may, in
fact, enable globalisation. People cannot easily be assigned to roles of
'promoting' or 'resisting' globalisation and, therefore, an analysis of their
situations within webs of power relations is better equipped to reveal the
ambiguous and cross-cutting nature of affiliation and dissent.

3. *Social practice and the 'everyday'* – I have argued that it is in the realm of
everyday life that understandings, experiences, and meanings of globalisation and global restructuring are produced and reproduced. IPE inquiry
has for too long assumed that the 'everyday' is a parochial realm, one
which holds only secondary importance for inquiry. But what is the
'global economy', 'the market', 'the MNC', if it is separate from the
experience and knowledge of living in a world we call global? IPE has
tended to assume that we examine 'small scale' empirical details in order
to explain the bigger picture. Drawing on conceptualisations of the everyday, I have suggested that it is in this realm that meaningful global social
change takes place. From this standpoint, the 'restructuring of the state' or
the 'strategy of the firm' becomes concrete when viewed through the everyday social practices that may constitute or contest it. Of course, past practice
becomes institutionalised and constrains present and future actions, but
these institutions are not prior to social relations. Work, conceived as
everyday social practice, is one means through which representations and
concrete realities of globalisation are enabled, contested or confounded.

Notes

1 Strange (1984) emphasises the potential for 'openness' which is held out to the social sciences by IPE. This 'openness' constitutes both a willingness to consider the insights of a wide range of social groups, academics and practitioners, and an acceptance of the significance of a diverse range of subject matter, issues and concerns.

2 Strange's (1984) *Paths to IPE* represents a clear statement of the problematic of IPE inquiry. The chapters by Tooze and Strange mark out early divergences in the conception of the ontological and epistemological bases of the field.

3 The finance structure is defined as 'the sum of all the arrangements governing the availability of credit plus all the factors determining the terms on which currencies are exchanged for one another' (1988: 68). The security structure is the 'framework of power created by the provision of security by some human beings for others' (Strange, 1988: 44). The production structure is defined as 'the sum of all the arrangements determining what is produced, by whom and for whom, by what method and on what terms' (1988: 62). Finally, the knowledge structure 'comprehends what is believed ... what is known and perceived as understood; and the channels by which beliefs, ideas and knowledge are communicated – including some people and excluding others' (1988: 15). In each of the structures the emphasis is on 'who benefits' and who loses or is excluded from the arrangements.

4 See, for example, Hettne (1995), Gill (1995a; 1997), Bienefeld (1991), Birchfield (1999), Bernard (1997).

5 For discussions of the use of historical sociology in interdisciplinary and IPE inquiry, see Leander (2000), Skocpol (1984).

6 Hettne has it that Polanyi offers a 'historical' but not a 'historicist' route into IPE inquiry (1995: 5). The historical sociologists use of Polanyi similarly marshalls historical material, but does not 'historicise' this material. See, for example, Goldthorpe's analysis of what he terms 'grand historical sociology' (1996: 112). For Goldthorpe, the work of Skocpol and Hall, for example, engages with a debate about the use of history in sociology without actually employing a historical mode of thought. Hence, the historical sociologists rely upon comparative historical material on differences between societies, for example, but do not emphasise the role of interpretation in these cases.

7 See, for example Cox (1981; 1983; 1996), Gill (1990; 1993; 1995), Gill and Mittelman, (1997), Harrod, (1987; 1997a), Murphy (1994).

8 The concept of 'anti-globalisation strategies' has become common parlance in the new media. See, for example, Channel 4 (2001) 'Politics Isn't Working: The End Of Politics', 13 May.

9 Cox (1992b) describes the shift in the relationships of states to the world political economy in terms of a 'post-Westphalian' order.

10 Gill (1993) outlines a 'post-hegemonic' research agenda. Indeed, early IPE debates were rather dominated by the issues surrounding the possible demise of the Pax Americana and the shape of a future new world order (Gamble, 1995).

11 For Hettne: 'Judging from the current debate in IPE and IR theory, we live in a period of "transformation" or "transition". In historical studies of transition from one system to another, we have the record – that is, both the starting points and the end points are known to us. In studies of contemporary "transitions" or processes of transformation, we don't know the end points' (1995: 10).

12 I first raised these questions with others in the Newcastle IPE discussion group (Amoore

et al., 2000). I thus owe many of these points to discussions and writing that took place within the group.

13 Cox (1996: 27) explicitly outlines the 'influences and commitments' of his work. Under the broad heading of historicism, Cox highlights the work of Georges Sorel , E. H. Carr, E. P. Thompson, R. G. Collingwood, Giambattista Vico, Benedetto Croce, Antonio Gramsci and Fernand Braudel.

14 Ronen Palan comments that Strange does not allude to the 'authors of structural power', Poulantzas, Foucault and Mann (1999: 128).

15 Foucault outlines transversal struggles as 'immediate' struggles that are not limited to one country (1982: 211). Campbell extends this to suggest that transversal struggles 'not only transverse all boundaries; *they are about these boundaries*' (1996: 23).

16 Latour's (1991) stories of the use of weights to encourage the return of hotel keys, and the development of the Kodak camera demonstrate the contingency and displacement of apparently 'designed' strategies.

3

~

Producing hyperflexibility:
the restructuring of work in Britain

~

> Change is opening up new horizons; but there is fear of what may lie
> within them. Technology and global financial markets are transforming
> our economies, our workplaces, our industrial structure. Economic change
> is uprooting communities and families from established patterns of life.
> The way we live, as well as the way we work, our culture, our shared
> morality, everything, is under pressure from the intensity and pace of
> change … It can be exhilarating. But it is certainly unsettling … Politics
> is going global. All of us are seeking to make sense of, and manage, change.
> The key to the management of change is reform. The pace of reform has
> to match the pace of change. Societies that are open, flexible, able easily
> to distinguish between fundamental values, which they must keep and
> policies, which they must adapt, will prosper. Those that move too slowly
> or are in hock to vested interests or what I have elsewhere called forces of
> conservatism, reacting negatively to change, will fall behind. (Tony Blair,
> 2000a: 1, Speech at the World Economic Forum, Davos)

In his speech to the Davos meeting the British Prime Minister, Tony Blair, conjures a particular image of global change. On the one hand, he constitutes the problem of globalisation and restructuring as an imperative that is disciplined by 'fear', 'uprooting', 'pressure', 'unsettling' and 'falling behind'. On the other, he offers a best practice solution to the defined 'problem'. The message is that if the 'right' policy response is made to globalisation – one that is 'exhilarating', 'managed', 'open' and 'flexible' – then there is no need to be afraid. The speech goes on to state that Britain has made the 'right' and 'flexible' policy response at a pace that matches the speed of social change.

What we can see here is one face of the making of a particular kind of global restructuring, one that for many commentators is captured by a 'British model' of neo-liberal or hyperliberal capitalism. Yet, how can we make sense of a 'national capitalism' given, for example, the prevalence of German banks in the City of London, the Japanese multinationals on northern business parks and the migrant workers providing much of the 'flexible' labour? This conundrum has been discussed at the heart of the globalisation debate, with those who see globalisation as a process proclaiming the convergence of national capitalisms around a neo-liberal policy agenda (Strange, 1997b), and those who see a nationally defined 'project' declaring globalisation to be a 'myth' (Weiss, 1998). Neither perspective, however, actually problematises the dichotomous representation of a globalisation 'outside' and a national capitalism 'inside'. As is clear from Blair's speech, it can be highly politically expedient to represent globalisation as 'outside' and beyond effective control by governments, and to position a national policy programme as a necessary response.

This chapter challenges the opposition of globalisation and 'national capitalisms' by exploring the making and remaking of a 'British model' of hyperflexibility.[1] Through a reconceptualisation of 'models of capitalism' as shifting and circulating webs of power, I question how it has been possible to represent a flexible 'model', and why this representation has emerged as a best-practice that is lauded by international agencies such as the OECD. A particular set of meanings of globalisation are produced through the discourse and concrete interventions of a restructuring programme. Hence, globalisation and restructuring are not separable as 'outside' cause and 'inside' effect. Nor is the programme of restructuring ever complete, uncontested or without contradictions. Flexible workers and a flexible labour market rest upon an array of social practices that translate, enable or confound the policy programme. Viewed in this way, the British model is not bounded, rational and strategic, but the institutionalised face of ongoing contradictions, struggles and contests in everyday practices. I argue that such a view serves to break open the political usage of a 'British model' to discipline workers in Britain and elsewhere. A particular kind of globalisation is thus made and remade, and I argue that we should question how this has become possible, and why it has taken the form of hyperflexibilisation. The first section explores how national capitalisms have been understood within the globalisation debate and outlines an alternative understanding that follows from the IPE of social practice developed in chapter 2. I then go on to explore the making of globalisation in the British discourse of hyperflexibility and the historical representations of state, capital and labour that have made this possible. Finally, I discuss the contemporary restructuring of working practices in Britain, revealing the contests and contradictions that characterise the politics of the flexibility programme.

Globalisation and the 'national capitalisms' debate

In the debates surrounding globalisation and social change, the idea that national models of capitalism compete within a 'larger' global economy has served a particular heuristic function. For those who represent globalisation as an irresistible process, the argument that this bulldozer pushes previously unique national capitalisms onto convergent policy lines serves to bolster their globalist position. For a number of scholars, the denial of such convergence is simply nostalgic for 'times past' and neglectful of greater 'systemic trends' (see

Strange, 1997b; Radice, 2000). However, for the comparative political economists and historical sociologists who focus on national models of capitalism,
the salience of 'embedded' institutions and practices call the process of
globalisation into question (see Berger and Dore, 1996; Weiss, 1998; Hirst and
Thompson, 1996; Zysman, 1996; Crouch and Streeck, 1997; Hollingsworth
and Boyer, 1997). Hence, as Held and Mcgrew have it, the telling of a story of
embedded national culture has become the 'sceptic's resource' (2000: 4),
marshalled to show that 'the impact of globalisation … is best approached
through a firm grounding in the detail of individual national cases' (Coates,
2000: 20).

The polarisation of the 'process' versus 'national project' accounts of
globalisation, however, constructs a somewhat false dichotomy. The process
reading relies on an image of the global as a 'larger' system (Radice, 2000: 730),
and the state as 'in retreat' (Strange, 1996) – opposing the realms of global and
national. The national 'project' reading, by contrast, appeals to the 'mythical'
construction of the 'powerless state' to call globalisation into question (Weiss,
1998; Hirst and Thompson, 1996) – essentially favouring internationalisation
as an explanatory device. What both positions overlook and obscure is the
representation and reproduction of globalisation, in large part through the
debates taking place within and across national capitalisms. A central source
of the diversity and contestedness of globalisation is the differentiated meanings generated through the webs of power that constitute competing forms of
capitalism.

In chapter 2 I discussed the use of Polanyi's concept of embeddedness by
IPE, and in particular, the need to shed light on the tensions and contradictions present in the institutions of market societies. There is scope within
the national capitalisms literature for such contradictions to be captured.
Colin Crouch, in his review of David Coates's 'Models of Capitalism', for
example, comments that there is a need for 'accounts which take note of mixes,
incoherencies, contradictions within cases' (2001: 134). Coates and Hay
similarly present the British Labour Government's policy programmes as
'constructed and contested wholes, whose contradictions, internal consist-
encies and conceptual limits are as vital to their trajectory as are their axioms,
theories and content' (2000: 1). Yet, despite their critical contribution to the
national capitalisms debate, these studies fail to acknowledge the contingency
of representations of globalisation, almost as though all governments in all
state-societies were perceiving and interpreting the same external problem,
and only responding in different ways. Indeed, they declare their focus to be
'the character and interaction of foreign and domestic economic policy'
(Coates and Hay, 2000: 2), delineating 'foreign' from 'domestic', and 'politics'
from 'economics' in a fashion not dissimilar from orthodox approaches to
IPE. As a result, they do not probe the webs of power that make, enable and
contest globalisation in particular ways, and surround and suffuse the restructuring agenda.

Following the 'IPE of social practice', with its emphasis on historicity, contingency, shifting webs of power and everyday life, I suggest that the so-called models of capitalism are less coherent and more contradictory than they are commonly depicted. They represent particular realities that have been produced and reproduced over time, and which enable specific claims to be made about the nature of globalisation. In this sense they are 'imagined communities' (Anderson, 1983: 13), within which programmes of restructuring are not bounded or discretely 'national' phenomena. Rather, the programmes are fluid and historically contingent, and engage with transborder programmes across governments, firms, international organisations and social groups. The image of a coherent 'model' of capitalism is reconceptualised as a 'programme' in a 'world of programmes [that] is heterogeneous and rivalrous', and in which 'the solutions for one programme tend to be the problems for another' (Miller and Rose, 1990: 10–11). Miller and Rose's innovative use of Foucault's 'governmentality' allows us to see programmes of government as produced through networks of power relations that cut across boundaries of state/market, politics/economics and domestic/international:

> The classical terminology of political philosophy and political sociology – State v. Civil Society, public v. private, community v. market and so forth – is of little use here ... Operationalising government has entailed the putting into place, both intentionally and unintentionally, of a diversity of indirect relations of regulation and persuasion that do not differentiate according to such boundaries. (Miller and Rose, 1990: 8)

Programmes of policy designed to restructure social practices can thus be understood as incomplete, non-linear, and extending into and across the realms of state-society[2], workplace, family and community. Recalling the insights of Lefebvre and Foucault, 'we do not come to institutions alone. We live them in historically specific ways' (Kaplan and Ross, 1987: 4), and 'one must analyse institutions from the standpoint of power relations, rather than vice versa' (Foucault, 1982: 222). Following our 'IPE of social practice' perspective, then, viewing the restructuring of work as a *programme* is distinct from a coherent elite *project* because it analyses the means by which globalisation is constituted as a problem, and the rendering of the problem as manageable via interventions of flexibilisation. It problematises the reception of a policy programme into everyday life, highlighting the negotiations, contestations and translations that ensue. As Miller and Rose highlight: 'Technologies produce unexpected problems, are utilised for their own ends by those who are supposed to merely operate them, are hampered by underfunding, professional rivalries, and the impossibility of producing the technical conditions that would make them work' (Miller and Rose, 1990: 11).

In the light of a conception of programmes of restructuring as problematic, contested and unpredictable, the British programme of hyperflexibilisation begins to look less like a strategic 'best practice' project. The making of 'global Britain' is simultaneously a particular rendering of globalisation and a specific policy programme resolution of globalisation: the national and global become fused. In the remainder of this chapter I will explore the British programme of restructuring to reveal the historical practices that it rests upon, and the contemporary practices that interpret and give meaning to, enable or confound its existence.

Producing flexibility in 'global Britain'

In the preceding chapters I have argued that the construction of a discourse of labour flexibility rests upon the production of a particular mode of knowledge about globalisation and social change. The discourse of restructuring for labour flexibility in British state-society has depended upon a representation of globalisation and restructuring which is now widely understood to transcend individual governments and party politics (Hay, 1999; Smith and Morton, 2001). As a number of studies of neo-liberal policy programmes have demonstrated, drawing on Foucault's concept of 'governmentality',[3] government both discursively constructs a problem to be addressed, and structures specific forms of intervention to 'solve' the problem:

> All government depends on a particular mode of "representation": the elaboration of a language for depicting the domain in question that claims both to grasp the nature of that reality represented, and literally to represent it in a form amenable to political deliberation, argument and scheming. (Miller and Rose, 1990: 8)

This precisely captures the means by which successive British Governments have depicted a 'global' domain as a problem to be solved, claimed to grasp the 'imperative' nature of this problem, and rendered it amenable to the construction of particular programmes – among them the flexibilisation of labour. The depiction of globalisation that is dominant in British state-society has legitimated a programme of restructuring in work and labour. A central problem for a study such as this that seeks to politicise restructuring is that the representation of globalisation in Britain is 'naturalised' so that the politics of restructuring are nullified. The problem is presented as technical and open to rational solutions, rather than as contestable. Contrary to the conspicuous efforts to remove the politics from discourses of globalisation and flexibility, it can be shown that the programmatic attempts to transform working practices are contradictory, contingent and contested.

There is little doubt that Britain has become the embodiment of all that is presumed to be flexible in a 'global era'. The British Government itself advertises Britain as 'the most lightly regulated labour market of any leading economy in the world' (Blair, 1998: 1). The British media claims that Britain offers the most competitive location for inward investment (*The Sunday Times*, 8 July 2001). International organisations and institutions seize upon the British case as their example of flexibility par excellence (World Bank, 1995; OECD, 1994). Indeed, even academic commentators who are critical of the British neo-liberal engagement with globalisation concur that 'while the belief is that the UK is running to catch up, it has actually got far ahead of the game' (Hirst and Thompson, 2000: 336). The image that is created is one of a clear winner in a FDI 'beauty contest', where the major attraction is a deregulated and flexible location with 'no strings attached' that is 'as easy to exit as to enter' (*Observer*, 2 August 1998: 14). The significant question here, before we can even begin to consider the consequences of British hyper-flexibility, is how this representation of a deregulated and FDI-attracting 'model' has been made possible. Within this question, the first step is to consider the central dynamics of the meanings that have been attributed to globalisation in governing British state-society. A unique and particular set of stories about the 'global' arena are told and retold to enable a programme of hyperflexibility to be perpetuated.

The first significant face of the making of a 'global Britain' is, perhaps paradoxically, one in which government (in the sense of legislative and regulatory functions) is distanced from the structural dynamics of the wider world economy:

> The balance of risk in the world economy is shifting – with the slowdown in demand in a number of countries, especially Asia … These are prob-lems that can only be addressed together … Since 1996 the world semi-conductor market has slumped … As a result, companies in this sector have been closing and cutting back around the world. Fujitsu and Siemens were two casualties of this change in world conditions. As they made clear, world conditions, and those alone, caused these closures. It would be totally dishonest to pretend Government can prevent such decisions. I do not intend to do so. (Tony Blair, 1998: 1, Speech at Doxford Park, Sunderland)

In this speech given in the wake of two high profile FDI 'exits' from the northeast of England, the forces of global markets are presented as 'squeezing' state authority and closing down the space for governments to exercise 'com-mand over outcomes' (Strange, 1996: 3). It is just one example of a pervasive representation of globalisation as having 'inevitable consequences' that are beyond authority and control. Globalisation is clearly presented as a process whose origins are 'out there' and 'bigger than us' and beyond the control of mere governments. In effect, FDI capital has become the embodiment of globalisation in the British debate. Such a representation is laced with political expediency – the construction of an external threat enabling politicians to 'present their policy preferences as the more or less unavoidable consequence of forces over which they can have little or no control' (Moran and Wood, 1996: 140). As a result, highly political questions, such as the ease with which inward investor firms are able to exit Britain (Watson and Hay, 1998), become depoliticised through the exercise of constructing distance between global economy and national state-society. In effect, the governmentality of an environment to attract FDI is positioned as a legitimate realm of political intervention, while the withdrawal and closure of plants is positioned in the 'other' realm of the global economy.

The second face of the dominant British representation of globalisation is one in which global forces are embraced and harnessed through the 'rational' and 'sensible' policy measures of deregulation (see Department for International Development, 2000; Blair, 1998). Having located globalisation at a safe distance, the process then becomes something that must be 'responded to' in appropriate ways. Globalisation is thus constructed both as a problem that is out of governmental reach, and as a conundrum that is amenable to political intervention: 'My view is that the global market, in the end, is a good thing for us ... and the way to handle its consequences is to prepare and equip ourselves for the future. Not to try and resist it or ward it off or say it shouldn't exist' (Tony Blair in BBC interview, cited in Coates, 2000: 262).

The representation of the global market as an external and ambiguous threat/opportunity that must be 'handled' serves to discipline the range of political responses to be discussed. The implication is that 'resisting' or 'warding off' the consequences of globalisation is a futile act that looks nostalgically into the past rather than bravely into the future:

> This Government is firmly committed to embracing the changing nature of the international reality as a condition of domestic success. We do not want to cling to a Little England. We want to build a Global Britain. A country which accepts globalisation as an opportunity to be seized, not a threat to be resisted. (Robin Cook, 2001, Speech at the International Institute of Strategic Studies)

The image of 'building a global Britain' that is attractive to foreign industrial and financial capital is contrasted with one of 'clinging to little England'. The 'international reality' is not open to question in this representation, but is established as incontrovertible fact. The inherently political questions that are engendered by 'seizing globalisation' are effectively sealed off from discussion and contestation by the framing of the problem. The statement of what globalisation 'is' explicitly warns against any social or political negotiation that may delay the necessary response.

Finally, the British production of a flexible and deregulated labour market in response to globalisation is canonised and celebrated in the language of international institutions and organisations. The OECD, in its evaluation of member countries' restructuring programmes in labour and work, commends Britain for 'prominent structural policy reforms', including cutting unemployment benefit, reducing employment protection and liberalising industrial relations (1997, 9-10). The report concludes that 'improved labour market outcomes in the countries that have gone the furthest in implementing the Jobs Strategy, including the United Kingdom ... and deteriorating conditions in those that have not, is an indication that the strategy works' (1997: 15). There is notably less attention given in the report to the high drop-out rates from education that are exhibited by precisely those countries that are commended for their flexibility (1997: 22). Put simply the problems of an 'inflexible' labour market are defined in such a way that the negative effects of deregulation can be masked. The British 'model' of deregulation and flexibility runs seamlessly alongside the discourse of flexibility that is communicated by the World Bank (1995), OECD (1994; 1997), and CEC (1993), so that 'market friendly' programmes of restructuring are replicated (see Cammack, 2000). In this sense we can see the British representation of globalisation and hyper-flexibility as in a dialectical relationship with other transborder 'packages' of neo-liberal ideas. Yet, if we open up this 'package' we can see that hyper-flexibilisation is made possible through webs of distinctive historical and social practices through which power is exercised. The problematisation of British hyperflexibility begins with the identification of the uniqueness and peculiarity of the practices that tend to enable it. It is not that British state-society fails to exhibit contest over 'what ought to be' in the global restructuring debate, but rather that this contest is masked by the specific representations of state, capital and labour in global social change.

Historical representations of British capitalism

It is notable that over recent years, despite the ascendancy of governmental appeals to the building of a 'new' and 'global' Britain, there has been a simultaneous revival of attention to the histories of British capitalism. The Tom Nairn and Perry Andersen 'exceptionalism' debates in New Left Review[4] have been revisited in contemporary discussion of the historical tensions between financial capital and industrial capital in Britain (see Cox *et al.*, 1997; Ingham, 1984; Hutton, 1995). The suggestion that is made by these literatures is that Britain has historically oriented its political and productive practices towards 'external' capital and investment, while maintaining an ambivalence to the 'internal' regulation of capital and labour. For many of the national capitalisms school this dualism in the history of British capitalism is used to rebut claims to globalisation in favour of a world where national political economies remain key (see Hirst and Thompson, 2000). However, the historical representations of state, capital and labour in British state-society can be interpreted precisely to problematise the separation of a 'global' from a 'national' sphere. Representations of what the 'global' means are distinctively fashioned through debates in British state-society, drawing on historical practices and understandings, and reinvigorating past tensions and contradictions.

State and market

British programmes of governmental representation and intervention have rested upon the depiction of distinct and opposed realms of state and market. In accounts of British 'early start' industrialisation the process is described as 'market driven' so that 'by the end of the eighteenth century, government policy was firmly committed to the supremacy of business' (Lee, 1997: 210; Hobsbawm, 1975: 68). The state is described as 'permissive' in its role of safeguarding 'private interests and the liberation of private energies' (Gamble, 1994: 72-3). The webs of power surrounding and suffusing industrialisation are revealed to produce the 'individual' as the central actor in social change. The cotton industry appeared to require little in the way of state co-ordination, enabling small-scale private entrepreneurs to 'launch themselves' into an international marketplace (Gerschenkron, 1962; Hobsbawm, 1975).

> The cotton industry was launched, like a glider, by the pull of the colonial trade to which it was attached … In terms of sales, the Industrial Revolution can be described except for a few initial years in the 1780s as the triumph of the export market over the home: by 1814 Britain exported about four yards of cotton cloth for every three used at home, by 1850 thirteen for every eight. (Hobsbawm, 1975: 50)

The central actors in social change, as described here, are essentially individual entrepreneurs operating in an overseas market. The industrial revolution did not in some automatic and 'natural' sense produce the primacy of these realms, but it has created the possibility for the market to be depicted as an external sphere within which individuals privately engage in business. The state is thus legitimated as an actor that stands apart from the market and intervenes in order to 'harness' private initiative to the 'pull' of the international market. As Polanyi has it: 'economic liberals must and will unhesitatingly call for the intervention of the state in order to establish it (the market system), and once established, to maintain it' (1957: 149). This nineteenth century liberal construction of the market as simultaneously external and 'larger' than the state, and also an 'opportunity' to be seized, has been revived by contemporary British appeals to globalisation.

Finance and industry

The relative isolation of British financial capital from the process of industrialisation, its historical international orientation, and the short-term conception of time governing finance-industry relations, are all oft-cited and broadly acknowledged features of a peculiarly British capitalism (see Hall, 1986; Hutton, 1995; Cox, 1986; Woolcock, 1996; Hirst and Thompson, 2000). In the context of early industrialisation, Britain's manufacturing industries were financed privately from non-bank sources and, in particular, from accumulated profits. Financial expansion itself developed through individual private investors and foreign capital, leading to what Arrighi terms 'cosmopolitan finance capitalism' (1994: 162). The organised and universal banking system characteristic of Germany, for example, did not feature in the development of British industrial or financial capitalism (Arrighi, 1994: 163). Indeed, the City of London had established itself as the world's centre for commodity trade by the late eighteenth century, and was relatively decoupled from industrial production. As a commercial centre the practices of the City of London were reproduced to serve the short-term needs of commercial activity, rather than the longer horizons of indigenous production (Ingham, 1984). On the one hand, it became possible for industry and finance to be defined and managed as distinct and separate realms. Meanwhile, on the other hand, tensions and contradictions continued to surround the dual character of Britain as the first industrial economy and the world's major commercial entrepot (Ingham, 1984: 6).[5]

Ultimately, the contradictions of industrial and financial capital in Britain remain central unresolved tensions in contemporary debates. The building of 'global Britain' is a fragile and precarious exercise precisely because it rests upon the maintenance of the industry-finance tension. The attraction of financial capital to the City of London relies upon the maintenance of perceptions of Britain as a deregulated and open social space. As the Chairman of Citibank reminds us 'the Eurodollar market exists in London because people believe that the British Government is not about to close it down. That's the basic reason and it took you a thousand years of history' (cited in Ingham, 1984: 41). Just as London's status as an 'offshore' centre relies on historical perceptions, so the British governmental predilection for 'shareholder capitalism' (Seccombe, 1999) rests upon perceptions of the City's ability to secure high short-term returns on investment. Industries are thus locked into raising capital on the stock market with its emphasis on immediacy and flexibility. As a result, it is widely argued, British industry is preoccupied with financial soundness to the detriment of longer-term investment in skills and innovation (Woolcock, 1996). Contemporary claims that Britain's competitive advantage lies in its ability to attract FDI with a deregulatory environment can thus be seen as one manifestation of the concealed tensions between industrial and financial capital. Since 1979, outflows of industrial investment from Britain have consistently exceeded inflows (Economist Intelligence Unit, 1998), and redundancies in British-owned multinationals have far exceeded job creation in inward investor firms (Coates, 1999).

Labour

The distancing of state from market in British state-society is evident also in the historical understandings and practices that have shaped the role of labour in social transformation. In many senses it is difficult to conceive of a system of industrial relations in the British context because a 'system' has historically been avoided and constrained. Industrial relations have tended to be constituted through the everyday practices of work, and have generally not been subject to state intervention or legal constraint. A web of power in which workers have negotiated or contested their own individual contracts has, in effect, become part of a British 'common sense' understanding of industrial relations. In terms of organised labour, the early craft unions actively sought to admit only those workers within the same occupation, and to exclude less-skilled workers or the 'labouring poor' (Hobsbawm, 1964; Middlemas, 1979; Gospel and Palmer, 1983). The excluded workers organised their interests in more politically oriented general unions, representing workers from across different industries. This divisive and internally competitive system established the organisation of workers' interests at a subsector craft level, and at a transsector general level, but mitigated against the emergence of industrial unions such as those characteristic of continental Europe (Visser, 1995; Fulcher, 1991; Heise, 1997). The combined effects of the historical organisation of labour around the Trades Union Congress (TUC), a 'loose confederation with few sanctions' (Hall, 1986), the internal competition between unions themselves, and the lack of state co-ordination of industry-wide bargaining, have been to construct the workplace as the social space of industrial relations, and the individual worker as responsible for their own working terms and conditions.

> [A] common way of ensuring labour discipline, which reflected the small-scale, piecemeal process of industrialization in this early phase, was sub-contract or the practice of making skilled workers the actual employers of their unskilled helpers. In the cotton industry, for instance, about two-thirds of the boys and one-third of the girls were thus 'in the direct employ of operatives' and hence more closely watched. (Hobsbawm, 1962: 66–67)

The devolution of responsibility through supply chains and contract labour is evident in this depiction of labour discipline in early British industrialisation. I am not suggesting that contemporary discourse of deregulation and labour flexibility simply follows from historical practices in a linear or path-dependent fashion. The role of labour in an industrial political economy has of course been highly contested and constantly challenged and redefined. However, the location of responsibility for restructuring away from the state, and into the lives of individual workers within individual firms does recall historical divisions and fault lines. From this perspective the British programmes of restructuring have drawn upon a logic of 'pro-competitive disengagement' (Vogel, 1996: 263), whereby individual entrepreneurs and individual workers carry the personal risks of restructuring. The dominant stance of the 'externally oriented' British hegemonic state (Overbeek, 1990: 35), thus provides the language and assumptions necessary for the reproduction of the problem of globalisation: 'Even now, many in the UK ... hark back, sometimes unconsciously, to the "golden period" of the British Industrial Revolution and the years that followed, carrying in their minds lessons from the efforts of a few brilliant entrepreneurs' (Graham, 1997: 119).

It is possible to view the major themes in contemporary British restructuring debates as drawing upon historical understandings of capitalist organisation, contesting and rearticulating these past understandings in the light of contemporary questions. The contemporary debates that define the British programme of the restructuring of work continue to raise questions of the conceptions of state, market, finance, industry and labour that were unresolved in past practices. The tensions and contradictions of historical practices can serve to reveal the politics that is so often obscured by the technical and rational treatment of 'strategy' in the contemporary flexibility discourse.

The contemporary restructuring of working practices

The contemporary British debates about the restructuring of work reinvigorate some of the nineteenth century representations of state, market, finance, industry and labour. This is not to say that Britain has produced a form of labour flexibility that is 'natural' given its historical practices, but that the themes of individualisation, self-responsibility, the 'distancing' of state from industry and society, and faith in the entrepreneur have re-emerged in new forms with new tensions and contradictions. The implications are that Britain has a unique 'semantics of flexibility' (Lemke, 2001: 203) that is produced, contested or enabled through social practices and, therefore, cannot be offered as an unproblematic model of globalisation management. I am not claiming here to offer an exhaustive account of all of the policy debates and restructuring patterns in contemporary Britain. The purpose of this analysis is to explore key dimensions of the British restructuring programme, and to reveal the tensions and contradictions in its making. As a result, this should be seen as an exercise in politicisation, since in each instance the emphasis is on the contested and difficult nature of transforming the working practices of everyday life. The disturbances and tensions within the programme may be seen as potential gaps or spaces for alternative tactics, where Latour's 'translation' and 'displacement' of intended strategy takes place (1991: 105), and where the 'movement back and forth' of Scott's (1990: 191) 'infrapolitics' may be seen.

'Functional flexibility', training and skills

Representations of 'global Britain' have positioned so-called 'functional flexibility' centrally in the strategy of rapid response to global competition. As defined by the Employment Department, functional flexibility means 'having a labour force that is able to carry out a wide range of tasks' so that firms may possess 'adaptability in allocating labour between different parts of the production process' (Beatson, 1995: 1, 51). It is argued that the demarcated 'jobs' that make up a production process, for example mechanical, electrical, quality monitoring, cleaning or maintenance tasks, could become 'rigidities' that prevent firms from responding to shifts in markets. In this representation 'a premium seems to be placed on speed of reaction: on rapid product change and an ability to cut costs fast' (Crouch and Streeck, 1997: 6), so that the adaptability of firms becomes a key strategy. A central feature of task restructuring, for example, has been the debate on 'teamworking' within HRM circles (see Sengenberger, 1993). Working practices are reorganised into teams or 'cells' that become akin to individuals responsible for multiple tasks, and managers are able to redeploy teams 'flexibly' in the production process. At its root functional flexibility carries a discipline of 'replaceability' that strengthens employers' ability to dispense with particular production roles, and instils a pattern of self-management on workers.

While the discussion of how to create 'multi-tasking', 'multi-skilling' or 'upskilling' working practices has taken place transnationally (OECD, 1994; International Labour Organisation (ILO), 2000), state-societies have framed these questions differently and in the light of their existing and past practices. For countries with relatively protected and high-cost labour, the 'replaceability' discipline is constrained and the questions have tended to be about the skills and training of workers, often at a co-ordinated sectoral level (Culpepper and Finegold, 1999). The British questions, by contrast, have been about how to create a business-friendly functional flexibility in which, as the Employment Department defines it, employers have 'no constraints on how they organise work' within the firm (Beatson, 1995: 135), and also have access to an external pool of relatively unregulated agency or contract labour. Indeed, it is predominantly at the level of the firm that the defining and contesting of functional flexibility takes place in Britain. The absence of state institutions or societal interests mediating between the state and the firm on questions of training and skills (Lane, 1994; Rubery, 1993), including the absence of trade union consultation, has reinforced a web of power that enables employers to define a hyperflexible agenda, yet also mitigates against firm-level incentives to invest in training for fear of 'poaching' by competitors.[6] The result is that a low skills 'low road' of labour cheapening (Esping-Andersen, 1996: 17) has found easy purchase in the British debate, and functional flexibility has come to mean 'flows' of workers in and out of contracts, and in and out of different tasks.

The programme of functional flexibility in Britain exhibits tensions both in terms of its own logic and representations, and in terms of its wider implications for society. First, in terms of its own market rationality, the interventions that have structured functional flexibility have produced a 'fallout' effect that could be understood as uncompetitive and 'inflexible'. The dissolution of skills and training provision that accompanies the rapid flow of workers in and out of jobs/tasks/contracts has been identified as a central problem for British firms. In effect, the emphasis on individual access to a wider labour market of contingent labour has limited the scope for flexibility within the firm and led to talk of skills shortages in Britain (Marsden, 1995; Rubery, 1999). The ad-hoc and management-led character of the programme, coupled with the division of workers along skilled/unskilled and core/contract lines, has arguably stifled consultation and innovation in the workforce, producing a 'low trust' environment (Lane, 1997; Rubery, 1993: 11–12).[7] The in-built paradox here, even viewed from a neo-liberal or business perspective, is that skills flexibility within the firm requires investment in training, which in turn necessitates some level of state regulation or co-ordination of the labour market.

Finally, in terms of a wider and more critical picture of social inequality and exclusion, the British programme of functional flexibility has contributed to a shifting of responsibility and risk on to individuals. In the face of diminished collective provision, the responsibility for education, training and personal security is attributed to the individual. Skills become an individual possession to be traded in an open market, rather than the shared resources of a society. UNDP statistics show that the UK has among the highest levels of functional illiteracy in the OECD countries. The UK level of functional illiteracy is calculated at 21.8 per cent of all 16–65 year-olds, a level that compares to 20.7 per cent in the US, 14.4 per cent in Germany, 7.5 per cent in Sweden and 29.5 per cent in the Russian Federation (UNDP, 2000: 172). The blurring of the boundaries between secure and contingent work has also resulted in a gendered 'functional flexibility' that finds women providing contract services for cleaning, catering and domestic functions (Anderson, 2000). Inside the claim that competitiveness can be achieved via rapid response and adaptive functions, there are tensions and questions that will continue to resurface in the restructuring debate.

Working time and 'non-standard' employment

The debate surrounding the reorganisation of working time reveals a great deal about the negotiated and contested nature of social change in the sphere of work. For many commentators, the 'speeding' up of social change and the temporal rhythms of everyday life have transformed working practices beyond all recognition (see Rifkin, 1995). However, conceptions and experiences of working time are highly contingent and contested, and the restructuring of working time is a profoundly political exercise, and not an automatic techno-logical reality. The restructuring of working time for maximum flexibility is programmatically highly ambiguous. Consider, for example, the contingency of meaning applied to flexible working time: the possibilities range from the complete ownership and abuse of temporal experience by an employer, as in bonded or slave labour, to the 'family friendly' flexibility that may be a desire of working parents (Hewitt, 1993). At one extreme the sense of time is governed entirely by the slave-master, while at the other the sense of time is expressed by the worker in terms of the demands of their own experiences and everyday workplace and household lives. In this ambiguity there lies considerable space for social tensions and political contestation.

The British governmental making of 'hyperflexibility' asserts a duality of strategies for the managerial defining of working time flexibility: the management prerogative to liberalise the regulation of working time within the firm itself, coupled with the freedom to access an external labour market of part-time, fixed contract or agency workers to extend the possibilities of time organisation. On the axis of time within the existing practices of the firm, the emphasis is on the ability of employers to vary the hours worked by employees. Prior to the incorporation into UK law of the 1994 EC Directive on working time, approximately four million people worked more than the 48 hours per week set down in the Directive, a figure that represented one-quarter of the full-time British workforce (European Industrial Relations Review (EIRR) 275, 1996: 12). Successive Employment Acts of the 1980s and 1990s had enshrined in law the prerogative of individual firms to govern working time, leading the ILO to report that Britain had 'made a concerted effort to substantially deregulate working time' (ILO, 1995). The Labour Government's 1999 Employment Act does not reverse the deregulation of working time and represents an effort to reinforce a system that has 'minimal effects on managerial prerogatives' (Smith and Morton, 2001: 124). The maximum use of the exceptions and derogations in the EC Directive by the British Government allows the working time of 48 hours per weak to be spread into longer periods of average hours, and permits exemptions in many areas.

On the axis of temporal flexibility via the euphemistic 'non-standard' employment contracts (they are rapidly becoming 'standard'), the British programme has made a virtue of the ascendancy of contingent working practices:

> The UK exhibits a good deal of flexibility on the extensive margin, both in terms of the prevalence and use made of part-time and self-employed workers, and in the degree to which employers face constraints on their ability to change employment levels. While UK employers may face greater constraints on their behaviour than in the USA, these constraints and regulations are liberal compared to other EU countries. (Beatson, 1995: 134)

This excerpt from a report published by the Employment Department explicitly frames access to contingent labour in terms of competitiveness and the attraction of FDI. The virtues of the expansion of contingent labour are also expounded by arguments that Britain's low levels of unemployment are, in part, due to deregulation and the expansion of alternative and 'more imaginative' forms of work (OECD, 1997). Yet again here the emphasis is on the self-discipline of individuals who will accept disruptions to daily life in the form of unpredictable working time, in exchange for the relative security of a job. Indeed, the flexible labour represented by homeworkers linked by information and communication technologies is even presented as empowering and emancipatory (see CEC, 1997; Negroponte, 1995).

When the programme of flexibilisation of working time is opened up to reveal political and social practices, the picture that emerges is one of contradictions and contests. At one level successive British Governments have been engaged in a series of contests with the EU over the state's authority to determine the level of regulation of working time. The central provisions of the EU Working Time Directive regulate the working week to 48 hours, stipulate minimum rest periods and set a minimum level of annual paid holiday.[8] The British Conservative Government challenged the Directive on the grounds that it was introduced through the back door of qualified majority voting in the area of health and safety. Following the failure of their challenge to the legal basis of the Directive in the European Court of Justice (ECJ), the British Government issued a consultation document to the effect that 'implementation needs to be carefully tailored to the circumstances of British business so as to minimise disruption and avoid undue burdens' (cited in EIRR 276, 1997: 14). Tensions thus surround the defining of working time flexibility and the authority of the state to maintain a deregulated environment. In a further example of such tensions and contests, in June 2000 the High Court referred to the ECJ the case brought against the British Government by the TUC. This case was brought claiming the failure of the Government to fully implement the EU Parental Leave Directive. Again, in this instance the Government had sought to tailor the Directive to the demands of the market by limiting the entitlement of 13 weeks unpaid parental leave to parents of children born on or after 15 December 1999. While this dispute remains unresolved at the time of writing, it is illustrative of the contests that surround the making of a particular British hyperflexibility.

The contested nature of the restructuring of working time is evident also in the public debate in Britain on 'who benefits' from temporal flexibility. Despite the rhetoric of empowerment espoused in Labour's White Paper 'Fairness at Work' (Department of Trade and Industry, 1998), and the representation of Britain as the most flexible European location for business, in terms of everyday social practices Britain could be said to be the most inflexible working location in Europe. European surveys of worker views indicate that Britain is the least 'family friendly' state-society in the EU, and that the term flexibility is employer-defined in Britain (EIRR, 323, 2000: 14). The meaning of flexibility of working time is thus revealed to be highly contingent and politically constructed.

In the governmental framing of the restructuring of work we see the blurring of the boundaries between 'work' and 'no work', or as Deakin and Reed have it, a 'substantial churning between unemployment and low-paid, irregular and short-term work' (2000: 143). The question of whether Britain has been successful in reducing levels of unemployment, a claim that features prominently in transnational debates on work, is thus reopened. Historically low levels of unemployment in Britain (6.3 per cent on the ILO count in 1999), conceal a concentration of unemployment in 'workless' households.[9] A fundamental tension in the British restructuring of work is the simultaneous intensification of work and the denial of 'the right to work flexibly' for workers (*The Guardian*, 29 June 2001), while exclusion from work clusters in marginalised households. Questions are also exposed as to the nature of work that is generated in a 'low wage strategy' and a deregulated temporal context. A report funded by the Department for Education and Employment estimates job creation at 1.5 million over the next 10 years, with 50 per cent of these thought to be in the part-time service sector (cited in EIRR, 276, 1997: 14). The astounding growth of call-centres across Britain looks likely to form a key element of this jobs growth, currently accounting for 33 per cent of all call-centre work in Europe (IRS, 2000). The tensions and struggles that surround and suffuse this form of job creation tend to be concealed in the discourse on hyperflexibility. Two-thirds of call-centre workers are women, and 27.5 per cent are on part-time or agency contracts. Workers in British Telecom call-centres staged a one-day strike in November 1999 in protest against a 'culture of harassment and bullying' (EIRR, 312, 2000: 13). In order to circumvent the strike, British Telecom recruited temporary workers from an employment agency for one day only. The meanings of working time flexibility are thus displaced and contested, and have unpredictable or unintended consequences.

Wage determination and collective bargaining

A highly visible sphere of the debate surrounding the reorganisation of work has been the relationship between wage levels and the competitiveness of firms. Within this debate, the neo-liberal assumption has been that wages are most flexible and competitive where their determination is decentralised. Different national models of wage determination are commonly contrasted in policy documentation, and a competitive 'benchmark' established: 'In most countries where relative wages have been flexible (the US, Canada, UK, Australia), both the relative employment and unemployment rates of the unskilled changed little during the 1980s. In comparatively inflexible Europe, on the other hand, both relative employment and unemployment rates deteriorated' (OECD, 1994: 11–12).

In the discourse of hyperflexibility the benchmark is Anglo-Saxon political economies that have deregulated pay bargaining to the level of individual firms. The British programme of restructuring has embraced the logic that 'wage determination is best left to those economic agents most closely affected by market conditions' (Beatson, 1995: 70), and has become a key benchmark in international policy literature (OECD, 1997). Successive legislative interventions have deregulated wage determination, removing mechanisms such as wage councils, arbitration procedures and enabling the use of individualised contracts of employment (see Table 3.1). Recent legislation by the Labour Government in the form of the 1999 Employment Relations Act, though

Table 3.1 Key legislative reforms of industrial relations in Britain, 1980–99

1980 Employment Act
- Restriction of the closed shop, picketing and secondary picketing.
- Removal of provisions for compulsory arbitration for union recognition.
- Reduction of unfair dismissal provisions; and maternity rights to reinstatement.

1982 Employment Act
- Restriction of lawful union action; removal of immunity of trade unions against claims for damages in the case of an unlawful strike; restriction of definition of trade dispute to make solidarity action, sympathy strikes, and inter-union disputes unlawful.
- Further restrictions on closed shop (ballot required on existing closed shop and 85 per cent majority vote needed for its lawful continuation).

1984 Trade Union Act
- Members of principal executive bodies of trade unions must be elected by secret ballot every five years; unions lose immunity unless a secret ballot is conducted and won before strike action.

1988 Employment Act
- Post-entry closed shop is made illegal and unenforceable; no strike seeking to enforce post-entry closed shop is lawful.
- During a lawful strike, union members who cross the picket-line cannot be disciplined.
- Extension of secret balloting in union elections.

1989 Employment Act
- Various provisions which extend labour market regulation to the small firm sector are withdrawn; repeal of discriminatory provisions restricting hours of work for women and young people above school age; abolition of Training Commission – previously Manpower Services Commission – its functions being taken over by the Department of Employment; unions no longer represented on industrial training boards, which are downgraded to non-statutory status.

---

introducing statutory recognition procedures for trade unions, reinforces company-level bargaining.

The themes of individualisation, self-responsibility and freedoms for the entrepreneur are strong throughout the British debate on pay flexibility. Data from the Workplace Industrial Relations Surveys (WIRS) demonstrates that the percentage of workplaces with arrangements for collective bargaining fell by one-half over a 14 year period, from 60 per cent in 1984, to 42 per cent in 1990, and 29 per cent in 1998 (Millward *et al.*, 2000: 186). Over the same period, profit-related pay increased from 19 per cent of all workplaces in 1984, to 44 per cent in 1990, and 46 per cent in 1998 (Millward *et al.*, 2000: 214). The overall trend is toward a detachment of individuals from collective ties that

1990 Employment Act
- Abolition of all legal protection for the pre-entry closed shop; refusal of employment to non-union members made unlawful.
- Employers given greater freedom to dismiss workers taking part in unlawful strike action; immunity removed for union officials, including shop stewards, who organise support for persons dismissed for taking part in an unlawful strike; all remaining forms of secondary action made unlawful.

1993 Trade Union Reform and Employment Rights Act
- Workers given right to join union of their choice; employers allowed to offer workers financial inducements to leave the union.
- Employer must be given seven days warning in advance before official industrial action; all pre-strike ballots must be postal and subject to independent scrutiny; users of public services have right to seek an injunction against unlawful strike action.
- Withdrawal of support for collective bargaining (removal of requirement for Arbitration Commission to encourage collective bargaining).
- Removal of all remaining minimum wage fixing (abolition of Wage Councils).
- Requirement for employers to give written statement of terms and conditions to full-time employees under regular contract; extension of jurisdiction of industrial tribunals to cover breaches of employment contract; extension of maternity leave for women and protection of pregnant women against unfair dismissal; protection of workers victimised over health and safety at work issues.

1999 Employment Relations Act
- Introduction of statutory trade union recognition and derecognition procedure.
- Clarification of existing legislation on industrial action and ballot procedures.
- Tribunal protection for workers dismissed due to lawful industrial action.
- Right to representation in disciplinary and grievance procedures.
- Parental leave and maternity provision amended.

Source: Compiled from Visser and Van Ruysseveldt (1996); Smith and Morton (2001); Deakin and Reed (2000).

might inflate wages beyond market values, and a simultaneous attachment of individuals expectations to the performance of the company. The focus of the wage determination debate has been the terrain of the workplace itself and has taken place in abstraction from discussion of working conditions. The flexibility of pay in Britain has been positioned at the heart of the 'competitive labour market' and is disciplined by the threat of job losses if demands become unreasonable or inflationary.

The British representation of the problematic of pay flexibility, and the interventions that are made in the light of the problem, harbour a number of distinctive tensions and contradictions. In common with other aspects of the restructuring of work debate, the inculcation of a culture of wage flexibility is contradictory both in its own market-centred terms, and in terms of tensions within everyday social practices. First, the business-friendly logic of wage hyperflexibility assumes that the 'low-road' of flexible and low-cost labour is attractive to firms and likely to increase investment in Britain. The assumption is that firms will be attracted by cheap labour and by an environment that enables them to structure incentives and disincentives through pay and rewards. Yet, the high-profile exit of inward investor firms from Britain, and their continued presence in perceived 'high-cost' locations raises questions of this assumption. In the wake of the announcement of closures by Ford in May 2000, and Motorola in April 2001, for example, trade unions have contested the British 'low cost' route to competitiveness. In both instances production from the British plants is to be transferred to German plants with higher labour costs. The pay flexibility programme that is manifested in Britain is highly controversial and contested and does not in any sense 'resolve' the conundrum of managing globalisation.

Finally, the fetishisation of flexible pay arrangements in the British pro-gramme of restructuring masks the divisions and inequalities that exist between different workers and their experiences of pay and collective bargaining. While the 1998 Minimum Wage Act and the 'New Deal' policy are presented in terms of 'tackling social exclusion' (Blair, 2000b), they embody an individualised discipline that reinforces social divisions (Gray, 1998). The minimum wage, established in April 1999 at a rate of £3.60 an hour, is differentiated for younger workers, with workers aged between 18 and 21 entitled to a minimum of £3, while workers younger than 18 are exempt. The level set also includes gratuities, affecting the wage levels of part-time and service-sector workers in particular. Early analyses of the effects of the minimum wage suggest that many employers continue to flout minimum wage legislation, while workers in precarious employment remain silent for fear of dismissal (TUC, 2001). The business-friendly exemptions that are built into the minimum wage tend to intensify divisions between workers along the lines of age, sector and gender. The New Deal programme has similar disciplinary features that, for example, remove entitlement to benefits where an individual fails to satisfy their 'welfare to work' contract (Krieger, 1999: 26). In sustaining the hyperflexibility pro-gramme in wage determination, British state-society is creating a social fallout that is simply shifted to other areas of welfare and social policy. At the time of writing, the OECD's most recent economic survey of the UK, while generally looking favourably at the UK's restructuring strategies, states that 'employ-ability remains wanting, as do work incentives for some at the fringes of the labour market. Against this background, poverty, including among children, is unacceptably high' (OECD, 2000: 17). A subtext of the British programme of restructuring sees the number of people on very low incomes, and the number of children living in poverty increasing (Joseph Rowntree Foundation, 1999).

Industrial relations

Within the hyperflexibility discourse, organised systems of industrial relations are represented as 'rigidities' that impinge on the competitiveness of state-societies and firms. In particular, organised trade unions are viewed as impediments to the flexible firm's responsiveness to global markets – limiting the scope for new working practices, driving up labour costs, disrupting production with industrial action and restricting access to contingent and contract labour. Thus, the neo-liberal assault on embedded systems of industrial relations taking place through the 1980s and 1990s is often explained as a necessary 'outcome' of the economic selectivity of globalisation (see Freeman, 1994; Blank, 1994). While some commentators remind us that transformations in industrial relations are highly political, exhibiting a strong national institutional character (Boyer, 1995; Abraham and Houseman, 1993), and representing an ongoing social creativity through contest and reaffirmation (Crouch, 1993), the hyperflexibility programme seeks precisely to depoliticise. Deunionisation is presented as a necessary process of depoliticisation and the workplace is reconstructed as a site of economic efficiency and individual responsibility.

The British programme of industrial relations restructuring has revived historical understandings of the relationship between state, industry and workers. British industrial relations institutions and practices historically developed out of an unregulated, decentralised and individualised process of social struggle at the workplace (see Lane, 1994). The regulation of bargaining, employment rights and worker organisation emerged out of norms, tacit understandings, customs and everyday workplace practices. Mechanisms of consultation, co-operation and negotiation have been weak, built on conflict lines and divisions that orientate to adversariality, both between management and workers, and between worker groups themselves. Contemporary restructuring has relied upon historical representations of voluntarist industrial relations so that 'a decade and a half of Thatcherism has only served to reinforce the voluntary nature of British industrial relations. The company, more so than before, now occupies centre stage' (Visser and Van Ruysseveldt, 1996: 78). The right to strike, for example, has existed in Britain only in the limited sense of immunity from damages claims, and this negative right has been removed in subsequent legislation that abolishes immunity and sees a 'return to private law' (Brown *et al.*, 1997).

Trends in the governmentality of industrial relations in Britain between 1979 and 1999 demonstrate that, with the exception of the implementation of EU Directives, the emphasis has been on restricting the influence of trade unions and devolving industrial relations to the level of the individual – recasting industrial relations as 'employee relations' (see Table 3.1). The transformation of rules governing industrial relations practices, and the use of complex disciplinary interventions on industrial action procedure, has been understood as the 'end of institutional industrial relations' in Britain (Purcell, 1993; Bassett, 1986), and the rise of 'new' workplace employment relations (Ackers *et al.*, 1996). The series data derived from the WIRS reveals that trade union recognition in British workplaces has fallen from 64 per cent of all workplaces in 1980 to 42 per cent in 1998 (Millward *et al.*, 2000: 96). In the private sector the last available figures (1998) are 29 per cent of all workplaces in manufacturing and extraction, and 23 per cent of all workplaces in private services. Alongside the process of union derecognition, the growth of single-union and no-union deals in new 'greenfield' production sites has exacerbated the trend to decentralised representation (Millward, 1992). There has been little evidence of a co-ordinated trade union response to the individualisation of industrial relations; indeed the debate has tended to occupy space that is managerially defined and fused with human resources discourse.

A central question for contemporary analysis of the restructuring of industrial relations in Britain is whether the election of a Labour Government in 1997 has reversed the trend towards the individualisation of industrial relations. The overwhelming finding seems to be that the Labour Government has reinscribed the individualisation dynamic with 'global' overtones (see Hay, 1999; Coates and Hay, 2000), and that given their 'enthusiastic adoption' it is 'inappropriate to continue to attach the label of "Conservative" to this legisla-tion' (Smith and Morton, 2001: 121). In terms of assessing the means by which the programme of restructuring is *exercised*, however, it is perhaps misleading to focus wholly on who is *wielding* the power to promote change. The legislative offensive on industrial relations in Britain cannot be viewed simply as the wielding of power by government and capital, and the disempowering of unions. Following a Foucauldian perspective on the productive capacity of power, it is important to recognise that the proclaimed 'death of industrial relations' is actually a reconstitution of industrial relations, with new tensions and contradictions produced and reproduced. In later chapters I will explore the dynamics of contest and collaboration that continue to make the workplace a political site: here I will confine myself to a brief comment on patterns of tension and contradiction in the British programme of restructuring itself.

The British programmatic interventions in industrial relations have relied on the representation of politics as the 'problem' that gets in the way of global competitiveness. Yet the manifest diminution of union influence has not squeezed out the political space for contest and dissent. There is little evidence to support the deregulationists' assumption that deunionisation creates a more peaceful and stable mode of industrial relations (see Table 3.2).

In terms of institutionalised industrial relations the numbers of workers involved in industrial action have declined at similar rates in neo-liberal and corporatist state-societies, with the Anglo-Saxon countries demonstrating no particular tendency to a benign industrial relations climate. If we look to less formalised modes of industrial dispute and dissent, British restructuring appears to be accompanied by ad-hoc expressions of discontent, with the

Table 3.2 Workers involved in strikes and lockouts (thousands)

	1980	*1990*	*1995*
Australia	1173	730	344
Canada	441	270	124
Germany	8451	257	183
New Zealand	128	44	31
Sweden	747	73	125
United Kingdom	834	298	174
United States	795	185	192

Source: Compiled from ILO World Labour Report, 1997–98.

Advisory, Conciliation and Arbitration Service receiving record levels of enquiries in 1998 (EIRR 305, 1999), and a TUC 'hotline' receiving devastating numbers of calls from call-centre workers with grievances (EIRR 328, 2000). The decentralisation of industrial relations to the level of the workplace has enabled firms to restructure rapidly and without consultation with workers. As the general secretary of the TUC, John Monks, stated in response to the Labour Government's 1999 Employment Relations Act: 'there is going to be a lot of fencing going on between unions and employers at the moment' (*The Financial Times*, 6 June 2000: 14). Meanwhile, there is scope for employers to contest statutory union recognition, and it has been suggested that this will spawn a new breed of consultants advising on anti-union corporate strategy (Smith and Morton, 2001: 133).

In sum, the British programme of hyperflexibility has structured a 'fast but fragile' approach to restructuring. Transformations in working practices are represented as inevitable responses to outside pressures, and the interventions made are not negotiated in any formal sense. Paradoxically, the reliance on legislative power and the failure to discuss or debate restructuring in a wider social forum has made the programme fragile in the sense that it is brittle and 'inelastic' (ILO, 1999a). Indeed, in response to a perceived lack of communication channels, some German companies with plants in Britain have developed employee representation arrangements to enable consultation with worker groups.[10] The current vogue for 'corporate social responsibility', fuelled in part by the publicity surrounding the anti-globalisation protests, reveals that firms are aware that they take social (or more accurately shareholder) risks in publicly excluding workers from restructuring decisions. While the corporate social responsibility debate may be a 'smokescreen to avoid statutory legislation' (David Coats of TUC, cited in *The Observer*, 8 July 2001), it is intriguing to reflect on why firms may consider this smokescreen necessary. The high public profile of issues such as the use of child labour in the supply chains of MNCs has led firms to consider the management of social and ethical risks, and trade unions to organise to expose such practices.[11] The decentralisation of industrial relations to the level of firms has paradoxically blurred the boundaries between industrial relations and wider social debates about work and labour, and raised some opportunities for organised labour to engage with these wider debates (Hyman, 1999b).

Conclusion

In this chapter I have argued that the British programme of restructuring has drawn upon distinctive representations of the roles of state, industry, employer, manager, worker and labour organisation, in order to normalise and depoliticise hyperflexibility. In a unique framing of the problem, globalisation is represented as dwelling above and beyond the realms of politics and society, safely lodged in a space that is removed from discussion and debate. At the same time, a discourse of 'harnessing' globalisation is constructed, on the basis of which interventions are made to individualise the risks and responsibilities of work and working life. Far from being a universal global 'benchmark' of neo-liberalism, the British programme rests upon past practices and perceptions of 'what ought to be' that are contested through complex webs of power. At the level of national debates the restructuring of work is politically and socially contingent. It cannot be understood as driven in a linear direction by exogenous forces, nor as a project defined by a coherent and identifiable global elite. In the archetypal neo-liberal setting of what is often described as Anglo-Saxon capitalism, the flexibility discourse is enabled by social power relations that are unique, shifting and contingent. We thus see a distinctive 'making' of flexibility along three central dimensions.

First, the terms that are used to define the problematic are distinctive – giving rise to a particular set of questions that remain essentially open to contest and dispute. The terms of debate in Britain have tended to surround the making of a location that is attractive to external financial and industrial capital. Within these terms, labour is represented as a contingent commodity, disciplined into the restructuring of working practices under the threat of failure to attract and maintain the FDI firms that provide employment. It is not simply the case that institutionalised forms of industrial relations are removed from the equation, but rather that a particular form of individualised relationship between employer and employee is enabled and reproduced over time. In essence, it is not that globalisation automatically depoliticises and codifies the workplace through restructuring imperatives, but that the globalisation debate is given a particular meaning, and that meaning legitimates deregulatory interventions.

Second, the programme of restructuring occupies a distinctive social arena in British state-society – with the workplace constituted as the central terrain of change. The risks and responsibilities of individuals are defined in the workplace, a domain that is carefully constructed as 'non-state', depoliticising the restructuring of working practices, making them 'corporate' and, therefore, 'essential' to competitiveness. The paradox is that the exercise of power in the workplace, expressed as creating a 'benign' industrial relations climate, has structured the kind of insecurity that makes the workplace a space of 'footdragging' resistance and infrapolitics, something that will be explored more fully in chapters 5 and 6.

Finally, the conception of time underlying the British debate is distinctive and reveals the making of a particular representation of globalisation. The hyperflexibility discourse is overwhelmingly constructed in terms of speed and flexibility of response to changes in global markets, and to the demands of consumers. In the opening paragraph of this chapter I cited Tony Blair's Davos speech in which he states that 'the key to the management of change is reform. The pace of reform has to match the pace of change'. The way that global change is constructed thus legitimates a particular style of reform, disciplined by the caveat that 'those that move too slowly will fall behind'. The making of a particular set of meanings of globalisation has enabled a programme of interventions to create an 'optimally flexible' labour market and concomitant 'optimally flexible' working practices. The economic expediency and rationality that is imputed to such interventions effectively attempts to close off restructuring from wider social discussion or debate, or to manage this through exercises in corporate social responsibility. It is this 'closing off' that paradoxically renders hyperflexibility fragile, and offers space for the framing of resistance or the consideration of alternatives. The vulnerability of the 'fast but fragile' programme has been manifested, for example, in a skills shortage and productivity problem (OECD, 2000), and in the high-profile exit of inward investor firms. These questions have been debated publicly, with attention drawn to the slippery nature of a deregulated and low-cost location from which firms can make a rapid exit. The creation of a shareholder society in Britain has served to legitimate much of the 'fast' discipline because it is perceived to be necessary to ensure returns on investment. Yet, the exclusion of the vast majority of people from this society, and their subjection to the dictates of shareholder short-termism, exposes a fragility that does contain spaces for struggle, and the politics of dissent and disaffection.

Notes

1 Hyperflexibility implies a discourse of flexibility that embodies a sense of rapidity and immediacy of response in social practices. In effect, this is the sense implied by most international economic institutions and by those state-societies that have embarked on a programme of what Cox has termed 'hyperliberalism' (1991/1996: 199).

2 Robert Cox argues that: 'Today, state and civil society are so interpentrated that the concepts have become almost purely analytical (referring to difficult-to-define aspects of a complex reality) and are only vaguely and imprecisely indicative of distinct spheres of activity' (1981/1996: 86). His use of 'state-society complex' captures this interpenetration and suggests that analyses of differences and contradictions in state-

societies can serve to open up the 'actions' that are so often ascribed to unitary states.

3 Examples of the use of 'governmentality' to understand neo-liberal policy programmes are abundant. Among the most prominent, see Lemke (2001), and Miller and Rose (1990). See also Foucault (1982) and Simons (1995).

4 For contemporary discussion of the British exceptionalism debate, see Nairn (1993) and Anderson (1991).

5 Interventions designed to reconcile the interests of industrial and financial capital have been made throughout the history of British capitalism (see Langley, 2002).

6 From 1964, the establishment of industrial training boards in Britain structured a clear framework of institutionalised incentives and disincentives within which the firm made its training investment decisions. State involvement in the form of levies raised as a percentage of payroll saw penalties put in place for firms who failed to develop effective training programmes, and structured rewards and incentives for firms who undertook quality training in the workplace. In the 1989 Employment Act, the demise of the industrial training boards was accelerated through the abolition of union representation on the boards, and the downgrading to non-statutory status.

7 The practice of teamworking, for example, while a long-established method of maximising skills utilisation and 'humanising' work in Germany, has become a management-defined method of weakening the boundaries between occupations in Britain (Ackers *et al.*, 1996).

8 It has been suggested that European labour law reflects, and is inspired by, national experiences of labour legislation. The EU Directive clearly follows a continental European approach to the regulation of working time and is in conflict with Anglo-Saxon liberal flexibility (Bercusson, 1997).

9 Deakin and Reed (2000) report that in 1998, 18 per cent of working-age households had no adult in work, a total of 3.15 million households. This figure compares with 8.3 per cent or 1.2 million households in 1979.

10 Insights gained from interviews with British components plants owned by German multinationals, July 1998 and October 1998.

11 Insights from interview with union officials from the AEEU, March 2001.

4

Producing flexi-corporatism: the restructuring of work in Germany

We support a market economy, not a market society ...
Modern social democrats want to transform the safety net of entitlements
into a springboard to personal responsibility...
Part-time work and low-paid work are better than no work...
(Tony Blair and Gerhard Schröder, 1999: 1–7)

The positioning of German state-society within the globalisation and restructuring debates is, in itself, highly contested between competing voices and claims. In a neo-liberal reading, evident across international economic institutions, academic analysis and media commentary, the 'low cost – low regulation' Anglo-Saxon programme is positioned as 'outcompeting' the 'high cost – high regulation' German social market (see OECD, 2001; Giersch *et al.*, 1992; *The Economist*, 8 July 2000). Some more critical social science commentaries have, perhaps inadvertently, reinforced the image of neo-liberal triumph by observing the dominance of a UK–US nexus of hyperliberal restructuring (Gill, 1995a; Van der Pijl, 1984), or by arguing that globalisation demands reforms from social democratic state-societies (Giddens, 1998). Gerhard Schröder's apparent embracing of the individualism and 'workfare' (Jessop, 1994) strategy of Blair's 'Third Way' in his 'Neue Mitte' concept may be read as indicative of an acceptance of the necessary restructuring imperatives of a global economy.

Yet, when we explore the debate taking place within and outside German state-society it becomes clear that the representation of Germany as a rigid and inflexible political economy in need of radical restructuring is by no means uncontested. An effective counter to neo-liberal claims is presented by those who emphasise the 'beneficial constraints' of close relationships between state, industry, finance and labour in 'Rhineland Capitalism' (see Albert, 1993; Streeck, 1992a; Soskice, 1996; Coates, 2000; Hutton, 1995). In this representation of Germany in a global era, the 'inflexibilities' and 'inefficiencies' of German capitalism are read as the resources of high innovation and high quality-based competitiveness. Put simply, perceptions of Germany in relation to globalisation, both inside and outside the state-society, are contradictory and contested. The media, for example, simultaneously proclaim that 'Tomorrow belongs to Germany', and that 'Germany is stalling' (*The Sunday Times* and *Evening Standard*, cited in Marsh, 2000: 76). Indeed, the images of Germany as inflexible 'laggard' and innovative 'leader' have even shared the same headline: 'The Sick Man of Europe Dances a Jig' (*The Guardian*, 12 August 1998: 15). What are we to make of the competing images of 'Modell Deutschland'[1] within the globalisation debate?

In this chapter I argue that 'Modell Deutschland' is being made and remade in contemporary times, constrained and informed by a range of historical institutions and practices, and exhibiting significant tensions and contradictions. As in the previous chapter on the making of a British programme of hyperflexibility, the emphasis here is on *how* it has been possible to represent Germany in particular ways within a debate on globalisation. The first section explores the multiple facets of 'Modell Deutschland' to reveal the competing meanings of globalisation that are constituted. The argument problematises the dominant modes of thought that see Germany *either* as 'squeezed' by global forces on to convergent neo-liberal lines, *or* as directly opposing neo-liberal restructuring, hence always either neo-liberal or non-neo-liberal. I then go on to explore the historical institutions and practices of state, capital and labour in Germany that have made possible particular contemporary programmes of restructuring. Finally, I discuss the contemporary restructuring of working practices in Germany, demonstrating the negotiated and mediated nature of reforms.

'Modell Deutschland' in the globalisation debate

In chapter 3 I argued that so-called 'models' of national capitalism are less coherent and more contradictory than they are commonly presented. In short, a 'model' of capitalism is imagined, produced and reproduced over time, enabling certain claims to be made about the nature of social reality, while impeding others. Drawing on a number of studies using Foucault's concept of 'governmentality', it was argued that governmental interventions (in our terms, programmes of restructuring) rely and rest upon the making of specific representations of a social problematic.[2] The representation of a 'Modell Deutschland', or a German model of capitalism, has been a particularly significant feature of the debates, both within Germany and from without, on what interventions are necessary in an era of globalisation. What is interesting about the 'Modell' is that it is not a singular, unitary or coherent entity at all, but a contingent metaphor that is made in different ways, drawing on a range of historical sources and points of reference. Given the competing representations of the Germany-globalisation relationship, the interventions that are discussed, proposed and implemented do not follow the deterministic logic of a global imperative of flexibility. Rather, they are paradoxical, convoluted and highly contradictory, displaying some affinity with hyperflexibility, yet also much that is anathema to that deregulatory and individualist schema.

In the contemporary remaking of Modell Deutschland, a central role has been played by the neo-liberal discourse that calls the institutions and practices of German capitalism into question. At the heart of the neo-liberal challenge is an appeal to the flexibility and speed of response required by globalisation, and to the rigidity and sluggishness of state-societies that seek to protect their welfare and labour market institutions. In the realms of production and work, embedded social institutions and practices become synonymous with structural rigidities that undermine the potential competitiveness of the labour market through disincentives to work and constraints on business management: 'Policies and systems have made economies rigid and stalled the ability and even willingness to adapt. To realise the new potential gains, societies and economies must respond rapidly to new imperatives and move towards the future opportunities. To many, the change is wrenching' (OECD, 1996).

The German strategy of 'diversified quality production' (Streeck, 1992a), lauded for its success in the 1980s and early 1990s, has had its sustainability questioned in the light of globalisation (see Streeck, 1997a; Zumwinkle, 1995). Commentators point to a number of factors to illustrate the incompatability of German capitalism with what they see as the 'global reality'. The lynchpin of the claims is that an inflexible labour market, combined with high production and labour costs, has made Germany uncompetitive. Commentators cite the high costs of German labour as the key explanation for the loss of the attractiveness of 'Standort Deutschland' (Germany as economic location).[3] A kind of 'Lexus effect'[4] is depicted, whereby German firms are under pressure to sustain their high-quality manufacturing in a context where they are making high cost social contributions in wages and taxes, and their competitors are closing the gap. In this context, much of the 'Standort' debate has focused on the exit of German companies to overseas production sites, with concern that high value-added manufacturing, such as the production of the BMW Z3 and Mercedes four-wheel drive vehicles, is moving to lower cost sites (Hancké, 1997; Gesamtmetall, 1997). With the unemployment rate at 8.3 per cent in 1999 (OECD, 2001), the neo-liberal case is bolstered by the argument that restructuring is required to loosen labour market constraints, reduce the employer cost burden and increase rates of employment.

Looking at the German programme of restructuring it is possible to find evidence that the neo-liberal logic of flexibility, drawing on the representation of the global conundrum I have outlined above, has taken hold. Following the election victory in September 1998, Gerhard Schröder appeared to embrace the market-friendly discourse of Tony Blair's 'Third Way'. Blair and Schröder's joint-authored statement appears as a direct manifesto for deregulatory reforms, in which globalisation is cast as an 'inescapable process' (Felhölter and Noppe, 2000: 241). Much of the text can be read as a direct challenge to prevailing German institutions and practices, pledging to 'accommodate the growing demands for flexibility' and to 'encourage employers to offer "entry" jobs to the labour market by lowering the burden of tax and social security contributions on low-paid jobs' (Blair and Schröder, 1999: 7). The 'Zukunfts-programm 2000' (Programme for the Future, 2000), and the 'Steuerreform 2000' (Tax reform 2000), do indeed appear to grasp some of the neo-liberal nettles, including a lowering of corporate and income tax rates from 2001 and a reform of 'pay as you go' pensions. Yet, the restructuring programme has been labelled 'disappointing' by the OECD (2001), 'insufficient' by the IMF (1999) and 'still too rigid and expensive' by *The Economist* (2000: 17). Presumably this lukewarm reception by the advocates of hyperflexibility indicates that we should exercise caution in claiming that Germany has embraced the deregulatory agenda. There is another story to be told in the Germany-globalisation problematic, one that suggests that 'Neue Mitte' and 'Third Way' take on particular institutional forms and meanings in their different contexts.

It is possible, however, to shed a different light on both the representations of German competitiveness, and the interventions made on the basis of these representations. In contrast to figures on unemployment and labour costs marshalled to urge neo-liberal interventions, figures can indicate that the German economy grew by 3 per cent in 2000, the strongest rate since 1992 (OECD, 2001); unemployment rates are falling (OECD, 2001); inflation is low (Harding and Paterson, 2000); Germany has become a role model in venture capital (Harding and Paterson, 2000); and the high pound has seen unit labour costs per unit of output fall to around 16 per cent below the level of those in the UK (Marsh, 2000). The merger of Daimler and Chrysler, the prominence of Deutsche Bank in the City of London, and the acquisitions of Bentley, Rolls Royce and Rover cast some doubt on the representations of lost German competitiveness on which hyperflexible interventions rely. In terms of the apparent 'Third Way' discourse adopted by Schröder, this has subsequently been put at a distance, not least because it was contested by organised labour, a group that have effectively been 'integrated' into the restructuring process (Ryner and Schulten, 2002: 1). 'Schröder is no Tony Blair, no third way-ist, and he almost certainly regrets bringing out with Blair the policy document on Social Democrat party modernisation' (Marsh, 2000: 75).

Not only has the German political programme sought to distance itself from UK-US-style hyperflexibility, but it has also debated the social effects of radical restructuring. The hostile takeover of Mannesman by Vodafone AirTouch provoked what was described as 'a heated debate about globalisation and Anglo-Saxon corporate aggression' (*Die Zeit*, 19 November 1999: 3). These alternative depictions of the German debate of globalisation and restructuring suggest that we are not witnessing the linear history of a convergence around principles of hyperflexibility. As Ryner and Schulten have it, 'the "hard neo-liberal line" could not prevail in any West-European country, except the United Kingdom' (2002: 12). While it is clear that Germany is engaged in a programme of restructuring, the conundrum of transforming the labour market and working practices takes on a unique form. In the context of social institutions and practices that have precisely sought to 'embed' the economy in society, the making of a neo-liberal discourse that 'renders the social domain economic' (Lemke, 2001: 203) is problematic. A central distinction between the British programme of hyperflexibility and the German restructuring programme is that a debate is actually taking place in Germany, among competing groups across state, finance, industry and labour, leading some to conclude that we are seeing the emergence of a 'competitive corporatism' (Rhodes, 1997) or a 'regulated flexibility' (Fuchs and Schettkat, 2000: 211). Thus, we see a number of competing meanings attributed to globalisation, and a negotiation and contestation of these meanings across state-society in a kind of 'flexi-corporatism'. A caveat to this apparent negotiation of globalisation and restructuring is that this debate is inclusive only in the sense that it includes core workers in a highly protected labour market. For the increasing numbers of people excluded from the core labour market in Germany, this is a debate that is closed to them and is unlikely to reflect their experiences.

Historical representations of the social market

Both the proponents and the critics of the so-called German 'model' of capitalism tend to make appeals to the historical development of the institutions and practices of the German 'social market' political economy. For the proponents, the embedded structures of concerted investment and co-determination make for a 'social infrastructure highly supportive of industry' (Lane, 1994: 174). Viewed in this light, Polanyi's 'fictitious commodities' of land, labour and money are actively embedded in a range of social institutions that ameliorate the effects of commodification (see Glasman, 1996). For the critics, the historical legacy of German social institutions has made the economy sclerotic and inflexible (see Giersch, 1985). In this neo-liberal reading restructuring is designed precisely to transform past institutions and practices and to render them more compatible with the needs of an increasingly competitive global market. Thus, whether proponent or critic, social democrat or neo-liberal, the historical representations of social order, and their reflection in prevailing institutions, have framed the terms of contemporary debate in Germany. Global restructuring has been debated in terms that are drawn from Ordo-liberal conceptions of a social market economy, so that even neo-liberal-style deregulatory strategies have been pursued in a manner that seeks to reconcile them with prevailing practices.

State and market

Much of the contemporary German programme of restructuring has rested upon a discourse of reconciliation between the pressures of globalisation and state-societal visions of a stable and negotiated order. Such a discursive management of the potential antagonisms of restructuring, in turn, draws on a framing of the state-market relationship that, in contrast to the British distancing of the state realm from a market realm of self-responsible individuals, sees a mutually constitutive relationship between state and market. The intellectual tradition of Ordo-liberalism that is credited with the building of a post-war 'Soziale Marktwirtschaft' (social market economy), provides a set of concepts and understandings that can be invoked to bring the market into the realm of political intervention and social dialogue.[5] Writing from the time of the crises of the 1930s, the Ordo-liberals sought to critique laissez-faire liberalism, arguing that a social market economy required protective social institutions to be created and sustained through state intervention (see Röpke, 1942; Eucken, 1949):

> Unlike this negative conception of the state typical of liberal theory in the eighteenth and nineteenth centuries, in the Ordo-liberal view, the market mechanism and the impact of competition can arise only if they are produced by the practice of government. The Ordo-liberals believe that the state and the market economy are not juxtaposed but that the one mutually presumes the existence of the other. (Lemke, 2001: 193)

This conception of a state-market relation that reconciles social needs and values to the dictates of the market is a recurring theme throughout German social history, and is reinvigorated in contemporary debates on the possibilities and limits of restructuring. The Christian Democratic Catholic philosophies pervading the German experience of late nineteenth-century 'catch-up' industrialisation provided a defence of the principles of subsidiarity and co-ordination governing the relations between state, capital, industry, labour and family (Gerschenkron, 1962; Weiss, 1998). As Maurice Glasman has it:

> ... a set of institutional practices embedded in daily working and religious life provided the ethical orientation which organised West German reconstruction. These were carried within the labour movement, Church and locality. No-one 'designed' post-war Germany, it was hewn out of more durable and sophisticated moral and ethical materials than those provided by economic theory or any other social science methodology. (Glasman, 1996: 55)

The durability of the social market economy conception lies in its capacity to be reinvented and reinscribed with new meanings in particular historical periods. In contemporary representations of the state and the global market, the social market is inscribed with a capacity to buffer the damaging features of globalisation. By way of example, in a BBC interview with the President of the World Bank, James Wolfensohn, and German Development Minister, Heidemarie Wieczorek-Zeul, the question of the relationship between society and globalisation was discussed and debated (BBC, 2000). Wieczorek-Zeul disagrees with the interviewer's suggestion that societies should be advised that 'globalisation is happening, here, get used to it':

> Globalisation should not become a situation in which the market economy decides everything in democracy, and social and ecological roles go down the river … within globalisation you have rules, you have social rules … we have a globalisation of markets, we have a globalisation of economy, of trade and what we also have, to a certain extent but have to develop further, is a globalisation of solidarity, a globalisation of values. (Wieczorek-Zeul, cited in BBC News, 2000: 2)

This debate depicted the tensions between neo-liberal conceptions of globalisation as an exogenous force that is 'larger than us', dictating terms to states and societies, and conceptions that render globalisation amenable to reconciliation with social values. I am not suggesting that the German conceptions of state and market are necessarily preferable to, or 'friendlier' than British conceptions, but that the differences are significant in that they reveal the political and social making of globalisation.

Finance and industry

The assertion of a close interrelationship between financial and industrial capital lies at the heart of explanations of the durability of German capitalism (see Hall, 1986; Hutton, 1994; Albert, 1993). Germany's rapid and late industrialisation is cited as the central driving force of bank-based 'state (monopoly) capitalism' (Gerschenkron, 1962; Arrighi, 1994: 163). While Britain's early industrialisation through textiles required relatively limited injections of capital, feeding a culture of individual entrepreneurship, and resulting in an 'industry-finance gap' (Coates, 2000: 67), Germany's industrialisation through heavy industries required the concerted harnessing of capital, framing an 'enabling' role for the state in structuring bank-industry relations. The capital requirements of indigenous industries – investments in production and materials, technologies, education and training – were legitimated as domains for state intervention (Hobsbawm, 1975: 41-45). During the period of post-war reconstruction, the tripartite relationships between state, banks and industries were revisited, with banks reinforced as the key providers of capital for industry and, indeed, given a function in the everyday decision-making of firms.

In contrast to the British making of the stock market as the legitimate source of industrial finance, the German financial system is historically founded on the principle of debt finance by banks (Woolcock, 1996: 183). It is through the lens provided by bank-oriented finance that contemporary questions of global finance are interpreted and framed. German banks have historically had a position on the supervisory boards of the firms in which they hold shares, also exercising proxy votes for shareholders who lodge their shares with the bank. As a result, it is often argued that German banks have competencies in industrial matters, playing legitimate roles in distributing regional development funds to firms, and holding knowledge resources for the benefit of clients (see Hutton, 1994; Albert, 1993), fostering a medium to long-term horizon in corporate strategies. When this industry-finance link is broken, as in Deutsche Bank's decision to sell its large stake in Deutsche Telekom in August 2001, the result is often fierce criticism and debate over the traditional role of German banks in holding shares and 'talking up' their corporate partners. The tensions between the short-term decisions fostered by the principle of shareholder value, and the consultative and longer-term dynamics of bank-based capital, have thus become central to German debates on the restructuring of bank-industry relations. As Michel Albert has it: '... in the Rhine model, the "golden boys" and their breathless exploits on the floor of the Stock Exchange are conspicuously absent. Banks, not stock markets, are the principal guardians of the capitalist flame in Germany' (1993: 106).

The primacy of bank-based finance, and the absence of the 'golden boys' has been challenged in contemporary debates surrounding 'Finanzplatz Deutschland' (Germany as financial centre) (see Story, 1997). The institutionalised relationships between banks and firms are brought into question by the ability of firms to move their production and their financial holdings between countries and to 'off-shore' sites. The large German banks have shifted their focus from credit to equities, reducing their stakes in firms and establishing a significant presence in the world's major financial centres. The shares in large German firms are increasingly in the hands of global institutional investors, and German society itself has doubled its individual share ownership from 10 per cent to 21 per cent over the 3 years to 2000 (*The Economist*, 8 July 2000: 28). Thus, on the one hand, we cannot say that there is no reform taking place in Germany, or that the deregulatory bias of neo-liberal restructuring has been entirely 'resisted'. Yet, on the other hand, we see that restructuring has taken on a particular form, with apparent concessions to neo-liberal flexibility matched by a shoring-up of prevailing institutions and practices – a defining feature of 'Finanzplatz Deutschland' (Story, 1997). For example, though major German MNCs have restructured in favour of equity financing and shareholder value, the vital small/medium size enterprise (SME) sector continues to be dominated by close relationships with the regional banks. Indeed, the OECD expresses its concern that the spirit of deregulated finance has not quite been grasped in the German programme, arguing that the state-owned banks should be privatised (OECD, 2001: 11). Far from abandoning past institutions and practices in favour of radical deregulation, the German debate revives past scepticism of shareholder value and renegotiates within a distinctive industry-finance frame of reference (see Schröder, 1996; Jackson, 1997; Moran, 1992).

Labour

IPE's engagement with labour in the global restructuring debate has tended to assume that, while capital 'promotes' globalisation, labour essentially represents a social force with the potential to 'resist' global dictates and to define alternatives. And, of course, labour has been a primary source of resistance and contestation to globalisation (see O'Brien, 2000; Stevis and Boswell, 1997). However, the role of labour in defining globalisation is somewhat more contradictory than a simple resistance strategy. While in the Anglo-Saxon 'hyperflexible' state-societies it may be more clear that labour is excluded from the defining of a programme of restructuring, the German programme is, at least in part, articulated through the institutions of organised labour.

Historical attempts to co-ordinate and mediate the capital-labour relation are revisited in contemporary German debates on the reorganisation of work. The German labour market has been constituted historically as a sphere that is delineated from markets in finance, goods and services, represented as a distinctly 'social' sphere, so that 'integration into the world economy was not accompanied by deregulated markets in labour and land' (Glasman, 1996: 51). Pre-war practices such as centralised wage bargaining and the institutionalisation of works councils, together with post-war practices such as the sectoral organisation of trade unions, have reproduced a co-ordinated system of labour organisation that positions core workers within decisions about production and changes in production (see Koch, 1992; Lane, 1994; Visser and van Ruysseveldt, 1996). The principle of 'Mitbestimmung' (co-determination) represents a legal intervention that establishes the right of organised labour to representation on advisory boards, and confers negotiative rights on works councils in corporate decision-making.

There is no doubt that Germany's system of labour organisation has been among the institutional aspects most criticised by neo-liberal commentators (see OECD, 1994, 2001). The centralised organisation of labour, the trade unions' ability to sustain a 'family wage' and job security, and the blocks on the development of a casualised work sector, have all been cited as responsible for uncompetitive wage levels, an inflexible labour market and high levels of unemployment. The OECD Jobs Strategy compares Germany, and other continental European state-societies, unfavourably with the UK, US, Australia, Canada and New Zealand, on the basis of its incremental restructuring programme 'at the margins': 'Instead of relaxing general employment protection provisions, some governments have preferred to introduce short-term contracts and liberalise employment protection for part-time workers in small firms (e.g. Germany, France, Belgium)' (OECD, 1997: 8). Despite some apparent concessions to the discourse of flexibility, seen for example in greater devolution of bargaining to the workplace and wage restraint since 1999, the German programme has continued to integrate core labour into the defining of programmes of change in the organisation of labour and work. Thus, restraint in wage bargaining has been secured via negotiations that effectively trade job security and employment creation in return for lower wage claims. The perceptions and realities of a historical interweaving of the institutions and practices of co-determination with German productivity and competitiveness have given rise to 'piecemeal' reforms (Vogel, 1996) that do not resemble UK-US-style hyperflexibility.

The contemporary restructuring of working practices

The contemporary German debates about the restructuring of work draw upon historical understandings of the relationships between state, market, finance, industry and labour. This is not to say that Germany has not felt the heat of neo-liberal exhortations to restructure its social institutions and practices, or that it has not engaged in a debate on the restructuring of work and labour. German state-society has negotiated the implications of globalisation and intensified competition *through* the frameworks of corporatist bargaining. This has not been an unproblematic or consensual exercise, and in most instances it is conflict and contestation that have limited or enabled particular restructuring interventions. Though I do not seek to offer an exhaustive account of the German programme, I am concerned to direct attention to the unique patterns of compromise and conflict that give shape to debates on restructuring work and labour. At the heart of German representations of the restructuring problematic there lies a fundamental tension with the neo-liberal image of hyperflexibility. Where Anglo-Saxon programmes have placed their emphasis on speed of response to global markets, and the self-discipline of individuals in an insecure working environment, the German programme has re-emphasised a protracted process of negotiation through national corporatist structures designed precisely to ensure security and stability for the social partners. I am not offering up the German model as a 'nicer' alternative to British hyperflexibility, or as a path-dependent system that cannot be transformed. Rather, I see the first step in a politicisation of global restructuring to be an exercise in identifying the distinctive webs of power that define the parameters of particular programmes. It is only through an understanding of these webs of power, of how they function and where their weaknesses lie, that we may open up potential spaces for critique, opposition and resistance.

'Functional flexibility', training and skills

The lean production discourse that has dominated much of the drive for flexibility, asserts the need for individual workers to 'multi-task', applying general skills across production, maintenance and quality functions. The rationale for this position is that globalisation accelerates the rate of change in market conditions, making it imperative that firms are able to respond rapidly and flexibly, changing the organisation of work through the reshuffling of production tasks. Despite an apparent thirst for the insights of lean production management models (the lean production 'bible', *The Machine that Changed the World*, made record sales in Germany), lean production and the functional flexibility it prescribes, has taken on a particular German form that is at odds with neo-liberal meanings (Benders and van Bijsterveld, 2000; Streeck, 1996). While UK-US-style prescriptions for functional flexibility emphasise a business-friendly environment in which employers define the necessary and useful skills within the firm, the German system of vocational training is concerned with occupations rather than discrete 'jobs'. The 'dual' system of training in public training institutes and in the workplace distributes the cost and responsibility for training among firms, governments and individuals (Culpepper, 1999). In contrast to the neo-liberal representation of skills and training as task- and firm-specific, German representations position skills as social resources. This has constrained the range of possible interventions so that, in short, nothing is restructured unless it can be agreed among a range of stakeholders – including local chambers of commerce, trade unions, works councils, employers' organisations and the Länder governments.

In terms of the everyday practices of training and skills deployment, there are fundamental tensions between the hyperflexible mantra of multi-skilling, multi-tasking and teamworking, and the negotiated occupational 'status maintenance' of the prevailing German institutions (Esping-Andersen, 1996: 67). Within existing arrangements there are constraints on the devolution of responsibility for skills and training to the level of individual firms, and on the blurring of demarcations between defined occupations. Rather than revising or deregulating existing legal frameworks and institutions, as in the British programme, in the German debate 'new' frameworks are added to existing regulations, negotiated with the social partners, often appearing to extend rather than limit the influence of organised labour – the antithesis of hyperflexibility. This 'restructuring by consensus' is characterised by the 'trading' of concessions between employers and organised labour. By way of example, during the 1980s the German metalworkers union 'IG Metall' conceded a reduction in the number of demarcated sectoral occupations from 48 to 6, conditional upon the demarcation of a new occupation of 'Anlagenführer' (equipment monitor) with overlapping competencies. It is precisely this general working function of quality monitoring and maintenance that the lean production thesis seeks to integrate into all working practices.

In contrast to the British skills flexibility debate, which has focused on the ability of an employer to access a flexible external pool of skills via subcontracting and outsourcing, the German debate has focused predominantly on the flexibility of the 'internal' labour market, arguably supporting a 'high-cost, high-quality' strategy (see Turner and Auer, 1994; Streeck 1992a, 1992b; Jürgens, 1991; Mahnkopf, 1999). The restrictions on 'hire and fire' practices, the embedded system of vocational training and the co-determination procedures that involve organised labour in the negotiation of change – all have combined to produce a distinctive web of power in the reorganisation of work. The German debate on teamworking (Gruppenarbeit), for example, has not inculcated the disciplinary individualisation of the British debate. Though teamworking is increasingly used in German firms, in practice it does not resemble the Toyota model, or the US management prescriptions for blurred boundaries between tasks founded on that model. The concept of teamworking was first defined in the German debate in the 1970s by trade union-led research into the 'Humanisierung des Arbeitslebens' (humanisation of working life). Though revisited and translated since then, the German trade unions have brought the issue of teamworking to the negotiating table of annual bargaining rounds, so that teams constitute semi-autonomous working groups with concrete involvement in the reorganisation of work.

The German debate on skills and training not only stands in tension with the hyperflexible dictates of the OECD's *Jobs Strategy*, but also exhibits unresolved tensions in its own terms. The negotiation of skills and training provision through corporatist channels does not result in a societal consensus around the programme. First, the mutual constitution of training arrangements between employers and core workers requires continuous reinscription and intervention. The influential trade union, IG Metall, for example, staged warning strikes in Baden-Württemberg in protest at what they saw as threats to their rights to consultation on training matters. At the time of writing the disputes had been resolved by an agreement between the union and the employers' organisation 'Gesamtmetall' that entitles all workers to represent their training needs, backed by a joint commission to resolve disagreement (EIRR 330, 2001: 7). The institutions and practices of occupational training do not simply remain static or natural features of German state-society – they are continually brought into question and rebuilt, and this is intensifying as the global discourse on flexibility gains ground.

Second, the greatest challenge to the prevailing programme of occupational status maintenance comes from the growing sector of German society that is excluded from the provision. The costs of the dual system intensify the exiting disincentives for German firms to employ new apprentices, exerting pressure on youth employment rates and giving rise to the possibility of a future skills shortage (Mahnkopf, 1999: 165). The training system itself was built on the tradition of a manufacturing-based 'male breadwinner' society. Unionised men who have experienced the dual system continue to exert their influence in sustaining it. Meanwhile, outside of this diminishing circle, women, unskilled and semi-skilled workers and migrant workers provide a buffer of dispensable labour within a web of power that excludes them. If Germany follows OECD (2001) exhortations to 'liberalise opening hours', removing some of the blocks on a private service sector, the tensions between insider, high-cost, high-skill manufacturing man, and outsider, low-cost, semi-skilled 'servicing' woman will be further intensified.

Working time and 'non-standard' employment

In a neo-liberal reading of flexibilised working time the emphasis is placed on the room for manoeuvre that an employer has to adjust working time within the firm, and to access a pool of contingent labour to stretch the temporal possibilities. For governmental programmes of restructuring this implies that the best practice is the deregulation of working time and employment protection to maximise employer freedoms. The temporal dimension of working practices, in this sense, is 'owned' and controlled by capital and not by the state, or by labour groups, or by workers seeking flexible hours to fit with family life. In the German debate, the statutory right to co-determination of working terms and conditions renders the deregulatory interpretation of working time highly problematic. Up until the 1994 Working Time Act, working time in Germany was regulated by legislation dating from 1938 (Fuchs and Schettkat, 2000: 235). The 1994 Act, reflecting consultation with the social partners, regulates working time to 48 hours per week, but allows flexibility in the calculation of hours so that up to 60 hours per week is permitted for a period up to 6 months. German firms are increasingly introducing 'working time accounts' that allow for flexible working within the statutory parameters, and German workers report increased use of flexibilised working time arrangements (ILO, cited in EIRR 274, 1996). Overall, what we can say is that a working time debate is taking place in Germany; what we cannot say, however, is that it converges on a neo-liberal reading of the imperatives of globalisation.

A central feature of the German debate on working time is its tendency toward a bargaining or 'trading' of firm-friendly temporal flexibility in exchange for job security for individual workers, and employment generation measures favoured by the unions. Within the parameters of prevailing institutions and practices that limit employers' access to external contingent labour, the practice of trading concessions has become a significant trend. A unique agreement at Volkswagen in 1993 established the terms of reference for flexibilising working time. Faced with a choice between large-scale redundancies, costly to both the firm and the workers, or a shortening of the working week, it was agreed that working time would be reduced from 36 to 28 hours, with a corresponding 12 per cent pay cut. The deal was extended to other firms in the engineering sector by IG Metall's 1994 bargaining round, arguably beginning a debate that has now been institutionalised in the 'Alliance for Jobs' programme:

> In a climate of high unemployment, threatened job losses and feared economic stagnation, the priority for trade unions has increasingly become the securing of job guarantees, usually as a trade-off against lower wage settlements and shorter working time with no or partial wage compensation. For employers, the main concern has been to increase working time flexibility in order to be able to respond to fluctuations in demand at minimal cost. (EIRR 268, 1996: 27)

Eight years on from the Volkswagen deal, the question of whether the firm's corporatist arrangements represent a 'vice or a virtue' in contemporary global capitalism remains a matter of much debate and controversy. The use of corporatist channels to negotiate 'flexibility deals' arguably has its own competitive benefits, though the same channels also 'break every taboo in the neoliberal code' (*The Guardian*, 19 June 2001: 12).

Where the German restructuring programme has engaged with the neo-liberal debate on the use of 'non-standard' forms of employment – part-time, contract or contingent work – it has done so through elaborate *reregulation* rather than direct *deregulation*. The regulations governing part-time working, for example, were redefined in 2001, extending the rights of part-time workers and giving full-time workers the right to move to part-time work. The legislation also codifies an ongoing controversy surrounding the use of fixed-term contracts of employment. The 1985 Employment Promotion Act relaxed the regulations governing fixed-term contracts, allowing their use for a period of up to 18 months. The controversies and contests that surrounded the reforms in effect put the brakes on restructuring. The regulation was revisited in 1996 when the permitted period for use of fixed-term contracts was extended to 2 years, and again in 2000 when the practice of concluding successive fixed-term contracts was curbed. The question of whether 'non-standard' employment should be limited in this way continues to be debated and contested – the German employers' organisations argue that the term of use should be extended to 5 years, while the trade unions oppose the use of fixed-term contracts in any circumstances. The OECD are uncompromising in their verdict that 'constraints on the renewability of fixed-term contracts reduces working time flexibility' (OECD, 2001: 9).

The German debate is in tension with much of the neo-liberal discourse on flexibility, with observers lamenting the government's 'cautious' approach to labour market reform, and Schröder's reversal of previous deregulatory strategies (Economist Intelligence Unit, 2001: 8; OECD Economic Outlook, 2000: 223). Aside from these ongoing tensions, the working time debate generates its own contradictions, and tends to conceal the experiences of marginalised worker groups. It is not at all clear that the working time deals that are made on the basis of job security and employment creation are actually having an impact on unemployment levels. Indeed, there is some evidence to suggest that the securing of working time deals by core labour groups could be further entrenching outsider groups in uncertainty and insecurity. For the approximately 6.5 million German workers in SMEs, and particularly for workers in the former East, the deals between the trade unions and employers' organisations are often inaccessible and do not shape the realities of everyday life in the workplace. Similarly, the working experiences of women tend not to be expressed in the working time debate. In a state-society where resources are channelled to social insurance and assistance rather than welfare services, the persistently low levels of women's participation in the labour market indicate that work in the home and caring roles provide an invisible temporal flexibility (see Anderson, 2000). The German debate on the restructuring of working time focuses exclusively on the corporate culture of manufacturing industries, concealing the work of women and migrant workers who provide much of the time flexibility, and excluding them from the debate on restructuring.[6]

Labour costs and collective bargaining

It is a central claim of the neo-liberal restructuring discourse that collective bargaining structures 'artificially' inflate labour costs, rendering a state-society uncompetitive in an era of footloose global capital. In essence, the devolved and deregulated bargaining structures of Anglo-Saxon state-societies are represented as more cost competitive than the dense regulatory constraints of German state-society. In a recent survey of the German economy, the OECD observe that 'labour market institutions are adjusting, but not yet sufficiently to cope with the substantial labour market imbalances persisting in Germany'. On the basis of this representation of the problem, they advocate deregulatory interventions, arguing that 'the authorities should support the process of introducing greater flexibility into the wage bargaining system' (OECD, 2001: 9). The debate over whether Germany can sustain its collective bargaining practices, and provide an attractive location for investment, the 'Standort-debatte', has replaced the 'Modell Deutschland' debate, drawing social democratic and neo-liberal commentators onto the common ground of 'location competitiveness'.[7]

When the terms of the Standortdebatte are explored, however, we find competing and contradictory discourses. On the one hand, we find the representation of Germany's collective bargaining structures as rigid, inflexible and uncompetitive:

> Now the emphasis is on the costs of regulation, bureaucratic red tape, high labour standards, short and inflexible working hours and high non-wage costs. Will Germany remain an attractive production location for global firms that can find highly skilled computer experts in India, hard working engineers in Scotland and low wages just across its borders in Poland, the Czech lands, or further east?' (Visser, 1995: 40)

In this reading total labour costs are argued to be uncompetitively high as a result of collective bargaining practices (see Table 4.1).

The German debate has certainly raised the question of whether any individual state-society can afford to sustain high-cost institutions and practices

Table 4.1 Average hourly labour costs in manufacturing industry, 1999 (DM)

	Wage costs	*Non-wage costs*	*Total*
Germany (W)	27.11	22.12	49.23
Germany (E)	18.70	12.50	31.20
USA	25.53	9.75	35.27
France	17.50	16.27	33.77
UK	23.21	9.56	32.77

Source: Institut der Deutschen Wirtschaft (2000).

in a 'beggar-thy-neighbour' world of regulatory competition. The German media has fed a strong discourse on the ability of German firms to 'shop' for cheaper labour and reduced regulation in Eastern European countries:

> Altogether, since 1990, German industry has invested around DM 216 Billion abroad, and created over half a million jobs – at the same time, in this country, around 2 million jobs were lost. For example, at the end of January, Porsche announced the future production of 5000 cars in Finland, resulting in 500 new jobs there. The lack of new jobs in Germany is caused by the unwillingness of everybody to accept flexibility. (Stern (1997) 7 April, own translation)

However, within the Standortdebatte a different set of representations can be made that legitimate more cautious interventions in the collective bargaining arena. Due in part to the weak Euro, 2000 saw German trade reach record levels, inward investment increase and outward investment by German companies decline (EIU, 2001). When productivity is taken into account and unit labour costs are calculated, Germany appears cheaper than either Britain or Norway, and only 10 per cent more expensive than the US (IDW, 2000). This 'performance paradox' casts some doubt on the confident claims that Germany is rendered uncompetitive by 'high cost' collective bargaining structures. Indeed, it is misleading to assess Germany against the hyperflexible criteria of Britain or the US, since the kinds of flexibility that are produced through corporatist structures are at odds with Anglo-Saxon practices. The Bündnis für Arbeit (Alliance for Jobs) initiative, discussed in greater detail in the section on industrial relations practices, has seen bargaining rounds since 1996 characterised by moderate pay increases, reflecting the trade unions' interests in bargains that extend beyond issues of pay, to include job security and employment creation.

Where programmes of restructuring in collective bargaining arrangements have been initiated in Germany, these have been negotiated and contested. The question of devolution of wage negotiations to the level of individual firms, a central feature of neo-liberal programmes, is not so straightforward in the German case. The German Government has adapted regulations so that firm-specific derogations from sectoral bargains can be made, though this has not been taken up in the way that the hyperflexibility thesis might assume. There are employers who resist firm-level negotiations because they fear that this will provoke wage competition between firms, manifesting in costs elsewhere (Fuchs and Schettkat, 2000: 224). Equally, there are works councils, particularly in the former East, who support firm-level bargains that allow them to secure the future of struggling firms.

Examples of what, according to a hyperflexibility logic, may seem unexpected twists in deregulation, abound in the German debate on collective bargaining. Regulations governing the provision of sick pay, for example, have vacillated back and forth as the social partners contest the programme. The

Köhl Government initially reregulated sick pay provision in 1995, reducing entitlement from 100 per cent to 80 per cent of net income. This was then subject to contest between IG Metall and Gesamtmetall, who finally agreed to restore the 100 per cent level in their sector. Viewed through neo-liberal eyes this is a bizarre example of firms agreeing to reject freedoms conferred on them by the government, ending finally in the Schröder Government's restoration of the 100 per cent level. The proposed reforms to the 1972 Works Constitution Act provide a further example of the non-conformation of German restructuring to a neo-liberal deregulatory model. Amid disputes with employers' organisations, the labour minister Walter Riester has proposed an extension of the powers of works councils, giving them a mandate beyond terms and conditions, to include consultation in the use of homeworking, subcontracting and outsourcing. The proposed Bill has provoked widespread criticism from neo-liberal commentators who see it as extending already 'protracted' decision-making structures (Economic Intelligence Unit, 2001: 17).

The maintenance (or even strengthening) of collective bargaining structures through the German programme has not merely provoked criticism from proponents of deregulation. The exclusivity of the 'bargaining club', as I have highlighted in the skills and working time debates, means that the image of a society-wide debate on the terms of restructuring is rather misleading. The trade unions have been anxious to extend collective bargaining across the whole of unified Germany, preventing the low wage 'undercutting' effect of the former East, but arguably also removing any chance of competitive advantage for these industries. As one commentator asked 'how would NAFTA have worked out for Northern Mexico if the US auto workers union had taken over the collective bargaining south of the Rio Grande?' (*The Guardian*, 19 June 2001: 12). The de facto reality for East German workers is that two-thirds of them are not receiving the wage increases agreed through sectoral bargaining, their employers having removed themselves from the agreement by leaving the employers' organisations (VSME, 2000).

The inequalities of access to the bargaining debate, though most acute in the divisions between East and West, are evident throughout German society. For the 'insiders', employed in traditional sectors with secure contracts and generous social insurance provision, the bargains struck in the course of restructuring reproduce an order that reflects their interests.[8] The overall trend is for secure and highly-paid workers to gain greater increases in bargaining rounds than their less secure and less well-paid colleagues. An increasing number of outsiders, excluded by virtue of their unemployment, their work in the informal economy or their fixed-term contracts, tend to be excluded from the German programme of 'restructuring within limits'. Birgit Mahnkopf identifies divisions between the interests and experiences of a nationally-rooted 'Arbeitsgesellschaft' (working society), and those of a globally-mobile 'Gesellschaft der Geldvermögenbesitzer' (wealth-owning society) (1999: 159–160). Yet, even within the working society, not to mention the extensive nonworking society, there are tensions and inequalities that are not resolved by the current restructuring programme. Ultimately, these divisions raise the question of whether, facing persistently high rates of unemployment, future government interventions in the rules governing the bargaining rounds will allow greater use of derogation. If the flood gates are opened on a feminised service sector, this is likely to create new inequalities based on insecurity, to replace the old inequalities based on unemployment.

Industrial relations and the 'alliance for jobs'

The German debate on the restructuring of industrial relations practices is tightly interwoven with the questions surrounding collective bargaining. However, I consider industrial relations here specifically in terms of organised labour's engagement with the programme of restructuring, and the debate on unemployment levels (see Table 4.2). In a neo-liberal reading, consensus-oriented industrial relations practices are held to inhibit competitiveness, growth and job creation. In a series of international reports Germany's high levels of unemployment have been linked to the bargaining power of the trade unions and the associated disincentives for employers to recruit new workers (OECD, 1994, 1997). Thus, for critics of the social market economy, prevailing institutions of industrial relations and collective bargaining inhibit job creation. In this sense, 'the crisis of the "German model" is, at its core, a crisis of the established system of industrial relations' (Mahnkopf, 1999: 161).

However, the industrial relations debate in Germany has not taken the form of Anglo-Saxon hyperflexibility in which trade unions are constrained in their activities and removed from many workplaces. In contrast to this

Table 4.2 Standardised rates of unemployment (as % of civilian labour force)

	1997	1998	1999	2000
Canada	9.1	8.3	7.6	6.8
France	12.3	11.8	11.2	9.5
Germany	9.9	9.3	8.6	7.9
Netherlands	5.2	4.1	3.3	2.7
New Zealand	6.6	7.5	6.8	6.0
Sweden	9.9	8.3	7.2	5.9
UK	7.0	6.3	6.1	5.5
US	4.9	4.5	4.2	4.0
OECD	7.2	7.1	6.8	6.4
EU	10.6	9.9	9.2	8.2

Source: OECD Economic Outlook (2001), compiled according to International Labour Office guidelines.

restructuring of industrial relations, the German debate has seen a *restructuring through* the corporatist channels provided by the social partners. The flexibilisation of labour and work is negotiated in a way that acknowledges the problems of global competitiveness and job creation, but seeks to reconcile these with societal corporatist (Rhodes, 1997). There is a notable absence of a clear-cut neo-liberal agenda of deunionisation, with employers unwilling to disrupt a system of industrial relations that imposes uniform constraints on themselves and their competitors, limits wage competition and promotes high value-added production (Tüselmann and Heise, 2000; Upchurch, 2000).

The Bündnis für Arbeit (Alliance for Jobs) initiative has provided a central terrain for the debate on consensus-led restructuring. First proposed in 1995 by Klaus Zwickel, leader of IG Metall, the programme began as a union initiative designed to promote job creation and apprenticeships and to limit practices such as overtime. The government, employers' organisations and trade unions engaged in a discussion of proposals designed to halve the rate of unemployment by the end of 2000. In effect the Alliance represents an attempt to achieve restructuring through compromise and accommodation – with the unions agreeing to wage restraint, the employers opening discussions on unfreezing recruitment and limiting overtime, and the government debating initiatives such as state-sponsored early retirement to take the pressure off the youth labour market. However, the Alliance is itself illustrative of the frictions and tensions that pervade a programme of restructuring (see Timmins, 2000; Fuchs and Schettkat, 2000). Though it has survived by adapting the agenda to lowest common-denominator agreement, it has stalled on several occasions when either the unions or the employers threaten to leave the table. The unions have contested what they see as a failure to match their wage concessions with job-creation initiatives. At the time of writing the unions are seeking 250,000 new jobs for 2001, and IG Metall warn that they will cease to exercise wage restraint in 2002 'unless there is evidence that pay moderation has been translated into new jobs' (cited in EIRR 327, 2001: 9). For their part, the employers' organisations threatened to leave the talks in 1999 in response to the unions refusal to define 'wage moderation'.

Overall, the German restructuring debate, conducted through industrial relations channels, is a highly contested and contradictory affair. On the one hand, for example, trade union membership has been in decline at around 4 per cent per year since reunification. This could support claims that organised labour has a diminishing role in the global political economy. On the other hand we find the launch of the new service sector mega-union 'Ver.di' in March 2001, suggesting that old style industrial relations practices are being revitalised for new sectors. The general secretary of the new union announced his intention to ensure that Ver.di adopted a 'fighting tradition', beginning with a series of warning strikes at Lufthansa to force a 3.5 per cent backdated pay settlement (EIRR 325, 2001; EIU, 2001). Though the unions have seized the opportunity, at least in their rhetoric, to reach out to workers who do not fit the archetypal industrial model, it is likely that tensions will continue to surface around excluded workers. The low-wage service sector continues to be neglected in the Alliance talks, raising the question of whether the restructuring agenda is simply 'co-opting' the unions and reproducing a 'Modell Deutschland' of working men in the manufacturing sectors of the West.

Conclusion

The discussion of Germany's programme of restructuring amidst globalisation has tended to offer two competing explanations. In the economistic readings of globalisation as inexorable 'process', the competitive flexibility of the Anglo-American models exerts a pressure that causes 'Modell Deutschland' to collapse, or at least to converge on neo-liberal interventions. For those who emphasise the national political 'projects' that shape responses to international pressures, by contrast, existing institutions frame somewhat path-dependent responses. Yet, despite their competing emphases, neither approach enables us to reflect upon how the notion of a 'German model' emerges over time, or on how this apparent model is negotiated, enabled or contested in the light of discourses of global restructuring. In neglecting the contingent historical making of the 'national' and 'global', the existing modes of understanding obscure the complex intertwining of these terrains of political life.

In this chapter I have used an IPE of social practice to shed light on the question of Germany's distinctive making of globalisation through programmes of restructuring. With regard to agency and the exercise of power in restructuring, I have argued that German state-society is not simply rendered *powerless* in the grip of global forces, as in the process reading. Nor is it the case that the social partners simply *wield* power in the political process in order to resist globalisation. Rather, a reading of the webs of power through which restructuring is exercised reveals a distinctive framing of globalisation, and a particular set of interventions made on the basis of this framing. In British representations of globalisation, there is a manifest 'distancing' of state from market, with the dominant restructuring question being 'in what ways can the state deregulate to allow greater market freedoms and attract inward investment?'. By contrast, the German programme represents markets as reconcilable with state and society, asking the question 'in what ways can the state-society restructure in order to enable German industries to compete more effectively?' Thus, it is not simply that national pathways of restructuring diverge, but that the representations on which programmes are based tend to reflect webs of power that are unique to particular social spaces.

In terms of the historicity that is highlighted by an IPE of social practice, the meanings that are attributed to globalisation and restructuring are framed by existing modes of understanding, prevailing institutions and practices. The historical framing of the relationships between state, finance, industry and

labour, for example, have provided the parameters for a negotiated programme of restructuring. In contrast to the 'fast but fragile' time-frame of
British hyperflexibility, the German programme is 'slow but sticky', pursued
through the webs of power of the social partners rather than conducted as an
assault on their known practices. This is not to say that the German political
economy is 'ignoring' or 'resisting' globalisation, nor that it offers a 'friendlier'
face of neo-liberalism. Instead, the pressures of globalisation are given a
distinctive set of social and political meánings in the German debate, and as
with the British programme, understanding how these have become dominant, and what their contradictions may be, is an important first step in the
politicisation of global restructuring. It is important that the 'automatic' logic
of restructuring is challenged and replaced by an acknowledgement of the
making and the contestation of particular programmes.

Finally, the IPE of social practice unpacks the 'German model' to reveal
the everyday practices that enable and confound its existence. Where the
British debate has actively sought to depoliticise restructuring by confining
the terrain almost exclusively to the level of individual workplaces and firms,
the German debate has been more difficult for political players to constrain
and limit. The German programme has relied upon the involvement and
participation of the social partners in a kind of flexi-corporatism of traded
bargains in order to embed restructuring within regulatory frameworks.
Where we see the formulation of apparently hyperflexible deregulatory
policies, these are subject to the tumult of industrial relations practices, and
are frequently abandoned or moderated beyond recognition. This regulated
and formal contestation within the parameters of collective bargaining
institutions forms one aspect of the contestation of restructuring in everyday
life in Germany. Arguably the most significant tensions of the German
programme, however, lie not in the practices of those who are included in the
debate, but in those of the excluded:

> The number of 'losers' is increasing. Now the working members of
> society sit in different boats, one of which quickly sinks, another sinks
> more slowly, while a third stays afloat. (*Stern* (1997), own translation)

This media comment on the fragmentary effects of global restructuring
foretells something of the future challenges of the German programme. For
the invisible and obscured workers in the informal economy, care and
domestic services, the former East, and other vulnerable groups, the terms,
time-frame and terrain of the restructuring debate are anathema. The terms
of the 'Standortdebatte' apply only to those who are directly engaged in core
financial and manufacturing businesses, the time-frame is much faster and
less secure for unprotected workers and the corporatist terrain is familiar only
to those interests who historically defined it. The working practices of the
unprotected groups are increasingly fundamental to the securing of the core
groups, in childcare and domestic work, for example, yet these practices

remain unacknowledged in the debate. The continued reconciliation of state and market will face the significant challenge of addressing the dynamics of the informal, tacit and unregulated markets that trade on the flexibility denied in the formal economy.

Notes

1 'Modell Deutschland', or the 'German model' was a Social Democrat election slogan from the 1970s. According to Mahnkopf, over time the slogan became a 'synonym for the consensual incorporation of corporatist interest groups into a ... "national economy modernisation" strategy' (1999: 153).

2 For some insightful examples of the use of Foucault's 'governmentality' to understand neo-liberal policy programmes, see Lemke (2001), Miller and Rose (1990) and Barry, Osborne and Rose (1996).

3 A number of agencies have marshalled comparisons of labour costs to caution against the maintenance of institutions and practices that may inflate labour costs. The Bank of International Settlements calculate costs in the UK manufacturing sector for 1995 at 45 per cent of costs in the same sector in Germany (cited in *The Independent*, 13 June 1996). The *Financial Times* focuses on labour costs in British and German plants of the same firm, Osram, a subsidiary of Siemens. Labour costs (including wages, taxes and related non-wage costs) are calculated at 66 per cent lower in Manchester, UK than in Augsburg, Germany (*Financial Times*, 21 March 1997).

4 In the year the Lexus car was launched, one model alone sold more vehicles in the US than the entire range of Mercedes models (Hancké, 1997).

5 The Ordo-liberal theory of the social market is broadly derived from the works of two groups of theorists: the Ordo-liberal economists and lawyers of the Freiburg school, notably Walter Eucken and Franz Böhm and the more sociological approaches of Alfred Müller-Armack, Wilhelm Röpke and Alexander Rüstow. The central contribution of these schools of thought is the notion that, far from representing a spontaneous and naturally efficient allocative device, the market requires state direction to encourage a decentralisation of decisions relating to social and economic life.

6 Brigitte Young argues that there is a 'flourishing black market' for domestic labour in Germany, predominantly provided *by* women and migrants from Yugoslavia, Turkey and Eastern Europe, *for* families with high income and little time (2001: 320). The unprotected and unregulated labour of domestic workers provides an informal working-time flexibility that is not addressed by the dominant German debate, though it undoubtedly plays a role in enabling the debate to take place.

7 This shift arguably follows Porter's (1990) influential work on the transformation from comparative to competitive advantage. IPE scholars have long argued that the nature of interstate competition has shifted from an emphasis on resources held – territory, raw materials etc. – to an emphasis on market share and the climate for business (Strange, 1988, 1996).

8 The 1999 agreement between IG Metall and Volkswagen, for example, secured 3.2 per cent pay increases, but failed to establish permanent status for the 6000 workers on fixed-term contracts.

5

~

The 'contested' firm: the restructuring of work and production in the international political economy

~

> no involuntary changes have ever spontaneously restructured or reorgan-
> ised a mode of production; … changes in productive relationships are
> experienced in social and cultural life, refracted in men's ideas and their
> values, and argued through in their actions, their choices and their
> beliefs. (Thompson, 1976/1994: 222)

The desire to comprehend, order and manage the dual dynamics of globalisation and restructuring has led to much attention being paid to the
actions and activities of MNCs. Academic commentaries in IPE, economics,
sociology and business studies have commonly singled out the MNC as the
central site of production and work for the global economy and, therefore, as a
leading agent of globalisation. As the primary vehicles for global forces, firms
are represented as *acting* to intensify competition, *reacting* to technological
imperatives and *transmitting* knowledge and practices of restructuring across
national boundaries. Media commentaries variously depict the multinationals
as 'a powerful force for good' (*The Economist*, 4 February 2000: 21), or as the
embodiment of globalisation with 'the whole world in their hands' (*The
Sunday Times*, 17 May 1998: 11). Meanwhile, for those who oppose or resist
globalisation, the logos of the MNCs – the Nike 'swoosh', the McDonald's
golden arches, the Shell emblem – have become the archetypal symbols of
global capitalism and the epitome of all that is wrong with globalisation. The
dominant understanding of firms in the GPE represents the MNC as a unitary,
coherent and bounded agent, pursuing global restructuring in a rational and
linear fashion. Paradoxically, both 'pro-globalisation' neo-liberal accounts,
and so-called 'anti-globalisation' accounts reinforce the image of firms as
abstract entities, thereby obscuring the webs of power and practice that
constitute sites of production – and limiting the potential for a politicisation
of the restructuring of work and production.

It is the contention of this chapter that dominant representations of the
firm within globalisation have underplayed the contested nature of the restructuring of work. Indeed, it has become the vogue to present globalisation
as actively decoupling the firm from its relationships with state and society,
rendering it 'footloose' and infinitely mobile. If we are to advance our

understanding of the webs of power that define global restructuring, and the implications for labour and social groups, then we must critically reconsider the assumed agency of the firm. How is it possible to delineate the agency of the MNC from, for example, the networks of shareholders, employers' and industry organisations or suppliers and contractors, within which it is situated? Defined in terms of a matrix of relationships that transcend ascribed boundaries – corporate managers, financiers, shareholders, suppliers and a diverse range of labour groups – the firm becomes a site of contest in the ascription of meanings and realities of globalisation.

The notion of contestation is furthered here at two interrelated levels. First, firms themselves are explored in the context of the competing social forces of which, and within which, they are constituted. Drawing on the restructuring experiences of British and German home-based multinational firms, the chapter suggests that the activities of globally-operating firms are less the outcome of unitary and unified actions than they are the result of a series of contests. If we understand the firm in this way, as a primary site of the experience of global change, then we are led to advance understandings of the contested nature of the restructuring of productive and working practices. We thus direct less attention to the firm as a vehicle of globalisation and become more attuned to the social experiences of global change that are played out within and around the firm. In this way, space is opened up for examination of the role of labour groups in the contestation and shaping of restructuring. Second, the chapter seeks to emphasise the contested nature of our knowledge of the firm within IPE. Capturing the potential position of the firm in the contestation of globalisation is thus posed as a challenge for the field of IPE, both in terms of its 'field of inquiry' and its 'set of assumptions' (Tooze, 1984). In short, it is argued that there is a need to emphasise contest both in terms of the social relations and practices within and surrounding the firm itself, and in terms of the contested nature of our knowledge of the nature and sources of globalisation.

The firm as a 'global agent'

The understanding of global social change that has dominated IPE has tended to reproduce particular conceptions of the relationship between states and markets. As I argued in chapter 2, the delineation and opposition of bounded states and markets has obscured the porous and interrelated nature of these domains. In accounts of globalisation as an 'inexorable process', the domain of the market is represented as encroaching on the domain of the state. For many, the 'footloose MNC' has become the visible face of global markets, wielding its power over national governments and changing the balance of political authority in the GPE. As a result, firms have come to be understood as essentially rational actors whose actions have created and sustained an intensification of competition in global markets. For IPE, a specific type of firm, the

MNC, has been cast as the key non-state actor in an increasingly inter-dependent world.[1] In this way, from the 1970s, the firm has come to represent the primary vehicle of globalisation as it creates restructuring imperatives for states and societies alike (Stopford and Strange, 1991; Porter, 1990; Ohmae, 1990; Sklair, 2001).

For many academics, policy-makers, business people, journalists and indeed workers, there is a sense in which understanding globalisation has become synonymous with understanding the actions of MNCs as they, in turn, react to productive and technological transformations. For Stopford and Strange: 'What is loosely termed "global competition" is the outcome of how individual firms have reacted over time to the changing balance of opportunity and threat' (1991: 65). The firm thus becomes understood as both absorbing and contributing to globalising forces so that it becomes decoupled from the institutions and practices of state-societies. It is understood as an agent of transformation in the global economy (see Sklair, 1998), whose authority challenges that of national governments. Where state-firm relationships do enter analyses, these tend to be defined as a kind of interdependent diplomacy (see Walter, 1998), particularly in terms of the state's attraction of FDI. Attention to firm-society relations is similarly confined to a focus on the imper-atives of restructuring for lean and flexible productive and working practices.

What are the limitations of this mode of knowledge about the firm? The idea that the firm has become a new unit of analysis in the study of the world political economy invokes, paradoxically, similar criticisms to those levelled at traditional international relations frameworks in their understandings of the state. The view of the firm as a coherent and identifiable actor in world politics has many parallels with the neo-realist view of the state as atomised, unitary and essentially rational. Susan Strange, for example, ascribes to MNCs some of the masculine qualities or a 'statesman' of diplomat with self-seeking expansionary ambitions. Firms are understood to be 'having to become more statesmanlike as they seek corporate alliances ... to enhance their combined capacities to compete with others for world market share' (Stopford and Strange, 1991: 2). The state and corporate actors Strange positions in relation-ships of 'triangular diplomacy' are presented as 'managers' of globalisation, resonant with Charlotte Hooper's 'frontier masculinity' in which business solutions are sought for global dilemmas (Hooper, 2000: 67; see also Hooper, 2001). Diplomatic practices, espionage and the activities of statesmen have defined what Hooper terms 'hegemonic masculinities' that now merge with business discourses to create images such as that of James Bond and Henry Kissinger 'sitting next to an Economist reading businessman on a plane' (Hooper, 1999: 485). Many IPE accounts of the firm reinforce such con-structions of atomised agency in which expertise, calculated strategy and rational action are at the cutting edge of globalisation.

The abstracted isolation of individual firms or businessmen as managers of globalisation assumes that these actors have a common voice and a single set of objectives. Yet, the social groups and interests within and around the firm itself are rarely cohesive. Restructuring is commonly characterised by conflict between, for example, managers and production workers, financial and technical roles at the corporate level, or between permanent and contingent workers at shop-floor level.[2] To present the firm as a unitary global 'power wielder' is to neglect to account for the webs of power of which, and through which, the firm is constituted. It is these webs of power that must be understood if global restructuring is to be repositioned as a social and political programme requiring particular representations and interventions, rather than as an automatic economic imperative.

Though the relationships between states and firms are explored and problematised to an extent in mainstream IPE literature, the contests within, across and around the firm itself tend to be neglected. In this way, globalising forces are treated as though they exist exogenously and are rarely considered as integral elements of a wider set of social practices. So, for example, much of the analysis of the relationship between technology and the firm adheres to some variant of the imperatives of lean production.[3] Womack *et al.* (1990) *The Machine that Changed the World*, for example, equated the loss of competitiveness in the European and North American automobile industries with the superior technologies and production processes of the Toyotist Japanese model. As critical approaches to the restructuring of production and work have demonstrated,[4] this simplistic construction of the interrelationships between states, firms, societies and social groups suffers from an 'unhealthy mix of analysis, description and prescription' (Ruigrok and van Tulder, 1995: 6). The firm becomes a disembedded entity to be studied outside of the realm of state and society, except insofar as it impacts on these levels through prescribed restructuring imperatives. Put simply, orthodox understandings of the firm in IPE tend neither to open up the firm to examine the social power relations within, nor to look at their extension into wider social contests.

Politicising the firm in IPE

As scholars have more actively explored interdisciplinary approaches to understanding global change, recent debates have begun to offer politicised alternatives to the study of atomised states and firms. In particular, the work of Karl Polanyi has been used to demonstrate the historical and contextual contingency of social action. From Polanyi's rich and diverse writings, contemporary IPE has drawn out the notion of the embeddedness of economic transactions in a web of social relations and institutions:

> ... man's economy, as a rule, is submerged in his social relationships ...
> Neither the process of production not that of distribution is linked to
> specific economic interests attached to the possession of goods; but every
> single step in that process is geared to a number of social interests which
> eventually ensure that the required steps be taken. (Polanyi, 1957: 46)

Contemporary interpretations of Polanyi's work have, of course, imported his ideas into a new context. The problematic of *The Great Transformation* was to explore the historical transformation of nineteenth-century liberalism and to explain the social effects of an imposed self-regulating market economy. However, Polanyi's ontological position has become increasingly useful in the development of critical positions on global social change. In essence, his work places society firmly at the centre of analysis, reminding us that '... normally, the economic order is merely a function of the social, in which it is contained' (1957: 71). For Polanyi, economic activities require social institutions to protect human beings and the environment and, indeed, to provide the skills and technologies necessary for production. To more fully understand the political economy of the firm, these insights suggest that there is a need to develop knowledge of the social institutions in which economic production is embedded.

Drawing on the Polanyian thesis, scholars have critiqued the notion of the firm as an abstracted global actor, and have sought to contextualise it within a set of political and social institutions. Pauly and Reich, for example, emphasise the enduring nationality of the firm, arguing that this reflects 'durable national institutions and distinctive ideological traditions' (1997: 1). Razeen Sally's (1994) institutional approach to the multinational enterprise, similarly explores the embeddedness of multinationals in broader networks of social institutions. From a different perspective, the 'societal systems' approach, applied widely to studies of industrial or firm-level change in the form of 'social systems of production', characterises the firm as a social arena (Maurice, Sorge and Warner, 1980). At the root of these analyses is some notion that the GPE is made up of an array of distinctive national capitalisms. Following, for example Albert (1993), Crouch and Streeck (1997) and Berger and Dore (1996), national models of capitalism arise out of a web of distinctive institutions and practices. For those whose focus is national models of industrial relations, it is these institutions and practices that condition and reflect the organisation of firms (Lane, 1996a; Rubery, 1996). The value of the 'national models' literature lies in their 'embedding' of the activities of the firm in the context of political and social institutions. In contrast to much of the economistic emphases on the corporate imperatives of globalisation, the firm is analysed in its concrete relationships with the institutions and practices of a particular state-society.

There are, however, a series of interrelated problems with the uncritical adoption of a societal embeddedness approach to the firm. First, there is a clear privileging of the notion of firms *existing within* sets of social institutions, to the neglect of the idea of firms as *constituted of* competing social relations, so that the most basic and fundamental everyday social contests are neglected. Many of the 'external' actors identified by this literature – for example trade unions, financial institutions and research institutions – cannot simply be considered to form the environment within which the firm is embedded. Rather, as we saw in the analyses of British and German restructuring programmes, they are an integral part of the social contests which extend into and across firms. Second, there is a tendency to overemphasise the coherence of the national system of production within which the firm is situated, and to neglect its historical making, and the contests which may potentially reinforce or undermine it. Finally, and a related point, the scholars who seek to raise the profile of the embeddedness of firms tend to do this through an emphasis on the institutions of the nation-state. It should perhaps be considered that the contests that characterise the restructuring of production and work may be simultaneously national and transnational (see Mizruchi and Schwartz, 1987). In sum, the embeddedness approaches to the study of the firm, though situating the firm within a political and social context, tend to present an image of static national path-dependency. If we understand the firm simply to be embedded within an array of fixed national institutions, then it becomes difficult to conceive either of how processes of change may occur, or indeed how transnational social forces may penetrate these institutions.

Taken together, and in a critical spirit, the broad thrust of the embeddedness approach is illustrative of a gap in the IPE literature on the firm and restructuring. In short, we are led to consider that the firm does not simply act and react to exogenous imperatives, but rather forms an integral part of a historical social environment within which globalisation and restructuring are perceived and experienced. The problematic at this point is to reinterpret these insights to characterise these meanings as socially bargained, negotiated and *contested*. Advancing an understanding of the firm as a site of contest serves to highlight the potential for individuals and social groups either to contest and transform embedded working and productive practices, or to challenge such a process of restructuring.

A reading of neo-Gramscian work on global transformation takes us some way towards viewing the firm as a contested site that extends into the domains of state, finance, society and labour. Though Gramsci's ideas have been interpreted in many different ways to explain diverse contemporary social change, we can identify a core of ideas that specifically illuminate the dynamics of production and work within the firm. First, society and social relations are positioned at the heart of understandings of processes of transformation. In this way, historical change is understood to be the product of competing social forces acting within the parameters of social structures (Gill, 1997: 17). In essence, such perspectives serve to counter economistic and teleological readings of globalisation and change, reminding us of the human and social roots of transformation. For those who seek to raise the profile of civil society, and labour in particular, in contesting and shaping global change, these insights have considerable utility. Globalisation and restructuring cease to appear as 'bulldozers' that destroy all potential alliances and resistances and, instead, become open to social contestation and redefinition.

Second, this range of approaches to IR/IPE has a strong and specific focus on the social relations surrounding production and work. Cox's (1987) and Harrod's (1987) seminal twin volumes explicitly explore the patterns of power relations within and around production. Both volumes contribute to a framework for understanding the social relations of production in a broad sense, acknowledging that societies may be constituted of several interconnected kinds of production within, for example, the firm, the household, the formal and informal economies. Production is conceived as ubiquitous in the experiences, perceptions and lives of human beings (Harrod, 1997a: 109). In terms of our focus on restructuring, attention is thus directed to the firm as a constitutive element of a broader and more complex web of social power relations[5] which are produced, reproduced or transformed over time.[6]

Finally, the neo-Gramscian analyses render visible the contested nature of social orders. Murphy interprets Gramsci's 'historical bloc' as a unified social order '... linked by both coercive institutions of *the state proper* and consensual institutions of civil society' (1994: 10). This approach directs our attention beyond institutional analysis which deals only with static, formalised public and private institutions, to expose the roles of informal and tacit social ideas, practices and institutions within, beyond and across states and firms. These ideas, practices and institutions will both reflect and inform the 'shape' of the historical bloc or how society should be organised or reorganised. Viewed in this way, restructuring becomes a process of contested definition and redefinition of social order. This has led some scholars to open up neo-liberal globalisation to the contests of 'labour and other subordinate social forces' (Stevis and Boswell, 1997: 93).

Despite the considerable critical contribution made by neo-Gramscian scholars to questions of power and production, transnational class, neo-liberal politics and social and resistance movements, the opportunity to expose the webs of power surrounding global restructuring has not yet been fully taken up. Caught up in explanations of the power held by elite transnational actors in the global economy, neo-Gramscians tend not to apply their analysis of political power to everyday realms.[7] Where ordinary and commonplace sites of struggle are identified, these are designated 'sites of resistance', and their relationship to programmes of restructuring (often highly contradictory), is taken for granted. The problematic becomes how to account for the commonplace contestation that gives meaning to the restructuring of production and work. The IPE of social practice perspective, developed in chapter 2, sheds light on the historicity, power relations and 'everydayness' of the restructuring of work.

An IPE of social practice draws our attention to the historicity and contingency of the restructuring of work. In contrast to essentialist accounts of the production structure automatically transforming in line with global dictates, a historical mode of inquiry highlights the capacity of human beings to apprehend their circumstances. Viewed in this way, the reorganisation of work within firms does not simply 'happen to' people, it is experienced and interpreted in the thoughts and actions of those within the production structure. The translation of techniques such as lean production into concrete transformations in working practices not only confronts a range of material constraints, but also structured social practices, shared understandings and frameworks of thought. Despite the managerial discourses that construct workplace relations as commodities, or 'human resources' that can be 're-engineered' in the manner of material entities (du Gay, 1997), the restructuring of work is conducted through a web of social power relations that extends within and across the firm. Much of the discourse of hyperflexibility, together with the interventions of lean production and TQM, relies upon a construction of the firm as a bounded entity that can be abstracted from wider social relations. Viewing the firm as a web of power relations and social practices effectively problematises the assumptions that underpin hyper-flexible programmes of restructuring.

In order to explore the webs of power that surround the restructuring of work, it is useful to conceptually 'freeze' a set of workplace practices so that the patterns and points of tension become visible:

> Ideal types 'stop' the movement of history, conceptually fixing a parti-
> cular social practice (such as a way of organising production ...) so that
> it can be compared with and contrasted to other social practices. To
> conceptually arrest movement in this way also facilitates examination of
> the points of stress and conflict that exist within any social practice
> represented by a type. Thus there is no incompatibility between the use
> of ideal types and a dialectical view of history. Ideal types are a part of the
> tool kit of historical explanation. (Cox, 1987: 4)

Research that seeks to interrogate the webs of power that draw elite and ordinary practices into the processes of restructuring, can usefully draw on this conceptual 'tool kit', effectively allowing us to 'crystallize a social practice' (Harrod, 1987: 13). Taken together with Foucault-inspired insights into the 'governmentality' of firms as matrices of power-knowledge, such a perspective challenges the conception of firms as bounded and rational agents. It becomes possible to explore 'work' as an everyday social practice through which the emerging social relations of globalisation are enabled or contested. The 'ideal types' of working practices in the British and German commercial automotive sectors, though in a sense artificially 'frozen', offer insights into the points of contradiction that may lead to transformation. The analysis that follows here is focused on three questions that probe the webs of power of programmes of restructuring.

1 *The state, the firm and social power relations.* How is the firm situated within a matrix of state-societal institutions and practices? In what ways does this matrix support and limit particular programmes of restructuring?

2 *Social power relations across the firm.* What is the nature and form of the
   power relations that characterise interfirm relationships, such as those
   between suppliers and contractors, and interinstitutional relationships,
   such as those between firms and banks?
3 *Social power relations within the firm.* What are the patterns of compromise
   and conflict between groups within the firm?

The state, the firm and social power relations

In explaining the distinctiveness of particular firms' strategies of restructuring, many commentators have appealed to 'national capitalisms' – conceived as rival forms of capitalist organisation, providing particular contexts
for firms' decisions (see Albert, 1993; Hart, 1992; Crouch and Streeck, 1997).
According to these institutionalist approaches, firms behave according to the
embedded institutions and practices of a nation-state, and restructure in
accordance with their contextual limits. Though, of course, in many senses the
firm is bound up simultaneously with social power relations that extend
beyond and across states, into world orders, and the everyday practices of
production and work (Cox, 1987). What is most significant in the restructuring of work within firms is the perceptions, mindsets and experiences that
participants have of their relationship to governmental institutions and interventions, and to debates about world markets and global competitiveness.
Thus, it is not that a national model of capitalism automatically dictates a
particular set of restructuring strategies, but that it provides one frame of
reference, among many that shape the contours of the reorganisation of work.
The 'social context of production' (Cox, 1987: 12), or for our purposes the social
institutions and practices within which, and of which, the firm is constituted,
condition what is produced how it is produced and who is engaged in
production via their work. British and German manufacturing firms are
differently inserted into state-societal debates surrounding competitiveness in
a global era, and the social groups within these firms are connected to the
social spaces of the workplace, state-society and 'global markets' simultaneously.
   Focusing on German firms broadly as ideal types, we are able to
conceptually fix a distinctive set of social practices to view their underlying
relationships and tensions. In the German case, historically the dominant
social practices tend to produce and reproduce a high value-added set of
answers to the 'what' and 'how' questions of production, transforming the
high cost of labour into a 'competitive factor' through a focus on quality
products (Wever, 1995: 69):

> Employers who find themselves permanently prevented by rigid high
> labor standards from being competitive low-wage mass producers may
> discover that what they *really* want to be is producers of quality-
> competitive, customised products, oriented towards markets in which
> the expensive social system of production that they have to live with may

not just be competitive, but may in fact be a source of competitive advantage. (Streeck, 1997c: 203)

The 'high value' production practices characteristic of German industries continue to represent the central terrain of dispute in the restructuring debate. The maintenance of the high cost 'quality factor' remains central to established firms: 'I cannot emphasise enough the importance of stability, continuity and strategic soundness. The idea that the customer is king is ridiculous. Sometimes what is good for the customer is not good for us' (Finance Director, German multinational).[8]

However, such views are contested by many of the smaller supplier firms in the chain, and indeed by the trade unions. The social power relations that sustain the dominant value-added production practices simultaneously give rise to the contradictions which may ultimately undermine them. Sustaining a set of high-cost production practices in a competitive global market places constraints on the creation of jobs in the dominant sectors, a key concern of the unions. The social relations in German firms, in a state-societal context where welfare services are relatively underdeveloped, are more likely to be part and parcel of the wider reproduction of the institutions of a 'family wage' society, paying relatively high wages and providing relative job security (Esping-Andersen, 1996: 75). In contrast to societies which have high social welfare service costs but which provide employment in these services, Germany's cost burden is in transfer payments which must be found by the social groups within the industrial firm, through employers' and employees' contributions. Given the relatively underdeveloped service and leisure sectors in Germany, the question of job creation on the one hand, and employers' cost burdens on the other, will continue to be the hotly debated and contested issues of contemporary restructuring.

In the British case, by contrast, the dominant social practices tend to produce and reproduce a low cost set of answers to the 'what' and 'how' questions of production, focusing on low-tech and service industry growth. The flexibilisation of work in the multinational manufacturing industries has not occurred in isolation from transformations in the SME supply chain, or indeed from the growth of a hyperflexible service sector. The growth of a casualised service sector has had a disciplinary effect on the demands of workers, and the SME sector is increasingly drawn into the restructuring of the MNCs through JIT production. Amidst a British programme that appears 'content to compete for jobs and for trade on the basis of low wage levels' (Rubery, 1993: 27), manufacturing firms are able to externalise their costs, and displace risks, through access to temporary and contingent labour. Firms pursue individual competitiveness via restructuring strategies that seek to 'benchmark' the competition, and transform working practices and 'cultural attitudes':

> To understand what needed to be done, we started back in the mid 1980s
> by benchmarking ourselves against similar firms with comparable

processes. Initially we looked at Japanese firms – they were our major competition. The benchmarking helped to identify some of the process and cultural changes necessary to close the gap. (Human resources manager, Anglo-American multinational)[9]

The state-firm relationship in British restructuring has effectively intensified the individualisation that is attributed to neo-liberal globalisation. Working practices are constructed as inherently malleable and open to competitive emulation, and firms are legitimated as the autonomous and efficient agents of restructuring. The costs and risks of restructuring are passed like a hot potato between different agencies, and risk-sharing, whether between firms for technological development, or between banks and firms for investment, or between groups of employees in consultation practices, is inhibited. Indeed, even in the context of a single management team, the process of individualisation results in a number of competing interpretations of global competition. During the East Asian crisis, for example, purchasing managers reported a competitive advantage in the low cost of imported components, while their counterparts in production and exports lamented the strength of sterling and the saturation of electronics markets. In the context of performance-related pay, targets and stock options, such tensions become a significant feature of restructuring. The perceptions and experiences of British and German participants in corporate restructuring indicate that they find themselves in a whirlpool of debates within which governmental regulation and deregulation, 'global' managerial debates, and day-to-day organisational questions represent currents that may tug in opposing directions.

Social power relations across the firm

An exploration of the restructuring debates in which firms are engaged demonstrates the interconnectedness of production and work *within* the firm, and social institutions, practices and ideas *across* the firm – extending into supplier and contractor firms (Lane, 1996a, 1996b). Contests and compromises in the reorganisation of work within a firm cannot be meaningfully abstracted from prevailing practices that are crystallised in institutions and agencies assumed to be external to the firm. Neo-liberal discourses of hyper-flexibility advocate the individualisation of the firm and the devolution of responsibility and autonomy to the level of immediate managerial production decisions. Indeed, it could be said that such discourses rely upon the abstraction of the firm from its wider relationship with state-society. The restructuring activities and debates within German and British manufacturing firms reflect and inform a web of power that extends seamlessly into banks, education institutions and civil society.

The webs of power that pull together the interests of German firms, banks and shareholders have historically reproduced credit-based finance, cross-shareholding and overlapping directorships. German banks held 10.3 per cent of total shares in 1997, a figure that compares with 2.3 per cent in the British case, where institutional investors are dominant (Deutsche Bundesbank, 1997). The resultant close ties between the finance, management, and ownership of firms, coupled with a high incidence of family-owned firms and state shareholdings have become the subject of much debate in the restructuring of German industries (Vitols and Woolcock, 1997). On the one hand, studies of management perceptions of restructuring indicate that the shared long-term time horizons reap benefits in terms of investment in training and innovation (Culpepper, 1999; Harding and Soskice, 2000). As one finance director put it 'we do not mind spending money in the short-term and we are prepared to wait three years or more to see the gains. We don't share the gambling mindset of the "casino" UK or US'. Social practices of education and training of engineers and technicians requires such investment, together with the maintenance of 'cooperation between companies, universities and research institutes' (Soskice, 1996: 17). Restructuring debates take place in clusters of agencies, with large export-oriented MNCs and supply SMEs, for example, sharing training programmes and product development costs. The full or part purchase of a supply firm by a MNC is much in evidence, the rationale explained in terms of control over quality and information flow.

The maintenance of close interfirm and firm-agency ties is not without controversy, however. The debate as to the virtues of shareholders versus stakeholders that rages within German state-society, for example, is evident in corporate debates, with divisions even within firms as to the appropriate relationship between financiers and managers. The emerging dualism between large equity-financed MNCs and the 'Mittlestand' of bank-based credit is reflected in divergent attitudes to the role of equities in the competitiveness of German firms (Deeg, 1997). So too, the restructuring of interfirm relationships has been subject to contestation, particularly where suppliers offer cheaper labour. An instance of subcontracting to a Hungarian supplier provides a case in point. The German MNC bought a majority share in a Hungarian firm which became a key supplier. Assembly functions have incrementally been moved to Hungary, meeting with resistance from the works councils. In an attempt to ameliorate the problem, the MNC began a series of 6-month long 'exchanges' between the plants, designed to inculcate a sense of 'shared identity'. Given the context of union concern over the creation of German jobs and apprenticeships, there has been little reconciliation. This is an illustrative example of the contested boundaries of German firms' restructuring programmes. Corporate managers are faced with a delicate balancing act between pushing the parameters of flexibility, while maintaining the cohesion necessary to sustain value-added production.

Turning our attention to the restructuring of work within British firms, the dominant relationships between manufacturing firms, banks and shareholders tend to be arms-length and fragmented, reflecting the centrality of the equity-financing and shareholder value. The concentration of shareholdings in the hands of institutional investors tends to produce and reproduce a separation of ownership from control, and a concomitant decoupling of firms from their sources of financial capital. Thus the dominant web of power characterising the relationships between a firm and its sources of finance tend to be profit-focused, privileging the short-term and, therefore, the support of entrepreneurial 'start-ups' and venture capital, while simultaneously reinforcing an environment of instability, insecurity and individual risk. As Jill Rubery has it 'British firms do not see themselves as producers but as asset managers' (1993: 10). Managers of production plants communicate a sense of 'distance' between their everyday production decisions (described as 'the real world'), and what they see as the arcane movements of the stock market (described as 'a cartoon world'). In response to this environment of short-termism, managers charged with restructuring plants paradoxically intensify the immediacy of responses. They shift the short-termism on to the relationships with suppliers, seeking out multiple sources of supply that can be changed at will, avoiding partnerships and alliances that 'tie in' particular orders. The effects of such displacement are explained vividly by the manager of an SME who described his relationship to the client MNC as 'like the milkman', where the placing or cancellation of an order could be as immediate as a 'note left on the doorstep'. The overwhelming insight coming out of the restructuring experiences of British managers is that they are making their own kind of global 'uncertainties', and passing these down the supply chain.

The tensions of 'arms-length' relationships are also evident in the skills debate within British management discourses. In the context of an unregulated and individualised training environment, where 'staff poaching' is feared, skills development is seen 'not as a productive investment ... but as an operating expense that depresses returns in the present' (Lazonick and O'Sullivan, 1996: 33). The competitive individualism that leads firms to rely on the labour market to provide skilled workers is further exacerbated by the growth in the use of temporary labour and the adoption of 'hire and fire' practices. The editorial of an engineering management magazine illustrates the problem to good effect: 'Some of industry has taken a careless approach to its skills base, seeming to believe it can discard and rehire people at whim, as if skills can be switched on and off like a light bulb. They can't, and the corollary is that skill shortages don't just occur at times when companies are recruiting: they are long-term too' (*Professional Engineering*, 11 February, 1998: 3). The debate was continued in the magazine the following month, with a former Land Rover worker contributing a letter:

> I asked my managing director why he had reduced the apprentice intake from 80 a year to zero. He replied that he could get all the skilled engineers he needed from other firms ... He would not accept that, by taking youngsters from school and sponsoring training he would sustain a core of staff both skilled in the company's requirements and possibly with that rare commodity, company loyalty. He was, at that time, the

managing director of Land Rover. (Letter, *Professional Engineering*, 11 March, 1998: 33)

In 1998, by this time owned by German BMW, the British-based car company announced it may recruit abroad, following 20 applications for 150 advertised skilled engineering posts. With Honda in Swindon reporting problems with skills shortages, it would seem that the British location is the most significant factor in enabling or constraining restructuring decisions. Now owned by Ford, Land Rover continues to exhibit the short-term relationships that are at the nub of contests surrounding British restructuring.

Social power relations within the firm

It is perhaps the social relations within the firm itself which are most self-evidently engaged in a process of bargaining and contest. Indeed, studies of industrial relations begin precisely from the point of observing such contests in their distinctive social settings.[10] However, within IPE debates there has been a neglect of labour relations, and where labour has been studied it has been viewed through the lens of changes in industrial relations practices. So, for example, Cox's (1971) early work on labour and transnational relations directly equates labour with national trade union organisations. More recently, organised labour has become a focus for the analysis of potential strategies of resistance to neo-liberal restructuring and globalisation (see Stevis and Boswell, 1997; O'Brien, 1997; IILS, 1999a).

There is little doubt that a focus on labour groups can go some way to counterbalance the preoccupation with finance and MNC power that globalisation has precipitated. A focus on organised labour clearly makes some contribution to a humanising of our knowledge of global change. However, it is important also to consider some of the problematics raised by a focus on organised labour. As emphasised by Hyman 'to be representative is to share the main characteristics of a broader population; but trade union and other employee representatives are never representative in this sense' (1997: 311). A focus on the changing shape of trade unions, for example, may not closely reflect the diversity of experiences of change in the workplace. In chapter 6 I will more fully explore the transformations in the meaning of work, and the implications for unprotected workers. However, here I am concerned with the webs of power that characterise the relationships between organised labour and the restructuring programmes of MNCs.

A starting point in the exploration of these webs of social power relations is to focus on the firm as a primary site of production and work. This leads us to ask critical questions about the relationships between different social groups within the firm, and about how these relationships inform processes of restructuring. How do the social relations within our ideal-type firms produce and reproduce specific social practices, and how might these practices be contested and transformed? For Cox, distinctive 'orientations to action' provide social groups with different ways of thinking about a problem: 'Specific social groups tend to evolve a collective mentality, that is, a typical way of perceiving and interpreting the world that provides orientations to action for members of the group' (Cox, 1987: 25).

The experiences different social groups have of embedded practices within the firm will be imprinted on the world view that informs their under-standings, actions and contests. For Pauly and Reich such ideas provide 'broad orienting frameworks or belief systems that, when combined with national institutions, define "collective understandings" of roles, beliefs, expectations, and purposes' (1997: 6). The social practices which rise to the top and become dominant in a process of contest between social actors are likely to reflect the relative power of social groups to engage with the debates surrounding restructuring, and to shape these debates in a way which reflects their interests and understandings.

The dual German model of trade union/works council industrial relations, with the unions sustaining two-thirds of works council seats, has led to a negotiated restructuring agenda, as discussed in chapter 4. Power within the firm is effectively diffused through formalised and institutionalised industrial relations practices, described by Maurice Glasman as 'the negotiated distri-bution of power' (1997: 22), and by Alain Lipietz as 'negotiated involvement' (1997: 4). Despite challenges from employers seeking greater regulatory freedoms, there is a broad acknowledgement that consensus has a value that is difficult to quantify, and risky to disrupt:

> If you believe that you can quantify labour costs and savings, this is nonsense. How do you calculate for skills developed over a lifetime? An example of this is our sickness pay issue, how do you quantify that? You may know that you reduce labour costs by 3%, but how do you know that the morale of your workers has not cost you 10%? You cannot know this, I doubt it very much. (Works Councillor, German multinational)[11]

There is a sense in which German employers insulate themselves from politically-sensitive negotiations, conducting these through formal channels. For example, in the introduction of new production technologies that reduce labour input, the works councils have played a role in negotiating the terms of the reorgan-isation of work and the retirement packages of redundant workers. In another case, a firm sought greater functional flexibility through an 'outsourcing' arrangement with an external supplier. Following negotiations with the works councils, a satellite 'job shop' was established, staffed by existing skilled workers, and designed to supply particular components on a 'client' basis, subsidised by business with other companies.

However, the shifting focus of the employer-employee relationship, in particular increased decentralisation to the individual firm, has been subject to considerable contestation. Employers organisations have experienced 'association flight' as firms have sought to define their own bargaining arrangements. As Werner Stumpfe, President of the leading engineering employers organisation 'Gesamtmetall' reports 'companies feel straightjacketed by the present agreements and want room to manoeuvre'. The question of the vulnerability of 'bargain bound' German firms to international competition from 'footloose' Anglo-American businesses remains a significant feature of the debate within German firms.

Focusing on the restructuring of work in British firms, the relationships between employer and employee are bound up with an intensified emphasis on the individual in society more generally (Williams, 1997: 498). In terms of production and work, the historical voluntarism of industrial relations implies a dual fragmentation, of the firm from its external social relationships, and within the firm between competing social groups. This decoupling of the experiences of work and production from a broader set of shared social understandings, has implications for the ways in which social groups seek to organise their interests. We can see several key mutually-reinforcing strands to the individualisation of the interests of social groups within British firms.

First, the lines of communication between employer and employee, historically represented by a 'single channel' of trade union-centred collective bargaining, are increasingly 'dominated by the employer, with no independent representation of workers interests' (Hyman, 1997: 314). There is a 'representation gap' (Towers, 1997) in hyperflexible state-societies that leaves six out of seven US workers, and two out of three British workers, without effective forms of representation at work. As a result, concerted negotiation has been rejected in favour of social practices that privilege ad-hoc concession bargaining and fragmented and individualised 'deals'. This process of decollectivisation has been paralleled by an increased emphasis on individual mechanisms of control and monitoring such as those inherent to systems of HRM, TQM and indeed many systems of 'employee involvement' (see Rubery, 1993; Moody, 1997). For example, a slide from a management presentation to production workers, entitled *The Process of Improvement*, positions the individual at the heart of the 'quality circle': 'a total quality approach must underly all business processes; especially management of change'. This requires quality to be built into every process and quality output expected from 'every individual in the company'. The language of the relationship between manager and worker is defined in terms of the imperatives of JIT, kaizen (continuous improvement), kanban (literally 'ticket', attached to product as moved though production process).

Where contestation arises in the individualisation of the employment relationship this tends to be presented by managers as an attitudinal problem, or a failure to grasp the imperatives of restructuring. As a human resources manager put it to me: 'One of the problems we have had here has been changing the mindsets and attitudes of older workers. This used to be a mining area and tinplate works. As those industries faded, people changed their jobs but not their attitudes, which were still strong unions and anti-management' (Anglo-American multinational).[12] The problem is thus associated with a collective mindset of shared past practices that is resistant to individualisation.

Second, the individualised nature of the employee-employer relationship has contributed to the fragmentation of the interests of employees within the firm. Corporate managers tend to divide workers into categories of wage structures and terms and conditions, fragmenting social groups into various degrees of 'contingent' labour using part-time and temporary contracts. Crouch has equated this recurring pattern with the dissolution of the concept of employment, 'replacing it by a series of contracts between a customer firm and a mass of small labour-contracting firms, temporary agencies or, in extreme cases, individual providers of labour services' (1997: 375). This effectively both externalises and individualises the social relations of production, with employers sustaining and reproducing a longer-term set of relations with a core of employee groups who are 'inculcated into a culture' and a larger group of contract workers who are 'outside that circle' (Crouch, 1997: 375). Indeed, this division of interests can be used to discipline core workers, with contract staff maintained at approximately 50 per cent of the workforce and distributed around the plant. As Herrigel describes it 'the old style firm disintegrates entirely into an infinitely recombinable set of roles and relations that the participants themselves reflect upon and restructure' (1994: 6). The governmentality of the hyperflexible British firm produces a form of self-management, within which workers pre-empt managerial intervention by restructuring themselves.[13]

Finally, this fragmentation has distinctive implications for the bargaining terrain of trade unions. The social relations within which trade unions organise are likely to reinforce their links with the 'insider' fragments of the workforce. British trade unions have sought to respond to this environment by becoming individual 'service providers', for their 'consumers' (Williams, 1997: 498), representing employees as individuals in disputes with employers. This process has, of course, further strengthened the role of certain social groups within the firm and placed significant constraints on the intermediation of contested interests. As a union official explains, in one sense the 'new workers' are lost to the collective focus of the union, and yet their interests and experiences remain common:

> It's a whole new ball game for the new generation of workers. They are expected to plan a life, a family, manage a pension, insurance schemes, while working on a temporary contract. Eventually something will capture the imagination of this group – which is, after all, likely to become the largest group of interests. (AEEU official)[14]

The patterns of social relations within British firms tend to be fragmented and individualised, providing the employer with unlimited access to ad-hoc contract relations with the 'external' labour market, while significantly limiting the potential for workers to organise their interests:

> ... the demands for increased labour market flexibility grow more strident by the day while assorted management gurus tell our young people that regular, life-time employment is a luxury they cannot expect to enjoy in this brave new world ... Paradoxically these demands are increasingly based on threats rather than promises. Wage reductions, the intensification of labour, the elimination of trade union influence, are all now said to be necessary in order to avert disaster and decline, rather than to attain greater prosperity. This shift is highly significant because the threat of decline constitutes a more compelling argument for change ... There are no gains to be distributed, only losses to be averted. The stick has replaced the carrot. (Bienefeld, 1991: 4)

In the case of British firms, the reorganisation of work has circumscribed the interests of workers in many sectors, and with varying skills and specialisms. Indeed, it has presented greater risks and insecurities across the spectrum of managers and workers:

> Some firms are seeking to discover how far they can proceed with a policy of 'eating one's cake and having it': seeking strong but unreciprocated commitment and loyalty from staff. Anxieties about the constant pressure to demonstrate to shareholders adequate achievements in down-sizing and delayering lead managers to do this, these managers themselves being vulnerable to redundancy through these processes. (Crouch, 1997: 375)

Current debates in the British management literature about the potential costs of disaffected labour would suggest that the 'loss of legitimacy' factor is recognised by those who seek to manage change. It is noted, for example, that 'employee-centred innovation' is limited in a low-trust atmosphere (*Independent on Sunday*, 19 October 1997: 6). The restructuring of work in British firms, with its nod to empowerment and employee involvement, and the concrete experience of disaffection and insecurity, is witnessing the emergence of a form of 'infra-politics' (Scott, 1990). Workers engage in footdragging and passive resistance in order to avoid the 'quality schemes' that, designed to reduce costs, ultimately are seen as leading to redundancies.

Taken together, the experiences and perceptions of restructuring within German and British firms demonstrate distinctive dynamics of contestation. Dominant social practices within German firms tend to favour the provision of legitimate 'vents' through the mandated channels of the trade unions and works councils, negotiating 'outcomes that are both mutually and socially acceptable' (Wever, 1995: 63). Hence, the diminishing sector of society in employment within core manufacturing find shared channels of communication for their interests. The pressures on these channels paradoxically come from employers seeking greater decentralisation, and from social groups who are excluded from such work. The dominant webs of power in British firms, by contrast, tend to reproduce managerial autonomy, dividing and excluding social groups within the workplace and externalising the employment relationship to outsourcing plants and external employment agencies.

In sum, viewing the firm as a key site of the contestation of global restructuring makes visible distinctive webs of social power relations. We are led to acknowledge that these social power relations may produce, sustain and potentially transform institutionalised social practices in ways that are distinctive and unique. Our comparative analysis of British and German firms demonstrates the contingency of social understandings of, and responses to, globalisation and restructuring. For those who seek to raise the profile of labour groups in the understanding and shaping of global change, these insights have considerable utility. It becomes clear that individuals and social groups do not simply accept globalisation and respond to its dictates with the restructuring of their working practices. Indeed, we may even question the notion of one clear and common process of globalisation in the sense that 'my globalisation is not your globalisation' since people interpret and experience the processes in diverse ways. Viewed in this way, strategies of hyperflexibility are not unproblematic or ubiquitous, but open to contestation and challenge.

Conclusion

The study of the firm in IPE has come to be closely bound up with understandings of globalisation. In many senses the firm has a rightful place at the heart of understandings of global transformations. It is, after all, through production and work that most people directly experience and interpret processes of globalisation in their everyday lives. In short, for academics, policy-makers, business people and non-elite social groups, the site of the firm has become a primary site of restructuring and change. While supporting the renewed emphasis on the firm in contemporary IPE for these reasons, this chapter has noted a lack of critical engagement with the political economy of the firm in orthodox accounts.[15] The chapter has taken a series of steps towards such a critical engagement by highlighting the webs of power and social practices that constitute and contest the firm as a site of work and production.

The first step has been to reflect upon and problematise our received understandings of the firm in the IPE. Much of the mainstream agenda in contemporary IPE has been dominated by studies of the relative and structural power of states vis-à-vis markets. For 'markets' much of the literature has substituted 'firms', drawing on models advanced by economics and business studies to develop a 'rational actor' view of the behaviour of firms. I have raised questions of this conception of the firm on the grounds that it ascribes the restructuring activities of the firm with a natural and automatic logic. In the opening citation, E. P. Thompson critiques the economic determinism of some historical accounts of social change, arguing that the thoughts, ideas, experiences and struggles of human beings in productive relationships are as significant as material factors. 'The restructuring of relations of power', he reminds us, 'has always been the outcome of struggle' (1976/1994: 222). Following such insights, representations of the firm as a unitary agent of globalisation, acting automatically to intensify globalisation, are subjected to challenge. The firm is opened up to reveal the contests and tensions that characterise changes in working practices, and their extension into the institutions and practices of state and civil society.

The second step has been to apply an IPE of social practice to the firm, with the aim of disclosing its political and social character. I have argued that programmes of restructuring within firms are context specific and historically contingent. Individual corporate groups, workers and unions do not simply respond to the imperatives of lean production and TQM. Rather, they experience, interpret and translate the meanings of restructuring programmes, and reflect on their implications in the light of immediate problematics and past practices. As a complex web of power-knowledge, the firm exhibits multiple restructuring discourses in its relationship with institutions, suppliers, contractors and worker groups. The power exercised by corporate managers is never simply a negative power of withdrawing influence from particular groups, but produces and reproduces particular relationships and disciplines, such as the individualism of the employment relation in Britain, and the formal channels of industrial relations in Germany. The contests and compromises that characterise restructuring in British and German firms serve to demonstrate that the reorganisation of work cannot, and should not, be presented as unproblematic or inevitable. Put simply, if firms are understood to have inevitable roles in intensifying globalisation, then the potential for states and social groups to regulate, challenge or transform these roles is restricted.

Finally, the paper has elucidated some of the implications of bringing contestedness to our understandings of the firm in knowledge terms. The political economy of the firm is itself constituted of contested knowledge: of what we know about the world, how we know it and how we might seek to change it. Dominant understandings of the firm within globalisation have tended to produce an image of the MNC as a market domain within which 'experts' direct strategy to maximise profits. The management programmes of labour flexibilisation are thus lent an air of legitimacy and rationality. The realm of everyday working practices is thus constructed as a realm of 'response' to 'higher' initiatives. By bringing the everyday into our analysis of the activities of MNCs we become more attuned to the making of global restructuring in and through social practices. While in some instances the threats and insecurities of contingent work discipline workers so that they 'restructure themselves' and monitor their own practices, in others the breaking up of past alliances clears space for new tactics. In broad terms, the concept of a 'contested firm' enables us to move beyond a focus on abstracted, exogenous economic transformations, to consider the ways in which globalisation becomes manifested in, and contested through, diverse social practices. In the chapter that follows, the relationships between workers within patterns of global restructuring will be explored.

Notes

1 The neo-realist and liberal debates surrounding 'non-state actors' tend to seek out new units of analysis or 'new things to look at', and new 'levels' of analysis or new places to find historical material (see Krasner, 1994; Keohane, 1984). From a different perspective, world-systems theorists tend to look at institutions and actors in addition to the state in order to understand capital accumulation, their basic 'level'. What these approaches do not do, however, is stand back from their assumptions to consider new ways of understanding the units or levels or, indeed, reflect upon how they have conventionally understood them.

2 For Ruigrok and van Tulder '... it is false to suggest that a firm or government has *one* strategy since it was top management that came to this decision, after an internal and external bargaining process. One should also consider whether it was a unanimous decision, which interests or departments or persons prepared the decision and which opposed it' (1995: 65).

3 The concept of lean production essentially combines the technological and productive labour elements of kaizen (continuous improvement), kanban and JIT, multi-skilling and teamworking, TQM, numerical and functional flexibility and outsourcing and supply-chain innovations. The key emphasis lies in the reduction of 'slack' in both materials and labour to reduce costs and increase management control.

4 For critical analysis of the use of the concept 'lean production', see Moody (1997), ch. 5.

5 An example of the inextricable relationships between the social power relations within the firm, and the broader social forces of society, is Harrod's insight into the ability of the firm to 'externalise' its costs on to society through, for example, the use of contingent labour. The actions of the firm, in this way, both reflect and contribute to wider social power relations (Comments made in discussion following paper presented at BISA 22nd Annual Conference, 15–17 December 1997).

6 Rupert, for example, in his study of the post-war hegemony of American Fordist mass production effectively raises the issue of power, critiquing approaches which neglect the 'crucial processes through which power has been produced, and the conflicting social relations which at once underlie and make possible that production, and which also make problematic its long-term reproduction' (Rupert, 1995: 1).

7 See Sinclair's (1999) work on the 'IPE of the commonplace' for a notable exception to this neglect of the ordinary features of power in the GPE.

8 Confidential interview with board members of key automotive components multinational, 3 September 1997.

9 Confidential interview with human resources department, electronic component multinational, 23 February 1998.

10 For Harrod the study of Industrial Relations as 'a field in which the focus was work and its relationship to production' has had much to offer the scholar of IPE through its focus on social forces as 'the identifiable social energy precipitated by production' (1997a: 109).

11 Confidential focus group with works councillors, Cologne, 27 August 1997.

12 Confidential interview with human resources department, electronic component multinational, 23 February 1998.

13 In one assembly plant visited, prominent posters showing the productivity and costs of Mexican workers producing similar components for the parent MNC, were displayed on the walls. In another plant, the cafeteria walls had been replaced with glass screens to enable workers who had returned to the line to clearly see those who had extended their break.

14 Confidential interview, 19 March 1998.

15 The renewed emphasis on the firm in IPE has led some scholars to make inroads into more critical accounts of the firm as both concept and social arena. See, for example, Eden (1991) and Tétreault (1999).

6

~

Globalisation at work:
unheard voices and invisible agency

~

The contemporary problematic of globalisation has encouraged a particular mode of knowledge to dominate explanations of social change. Academic and popular discussion of all matters 'global' have predominantly asked 'what is happening' type questions. It has become almost common sense to seek to explain the nature of the beast itself, making reference to technological and market structures as the driving forces of change. In this formulation the everyday lives of people are positioned passively outside the process, receiving the imperatives of global restructuring. For workers this implies that transformations in their everyday lives will follow essentially, necessarily and automatically from new production technologies, the competitive impulses of global markets and the demands of shareholder capitalism. Where agency-centred questions have been raised in the globalisation debate, these have tended to focus upon the decisions and actions of powerful transnational, state or corporate elites. Here the actions, experiences and articulations of workers are simply contained within corporations, transnational trade unions and state formations as sites of global restructuring. Taken as a whole, the globalisation debate has tended to reproduce an implicitly 'problem-solving' mode of knowledge, one that emphasises the explanation of, as opposed to the understanding of, global social change (Cox, 1996: 88; Hollis and Smith, 1990: 1).

This chapter argues that the dominant representations of global restructuring have rendered the voices, experiences and practices of workers, and particularly unprotected or unrepresented workers, unheard and invisible.[1] Not only does this invisibility produce a serious deficit in our understandings of the dynamics of global change, but it also causes us to avert our eyes from the very sites where work and political contestation is taking place in the global political economy. As MNCs increasingly outsource their production and services, they become fractured into loosely connected sites, many of them employing unprotected and precarious workers. The programmes of restructuring in the advanced industrialised countries (AICs), whether 'hyperflexible' or 'flexi-corporatist', run in a seamless web of power with the practices of unprotected workers in the less developed countries (LDCs) of the 'South', and with the 'invisible' work undertaken in the informal sectors of the 'North'. For a contract worker in a British production plant, the everyday practices of Mexican workers producing the same component for the client corporation may be far more proximate than geography would dictate, and may be expressed ambiguously in terms of competition and insecurity, or in terms of identification and solidarity. For a Bolivian live-in domestic worker in Berlin, the practices of her globally mobile management consultant employer constitute yet another ambiguous and contradictory global working relationship. On the surface they could be depicted as women working flexibly in a global economy, yet their experiences are in tension and their relationship is fundamentally unequal.

As a consequence, if we are to understand work in the GPE, we need to look beyond 'states and firms' to consider the political, geographical and social relationships that workers have with one another, and to the GPE, and how these relationships are historically and discursively constituted. In line with an IPE of social practice, this chapter explores the everyday practices of work that variously enable, contest or confound the emerging social relations of globalisation. The chapter is organised in three parts. The first explores the representation of transformations in work and work organisation within the dominant expositions of globalisation. In what ways are workers rendered invisible by the globalisation discourse? In the section that follows, the treatment of production and work within IPE is discussed. Where workers are made visible in analysis, which workers feature and which remain excluded? Finally, a social practice approach to work is outlined and insights are drawn for the repoliticisation of work in IPE. It is argued that in order to restore and capture the social conflicts, tensions and compromises of the restructuring of work, it is necessary to address the concrete experiences of workers who are differentially positioned in the IPE of work. Given the explosion of working practices into multiple domains, it is increasingly problematic to delineate those practices that are contemporaneous with particular state-societies. Throughout this chapter, I draw on illustrations of working practices that connect to, yet extend beyond, the flexibilisation of work in Britain and Germany.

Global restructuring and the invisibility of work

The concept of globalisation has been variously described as 'vague', 'ambiguous', 'the cliché of our times' and 'wishful' (Jones, 1995: 3; Held *et al.*, 1999: 1; Scholte, 2000: 1). It is perhaps the empty and mythical nature of the concept that has endowed globalisation with such seductive power, inviting people to fill the void with distinctive meanings. The dominant representations of globalisation celebrate a process of change that is the inevitable outcome of the expansionary ambitions of a global economy and transborder technology, and deplore the politicisation of the process: 'Lately, technology has been the main driver of globalisation ... It would be naïve to think that governments could let integration proceed mainly under its own steam, trusting to technological progress and economic freedom, desirable as that would be. Politics could never be like that' (*The Economist*, 23 September 2000: 19). In this reading states, societies and political activities 'get in the way' of an economic and technological process of transformation. A kind of 'no alternative' logic prevails, whereby it is assumed that practices will be restructured to conform to a hyperflexible Anglo-Saxon model. Political and social aspects of change are abstracted from the economic and technological imperatives so that particular governments, trade unions and welfare institutions, for example, are cast as obstructions to successful transformation. The social costs of global restructuring are commonly perceived as temporary by-products of adjustment to the imperatives of change. 'People' generally, and non-elite groups specifically, are rendered invisible in such readings of globalisation. People are positioned as passive receptors of global imperatives who, if they are sensible, will seize the opportunities of a globalising world economy.

Representations of the globalisation of production, whether framed in terms of post-Fordism (Hirst and Zeitlin, 1989; Lipietz, 1987), transformations in competitive strategy (Strange, 1996; Porter, 1990) or grand-scale shifts in the organisation of capitalist societies (Rifkin, 1995; Toffler, 1980), all tend to emphasise the common effects of transformation in different places. The restructuring of work is presented as a unidirectional and universal outcome of restructured production, with global forces determining changes in everyday practices as though workers were simply passive observers of a 'bigger' process. Such analysis tends to feed an economic management logic that says that all work must become flexible, casual, contingent, feminised and service-oriented if the opportunities of globalisation are to be seized and the forces of global production successfully 'harnessed'. 'Making globalisation work' has thus received a dialectical double meaning in recent times. On the one hand it has been used to indicate that globalisation has a 'friendly face' that can 'work', and on the other, the restructuring of work itself is presented as a panacea with the potential to ameliorate the pain of globalisation.[2] The surface-level shifts of new production technologies and management techniques are highly visible in such accounts, but the contradictory currents below the surface remain obscured from view. While the introduction of ICTs to the workplace, receives a high profile in accounts of the flexibilisation of work, the temporal practices of work and home life that make their introduction possible are less visible: 'In stressing the shared patterns of global processes, there is a tendency to underestimate how the conditions and relations of everyday life constitute processes of economic and social reorganization' (Feldman and Buechler, 1998: 623).

The everyday experiences, practices and contests of workers are overlooked amidst a flurry of activity in pursuit of the definitive understanding of 'large-scale' transformations. Indeed, international economic institutions have cast labour as a commodity that is simply moulded to fit prevailing economic conditions. The World Bank acknowledges that change is 'difficult

and frightening' (1995: 11), and the European Commission that 'the reorganisation of work often causes uncertainty' (CEC, 1997: 8). Yet, the overriding
assumption is that the globalisation process is a given reality, essentially
separate from the social and political restructuring that is undertaken in its
name, and entirely independent of the everyday thoughts and actions of
workers. Indeed, in the effort to construct a discourse of opportunity and
manageability, such interventions represent the agency of workers as a
problem to be overcome on the path to a more adaptable and flexible workforce. Put simply, there is an implicit warning that the organised actions of
workers will incur the wrath of the not-so-friendly face of globalisation.

Agency uncovered: perspectives from IPE

Critical IPE accounts of globalisation have tended to expose and counter the
dominant discourse with an emphasis on the power of particular individual
and collective agents to drive or resist global change. It must be said, however,
that these agents are identified predominantly in terms of production
structures at transnational and national levels. In short, IPE has appeared
comfortable with production and the empirical study of the firm, and much
less comfortable with the study of labour and work, resulting in the 'deafening
silence' that is the 'almost total neglect of labour' (Denemark and O'Brien,
1997: 232). As I have shown in my discussion of the firm, transformations in
labour and work are variously given their agency through a focus on the
actions of MNCs as key actors in production (Stopford and Strange, 1991;
Sklair, 2001); the power of the disciplinary forces of neo-liberalism (Gill, 1995);
and, much more rarely, the actions of fledgling global trade union movements
(O'Brien, 2000; Cox, 1999; Radice, 2000). Meanwhile, others point to the
'embeddedness' of MNCs in national structures (Sally, 1994), and to the
competing models of national capitalism, particularly industrial relations
institutions and systems of production, that give distinctive character to
divergent patterns of change in forms of work (Crouch and Streeck, 1997).

The approaches outlined provide a valuable antidote to the techno-
economic determinism of the dominant globalisation discourse. They provide
us with insight into the individuals and groups whose actions, knowledge and
power are intertwined with global transformation. However, taken together,
they sustain a separation of labour and workers from the restructuring of states
and firms, highlighting the experiences of workers solely in terms of their
relationship to production, narrowly defined. As Peter Burnham has compell-
ingly argued, the category of 'labour' is explored only insofar as it equates with
'trade union bargaining power' (1999: 3). It is not difficult to see how even
critical accounts of hyperliberal restructuring could feed a depoliticisation of
labour by reinforcing the image of a spent force. The prevailing common sense
begins to see the elite-level actions of national governments and corporate managers as the sole legitimate 'researchable' agents in the restructuring of work.

In subsuming work into understandings of production and capital, IPE analysis does tend to treat labour as a singular force, and workers as a naturalised category of class that maps on to a global proletariat. As E. P. Thompson noted: 'There is an ever-present temptation to suppose that class is a thing' (1968: 10). The insights of his historical mode of thought are particularly significant given the way the problem of class consciousness is framed in the light of contemporary changes:

> One of the most puzzling developments of the closing decades of the twentieth century has been the precipitous decline of working-class consciousness and organisation at a time of great numerical expansion of the world proletariat ... It was not unreasonable to expect the capitalist crisis of the 1970s would enhance rather than dampen the class consciousness of the expanding world proletariat. (Silver and Arrighi, 2001: 53)

To take seriously the historical contingency of workers' consciousness and experiences is to problematise the above assumption that 'class consciousness', as a monolithic entity, rises and falls in response to capitalist shifts. Workers express a multitude of contradictory and contingent 'consciousnesses' in the deciphering of their experiences of restructuring, and are differentially inserted into relationships with one another, and with global fractions of capital. The contradictions and compromises of workers' experiences thus provide a window on the tensions and inequalities of globalisation. Some intraworker dynamics and relationships actually intensify and enable the programmes of hyperflexibility that are enacted in the name of globalisation. As Dimitris Stevis has it, there are 'competing experiences and expectations depending on the "position" of the worker in the political geography of work', so that even 'formally protected workers may be well protected citizens through other means' (personal correspondence, 2001). To assume that workers represent a singular and coherent group of potential 'globalisation resistors' not only seriously underplays the participation of some workers in enabling hyperflexibility, but it also underestimates the concrete acts of resistance that emerge in the interstitial spaces outside of formal organised channels. Trade unions themselves increasingly acknowledge both the importance of unprotected sites for global campaigns, and the potential contradiction within the sites' relationships to other workers.

In essence, state-societies, firms and 'classes' are too often assumed to 'contain' workers, and are rarely unpacked to reveal the political and social forces engendered by these workers (Amoore, 2000; Vilrokx, 1999). Where labour is acknowledged in analysis, this is conceived as an oppositional force of resistance, embodied in the form of organised and represented workers in trade unions. As a result, while the invisibility and obfuscation of agency in the hyperflexibility discourse is challenged, alternative sources and forms of invisibility emerge in IPE inquiry. The need to address new sources of the invisibility of workers is rendered all the more acute by the very restructuring process itself, which serves to fracture the firm into a myriad of loosely connected or contracted fragments. As a result, an exploration of the restructuring of work in particular social spaces cannot meaningfully abstract the workforces of individual firms from their relationships with the practices of agencies, satellite plants, workshops and households. There are a number of dimensions to this fragmentation, each of which contributes a layer of invisibility.

First, the rapid growth in outsourcing,[3] contracting out and the use of temporary employment agencies has moved production to sites that are not immediately visible if the firm is treated as a bounded entity. As a result, the contemporary study of MNCs must confront the problem that new flexible working practices do not sit neatly within the bounded firms that tend to be the focus of IPE inquiry. As a MNC outsources some of its core and most of its non-core activities, understanding the social practices of the workplace extends to the practices of homes, sweatshops, supply-chain workshops with a contract workforce, and other ad-hoc and unprotected sites of production. The use of unprotected labour in production for the global economy has led scholars to focus on the increased use of child labour[4] and bonded or slave labour in the LDCs (see Bales, 1999; Klein, 2000). In the OECD countries, the growth of precarious and unprotected forms of employment has pushed workers towards forms of individualised flexibility that carry high levels of personal risk (Moody, 1997; Coyle, 1997; Beck, 2000b).

The trend towards a fractured firm that outsources production and business activities intensifies a second key layer of invisibility, that of gender. As corporations replace full-time protected workers with part-time, temporary or contracted unprotected workers, they also tend to replace men with women (Corporate Watch, 2000). The invisibility of the role of women in IR, IPE and Industrial Relations scholarship has, of course, been widely documented by feminist scholars (see Enloe, 1989; Marchand, 1996). However, the feminisation of work that has accompanied global restructuring makes it particularly important that we 'see women' as actors in global restructuring, and that we 'recognize gender' in terms of the webs of power at work within the process of change (Murphy, 1996; Marchand and Runyan, 2000: 225). At one level, then, this implies making womens' experiences and activities visible in our analyses: '$16 trillion of global output is invisible, $11 trillion produced by women' (United Nations Human Development Programme, 1995: 97). Here it is the non-monetised care, family and community, agricultural and domestic work of women that is absent from our understandings of the GPE. At another level, however, making gender visible is about revealing the gendered nature of the power relations surrounding the global restructuring of work. A focus solely on firms and trade unions as somehow representing and 'containing' workers perpetuates a gendered invisibility that sanitises and naturalises processes of restructuring.

Finally, and related, an invisibility persists with regard to the reconfiguration of public and private within the restructuring of work. Janine Brodie depicts restructuring as a 'recoding' and 'renegotiating' of the boundaries between public and private (1996: 387). In people's working lives, this recoding is manifested in the permeability of the boundaries between 'home' and 'work'. The private realm of home and household is increasingly a site of production for the global economy. The ILO report rapid increases in the numbers of homeworkers providing 'optimal flexibility' in the industrialised and developing countries (2000: 114). Households in both 'advanced' and 'developing' regions are simultaneously sites of production and consumption. The clothing industry, electronics and assembly sectors, together with 'non-core' activities such as catering and repairs have found their way into homes. As sites of production, homes are predominantly low paid and unprotected, based on piecework with no formal contract of employment. Households also represent the sites in which the global growth in domestic services has taken place. A 'new domestic labour' is said to be 'flourishing' (Ibarra, 2000: 454) in a climate of 'deliberate economic interventions' by the AICs to individualise and privatise care services (Chang, 2000: 3). Given IPE/IR's predilection for data on change in production and work, it is perhaps unsurprising that the work of, in particular, immigrant domestic workers remains 'hidden'. The ILO standard classification of occupations fails to describe the roles of migrant domestic workers and does not provide data on the extent of this work (Anderson, 2000: 15). As a result, what Chang and Ling (2000) refer to as the 'global feminization of labour intimacy' is seriously underestimated and distorted.

As a consequence of these layers of invisibility, there is a serious obfuscation in representations of the power dynamics of the global restructuring of work. A growing gap between the 'two IRs' of international relations and industrial relations has concealed the connections between workplace and world order (Harrod, 1997a: 105), making an IPE of labour and work ever more necessary, yet problematic within prevailing ontologies.[5] The legacies of positivist IR/IPE inquiry persist in the tendency to view power 'as resource' in our studies and to seek out 'power-wielding' people as the subjects of our research. Work is thus equated with monetised economic activity, and workers are conceptualised as a commodity, so that for those whose working practices are unprotected or subordinate, there is little or no recognition in IR/IPE research. In a sense, it is assumed that those who do not possess power as a resource are not significant to understandings of the GPE. Unprotected workers are the passive victims of someone else's power. It is this 'someone else' whom orthodox (and some heterodox) IPE feels it should be concerned with, whether international organisation, MNC, government or transnational class. So, to be a significant, research-worthy global agent, one needs to have the ability and resources to transcend distance – mobility, flexibility, distance-shrinking telecommunications and portable skills. At a time when work is increasingly undertaken in a range of unprotected spaces, addressing the blind spots in existing IPE research is rendered all the more important.

There is currently a relative invisibility with regard to the meanings and concrete experiences that workers, and particularly unprotected workers without formal representation, themselves ascribe to the pressures and trans- formations of globalisation at work. The IPE of social practice perspective developed in chapter 2 opens up a number of avenues into the recapturing of worker experiences, and the repoliticisation of work in a global era. To explore work as a set of structured social practices is to render visible the webs of power within which differential experiences of restructuring are played out. The 'hyperflexible' governmental and corporate interventions rely upon a process of individualisation that breaks up shared understandings and affiliations. Attendance to the experiences that workers have of restructuring reveals that patterns of inclusion and exclusion are formed, challenged and reformed over time, constructing and corroding social alliances and recon- stituting webs of power (Sinclair, 1999: 158). It is important to understand these divisions and alliances, and to reveal the 'minor' everyday 'silent resistances' that result (Cheru, 1997: 153). While it is undeniably the case that formalised worker representation is being broken up in many state-societies (as in Britain), and represents an 'exclusive club' in others (as in Germany), it is not the case that 'outsider' worker groups are passive and fungible individuals. The insecurity and uncertainty of contingent work is increasingly a shared experience that brings its own foundations for informal organisation, as in the example of the 'Homenet' organisation for homeworkers. The incorporation of the theory and practice of everyday life into our understandings of the restructuring of work can serve to heighten the visibility of workers who have been obscured from view. I do not propose that attention should cease to be paid to the strategies of organised labour, such work is highly significant (see Hannah and Fischer, 2002; Gallin, 2002; O'Brien, 2001). However, organised labour groups must be explored in terms of their power relationship to discourses of restructuring, and to unprotected and informally-organised workers. Thus, underpinned by an ontological commitment to understand work in the broadest sense, as social reproduction, and labour as a diverse grouping that is neither a 'commodity' nor the unified voice of 'civil society', it is necessary to reveal the practices of organised and unprotected workers as they enable, contest or confound the emerging social relations of globalisation.

Contradictions at work

A focus on work as sets of structured social practices reveals a series of contradictions within hyperflexible representations of a benign and uncon- tested process of restructuring. Such representations conceal the tensions and inequalities of restructuring through an assumption that flexible forms of work and employment are compatible with human security. Indeed it is claimed that a failure to deregulate labour markets and seize the opportunities of new forms of work will result in a loss of security through increased unemployment and diminished competitiveness (OECD, 1997; World Bank, 1995). Where it is acknowledged that there may be tensions between flexibility and security, the problem is presented in terms of 'striking the right balance' so that employees can enjoy 'greater involvement in their work, more job satisfaction and the possibility of developing skills and long-term employability' (Commission of the European Communities (CEC), 1997: 8). This representation of the 'benefits' of flexible work appeals to images of autonomous workers in an information society, while obscuring the concrete experiences of workers for whom flexibility means acute personal insecurity. The European Commission's Green Paper, for example, focuses on the balancing of work and home life via teleworking, but makes no reference to homeworkers or domestic care workers, whose working time flexibility is more immediate and uncertain.[6]

A focus on the tensions between hyperflexibility strategies and everyday social practices reveals that general deregulation and new forms of work organisation replace one identified problem of poverty (unemployment) with other, less directly visible forms such as income inequality, insecurity, financial exclusion and indebtedness (International Labour Organisations (ILO), 1995). Indeed, implicit within OECD figures there is a correlation between those state-societies that have 'implemented the jobs strategy' and those that have high drop-out rates from education, widening income inequalities and a growing disadvantaged social group (OECD, 1997). The experiences that workers have of hyperflexible forms of work reveal the tensions between flexibility and security. In its most contingent form, flexible working rests upon and requires acute insecurity and instability on the part of the worker (Milkman, 1998; Pollert, 1999).

Second, there is a contradiction between processes of deunionisation and levels of contestation. The restructuring of working practices along UK/US-style hyperflexible lines is widely associated with an assault on traditional industrial relations practices. Direct admonitions to deregulate collective bargaining to the level of individual firms assume that the contests of centralised industrial relations can be minimised. However, an exploration of the ways in which concrete industrial relations practices are challenged by restructuring, reveals a different picture. The loss of formalised channels of collective bargaining in the 'radically restructured' workplaces does not result in a diminution of contestation and dissent.[7] Rather, the traditional channels are replaced with less organised and more fragmented tacit forms of resistance and challenge based on common experiences and feelings. Nor can the neo-liberal assumption that trade unions distort labour markets, inflating wages and creating income inequality and unemployment, be upheld. As Coates has it, 'inequality is not a product of trade unions. It is a product of unregulated labour markets' (1999: 133). Where unions and other civil society groups are involved in negotiating the shape of future forms of work, such as in the German Standortdebatte,[8] the result has been a focus on skills and job security rather a direct stand-off over pay. A focus on working practices suggests that the experiences of transformation in industrial relations are simply not universal: they are contingent upon a worker's position in the networks of employment, family, welfare, and so on. As formalised traditional forms of industrial relations practice are diminished, it is important that we open up our analyses to reveal new relationships that emerge within the firm and extend into unprotected workspaces (Anderson, 2000).

Finally, there is a contradiction between the global image of empowerment and the concrete realities of increased control. Images of empowerment abound within global blueprints for new forms of work and work organisation. In an elite group are the 'symbolic analysts' whose new 'weightless' portfolio careers in web design, business consultancy or financial services appear to offer flexible alternatives to traditional working practices (Reich, 1991; Coyle, 1997). Yet even within the ranks of these apparent 'free agents', the concrete experience can be 'net slavery', when 'the stock options turn into pink slips when the company goes belly up' (Ross, 2001: 81–82). Then, there are the workers for whom teamworking, quality circles and working time flexibility are said to offer empowering alternatives to the Ford-Taylor scientific management. The experiences of hyperflexible working, as expressed by workers, have much in common with the monitoring and surveillance of Taylorism, intensified by the use of self-monitoring and team 'targets'. At the 'ends' of the supply chain, in the maquiladora factories and export processing zones (EPZs) of the LDCs, are the predominantly women workers for whom images of empowering participation in the workforce are played out in the realities of abuse, exploitation and personal injury (Lui and Chiu, 1999; Soldatenko, 1999).

The disparities in workers' experiences of production in a global era will be explored further below. Here the purpose is to emphasise the common patterns of control and power that lie behind the images of empowerment for many worker groups. In terms of everyday working practices globalisation has come to be associated with a hiving off of peripheral activities into branch-plants, micro-firms, households or the informal economy. This is the concrete reality behind the much-hyped promise of a flexible and productive global workforce. In a very real sense production has exploded into a galaxy of stratified, loosely connected workspaces that are, nonetheless, closely controlled through webs of corporate power. In the example of teamworking, presented as a potentially autonomous and innovative experience, workplace studies demonstrate the reality of monotony, repetition, diminished skills and increased surveillance and control (Danford, 1998; Pollert, 1999).[9] At the heart of expressions of change in everyday working practices is the experience of increased individualisation, intensified risk and heightened tensions between individuals and groups. The image of individual empowerment emerging out of globalisation and flexible forms of work is a constructed discourse that inhibits workers' efforts to organise.

Divisions at work

Alongside the contradictions outlined above, a practice-centred perspective also reveals patterns of inclusion and exclusion that are significant to the restructuring of work. New forms of work organisation and the rise of flexible and mobile forms of work imply challenges to past practices and a reconfiguring of working relationships. However, an assumed to be emerging 'global consciousness' (Scholte, 2000: 85), or indeed a 'class consciousness', is not necessarily a unifying characteristic. Within what may be considered to be a single 'class', there are vastly different worker experiences, and differential opportunities to organise. There are also significant commonalties of experience that, though they may be uneven, extend across a range of social groups. Such commonalties include the association of globalisation with increased risk and short-termism, the intensification and speeding up of work and feelings of individualisation and acute competition: 'Flexibility means a redistribution of risks away from the state and the economy towards the individual' (Beck, 2000b: 3).

Within the contemporary intensification of risk and individualisation, as in past practices of collectivised industrial relations, the sense of a common experience and struggle has to be 'made', through actions, exchanges, ideas and interpretations. Leo Panitch, in his incisive discussion of the potential for labour to 'strategise' in response to globalisation, is concerned with the abandonment of 'class analysis' in favour of 'civil society'. He argues that leftist scholarship has moved to a pluralist concept of civil society, and in so doing has tended to leave out labour, affording 'almost no vantage point for observing that arena of non-freedom within civil society, the work-place' (2001: 367). Yet, given the fragmentation of the workplace into a myriad of contracted relationships, we have to question whether 'class' can adequately capture contemporary working experiences. The hyperflexibilisation of work cuts across conventionally held 'class' boundaries so that an effective labour strategy would have to engage in a dialogue across groups.

If workers come to know and recognise change in the global economy through the lens of their own experiences, and via their relationships with other workers, this changes the picture somewhat. There is now a need to explore the stratified social practices of different groups and individuals, and to avoid the assumption that these necessarily represent a 'class experience', or an expression of the general interests of civil society. I discuss these here in terms of insider, intermediary and outsider practices, though of course, many groups cut across these ideal-type boundaries and there are important patterns of inclusion and exclusion within the groups. The divisions at work are overlaid by other social divisions and inequalities so that, for example, some workers' experiences of increased risks are ameliorated by financial security, and by inclusion in the defining of the terms of flexibility. For others, the risks of flexibilisation are exacerbated by social exclusion and poverty.

Similarly, a worker's position in terms of state-society, firm and legal status will condition a particular relationship to programmes of flexibilisation. In essence, programmes of hyperflexibility in Anglo-Saxon state-societies are concerned with expanding the ranks of the 'outsiders', making these involuntarily contingent workers the key group, and giving employers open access to this pool of labour. Flexi-corporatism, by contrast, reinforces the status of the 'insider' workers, using them to define and legitimate restructuring, and containing the outsiders by denying them access to the restructuring debate.

Insider working practices

Insider workers predominantly take on one of two central roles in the reorganisation of work. The first is a direct participatory role in defining the terms of new forms of work and work organisation, and in reinforcing the global image of flexibility and mobility. These 'portfolio people' (Handy, 1995) represent a managerial elite, to include business analysts, policy advisors, consultants and auditors and marketing and advertising agents. The intensified 'risks' taken by these groups, such as their eschewal of company pension packages and job security, are matched by the potential rewards – working autonomy and high renumeration. As Coyle argues, there is a stark contrast between those working in the 'weightless industries' who can use the new flexibility to 'turn themselves into stars', and those people for whom flexibility 'boils down to being exploited' (1997: 91). For the insider groups an increasingly mobile and flexible lifestyle serves to reinforce their own security. Indeed, as Beck (2000b) suggests, the security and mobility of these groups rests upon the relative insecurity and immobility of other groups who are excluded from a defining role. Stability is not experienced by insider groups in terms of a single workplace, but in terms of the ability to enter multiple workspaces, as consultants, commentators and managers of change. It should not be assumed, however, that such elite groups do not contest the demands of working arrangements on their lives. For instance, after Merrill Lynch made *Working Mother* magazine's 'best employers' list in 2000, a group of women stockbrokers, who had sued the company for sex discrimination, campaigned by hiring light aircraft with banners and storming a shareholders' meeting (*New York Times*, 30 January 2001: 3).

The second key group of insiders is the core skilled workers whose working practices enable restructuring, though perhaps not as consciously as the first group. The highly skilled German craftspeople in manufacturing, and the software programmers in the British service sector, for example, have become wrapped up in the discourse on restructuring. Their stock options, bonus-led pay structures and performance-related pay, together with the nature of their work, ties their interests into particular programmes of flexibility. In the examples of the UK, US and to a lesser extent Germany, there is a common trend towards skilled workers 'playing the labour market' in a way that mirrors the 'leanness' of corporate organisations: 'Well-paid technicians, engineers, and designers became independent contractors ... "Employees without jobs", they moved from company to company, "pollinating" the seeds of innovation, according to the new flexible style of corporate organization' (Ross, 2001: 79). As core worker-stockholders and mobile skill traders dominate the 'high' end of the contingent workforce, they become emblematic of the possibilities of flexible work, featuring heavily in governmental reports and media images. The threats of globalisation and the demands of everyday working life are more comfortably reconciled and interchangeable for insider groups than for those working at the margins of the spaces they so fleetingly occupy.

Intermediary working practices

Intermediary workers can be understood as those whose practices provide a 'buffer' function at the interface between the demand for flexible labour and the need for employment and work. In essence the intermediaries insulate the insiders from responsibility for the risks and reprisals of the reorganisation of work. They take radically different forms, from the proliferation of recruitment and employment agents, through informal subcontractors, to the individuals and gangs trading in the supply of undocumented, unprotected or slave labour (Bales, 1999). At one end of the scale management and human resource consultants move fluidly between insider and intermediary functions, maintaining the 'expertise' of an 'external agency', necessary to legitimate their role in prescribing work reorganisation and to lend an air of objective neutrality to restructuring. Currently, for example, there is a trend towards the use of British management consultants on short contracts to oversee the privatisation of industries in Continental Europe. Similarly, Pricewaterhouse-Coopers and Ernst and Young have contracts to monitor the implementation of labour codes of conduct for garment and electronics multinationals. Their 'independence' as intermediaries has been questioned by international trade union confederations, though it is clear that for their corporate clients they diffuse the risks and responsibilities of outsourcing. As the chairman of Ernst and Young describes it, the professional service firms 'provide a more complete solution' (*The Economist*, 7 July 2001: 87), by engaging in both 'audit' and 'non-audit' activities.

While professional service workers are situated at the boundary between insider corporate interests and a pool of human resources, intermediaries may also take the form of traders and buyers of the services of unprotected outsider groups. One such group are subcontractors who buy in contingent labour for a specific contract with a client corporation. In the automotive component, electrical and garment manufacturing sectors, and in service sectors from logistics and transportation to cleaning and catering, such practices surround a larger client MNC and serve to absorb the slack in a lean production system. Intermediary contractors diffuse the responsibility for stock inventory, terms of employment and labour costs 'down the line' to SMEs, 'shop houses' and homeworkers. As one contract production worker for an automotive component supply firm explained: 'In a lean system, someone somewhere has to take up the slack. It is usually the weakest link in the chain'.[10] Not dissimilarly, Naomi Klein argues that trade liberalisation and labour law reform has enabled large MNCs to 'no longer produce products… but rather buy products and brand them' (2000: 5). The result has been a proliferation of subcontractor roles, and an arms-length relationship between the 'insider' corporate managers of the client MNC and the workers producing for a subcontractor: 'Larger firms spread their risks of production by subcontracting. Subcontractors, in turn, pass on the risk by contracting out to homeworkers. The latter … are not considered as employees and thus fall outside the scope of labour protection' (Lui and Chiu, 1999: 171).

The growth in outsourcing and contracting out production and services, as documented by Lui and Chiu in Hong Kong and Taiwan, effectively diffuses risk disproportionately along a supply chain, reducing the responsibility (or perception of responsibility) the customer firm has for work done in its name. In terms of working practices, the intermediary traders and buyers will outsource to sites that demonstrate a higher instance of poor pay and intensified work loads, and greater use of temporary, unprotected or illegal labour than the MNCs they supply (European Industrial Relations Observatory (EIRO), 2000; Klein, 2000). Research into the roles and practices of these intermediary actors is almost totally absent from the contemporary agenda in IPE. And yet a focus on the diffuse webs of production and supply begins to reveal an array of complex relationships between worker groups. The experiences of the 'outsiders' among them remain relatively invisible in our understandings of the contemporary GPE.

Outsider working practices

Outsider groups are those who are excluded from a formal role in defining the terms and nature of new forms of work and working practices. This is not to say that their working practices do not play significant roles in shaping or contesting transformation. Though we may not consider them to 'wield power' in a direct sense, their practices and relationships lie at the heart of the webs of power that constitute contemporary restructuring. The much-prized labour mobility and flexibility of the insider 'portfolio people' is reproduced through the practices of outsider 'precarious people' (Cox, 1999: 87) – a reserve army of contingent workers in factories, offices and homes. The 'outsiders' cannot be defined in terms of a single class, and indeed the overwhelming trend is towards a fracturing of common working identities, a 'patchwork quilt characterised by diversity, unclarity and insecurity in people's work and life' (Beck, 2000b: 1). In this sense the outsiders are themselves divided into an array of disparate individuals and groups precisely in order to destabilise and disrupt the potential for organisation and to provide optimal flexibility:

> Every corporation wants a fluid reserve of part-timers, temps and free-lancers to help it keep overheads down and ride the twists and turns in the market ... One thing is certain: offering employment – the steady kind, with benefits, holiday pay, a measure of security and maybe even union representation – has fallen out of economic fashion. (Klein, 2000: 231)

Thus, though outsider groups are fluid, segmented and difficult to iden-tify, it is precisely for these reasons that they need to enter our understandings of global restructuring. The 'rise of the permatemp' documented by *Time Magazine* is indicative of the ironic permanence of temporary and contingent work (12 July 1999). Despite barriers to the formal organisation of their interests, and direct efforts to position workers in competitive rather than collaborative relationships with one another, the experiences of outsider workers exhibit common patterns and conflicts that must be understood if meaningful dialogue between protected and unprotected workers is to take place. First, there is an expression of a consciousness of individualism and 'hypercompetitiveness' (Vilrokx, 1999; Sinclair, 1999). The use of HRM tech-niques such as the benchmarking of the performance of production plants,[11] coupled with the 'storming' effects of JIT production,[12] leads workers to feel that the greatest threats exist within the supply chain itself. The volatility and irregularity of production that is commonly associated with efforts to respond to the perceived demands of global markets, is understood by workers to be created by the manipulation of orders to fit JIT, to suit shareholders reports, or to respond to 'last minute' short-run contracts. Similarly, outsider groups associate the use of quality circles and teams with attempts to encourage them to compete with one another, and this is resisted via tacit and non-direct means (Rubery, 1996; Danford, 1998; Moody, 1997). Such heightened compe-tition between individuals often takes on a gender dimension in which women in precarious working situations both sustain neo-liberal restructuring and pose a threat to traditional masculine working roles (Hooper, 2000: 60; Chang and Ling, 2000).

Second, and a related point, outsider groups widely associate globalisa-tion with a diminution of collective identities and group representation (Towers, 1997). This is, of course, a phenomenon that is widely documented by industrial relations scholars in their studies of deunionisation. However, the changing practices of the unions themselves reveal much about the character of contemporary change in the workplace. UK and US trade unions have responded to challenges by becoming individual service providers for their 'consumers', thus reinforcing individualisation and excluding contingent and non-standard workers (Williams, 1997). Stabilising and protecting core workers has the effect of further destabilising the already precarious contract workforce. For a flexibility-seeking corporation, a protected and stable core of workers increases the incentives to create a buffer of temporary or outsourced working practices. This contributes to the polarisation of a core group of workers who may organise to protect themselves from restructuring (or to negotiate an insider role in the form of restructuring), and a larger group of workers in contingent, outsourcing or homeworking roles whose practices may undermine these efforts, making dialogue problematic (Gallin, 2001). The polarisation of worker groups is taking place in close spatial proximity, so that it cannot be understood purely by reference to geographical development divisions. Research has shown, for example, that restructuring has produced dramatic increases in socioeconomic and spatial inequalities within the cities of the developed world (Sassen, 1994; Enloe, 1996). Feelings of belonging and alienation transcend distance so that precarious workers in the advanced industrialised world may share some of the characteristics of workers in developing countries working in the same supply chain.[13] Indeed, their practices may be remarkably similar and they may feel that they compete directly for their personal security.

Finally, the social practices of paid work are perceived to become increasingly similar to the social practices of unpaid work in the home. The British media has observed this trend in terms of 'family life mirroring the workplace' as 'services such as cleaning, cooking, childcare, DIY and laundry are "contracted out"' (*The Guardian*, 6 February 2000). Thus, as Brigitte Young argues 'the growing participation of professional women in the labour market is accompanied by the largely "invisible" development of paid work in the private household' (2001: 316). To trace the webs of power in the restructuring of a large European or North American MNC is to cross the permeable boundaries of public and private, to see the relationships between 'flexible' professionals and the 'flexible' cleaners and childminders working in their homes.

Meanwhile, for the most 'flexible' contract workers, the 24 hour instantaneous demands of care and household work are contemporaneous with the demands of production for the global economy. These 'precarious workers' (Cox, 1999: 87) convey acute experiences of what one woman working in electronics assembly termed 'knife-edge flexibility' in paid working practices and absolute rigid constraints in unpaid family work. Commenting on her husband's opposition to new working time arrangements, an agency cleaning worker indicates no clear boundary between paid work for the MNC, and the unpaid and informal work 'outside': 'I don't know why they fuss on so much about the new hours. I have worked like this as far back as I can remember. It is the same here as at home'.[14] In industries such as textiles, garments and electronics, where the production chain runs deeply into unprotected sites, women at this ultimately flexible end of production take on acute personal risks. Their labour is a complex blend of private household and public enterprise production and, as a result, they are often not legally acknowledged to be employees. Work that takes place in ad-hoc workshops and in family living rooms or on kitchen tables tends to be both unprotected and invisible

(Sassen, 1994: 115; Hsuing, 1996). The rise of the 'multi-activity society' (Beck, 2000a: 42) interweaves the social practices of work, family, leisure and consumption, giving rise to new political questions and potential sites of political organisation.

Politics at work

A focus on the contradictions and divisions that arise from the restructuring of work demonstrates that work and workers need to enter the globalisation debate on a level that reveals the political nature of changing practices. Is it possible to sketch the terrain of an emergent politics of transformation in working practices? As large firms fracture their activities and workers experience intensified insecurity, can we identify spaces of potential political organisation? At one level the most visible political contests could be said to be the strategic activities of nationally or transnationally organised trade unions (O'Brien, 2000; 2001). Here the contradictions of globalisation may create the pressures and opportunities for 'global social movement unionism' (Lambert, 1999), and extend IPE inquiry into the political economy of labour (Harrod and O'Brien, 2002). The roles of trade unions in forming alliances with non-governmental organisations (NGOs), partcipating in the highly visible 'anti-globalisation' protests (Waterman and Wills, 2001), and adapting to engage with workers in the informal sectors, suggest that 'organised' labour could become a more open political mechanism for a global civil society (Somavia, 1999; IILS, 1999a).[15]

However, at the level of social practices the study of firms, unions and organisations as primary sites of political activity in the GPE is problematic. Put simply, the fracturing of traditional sites of production leads us to question the representativeness of trade unions and other institutionalised political agencies. In a report for the ILO, Richard Hyman captures the 'gap' between the image of a homogeneous labour internationalism, and the concrete experiences of different worker groups:

> It is evident that the traditional core constituency of trade union mem-bership has dwindled, while there has been expansion at two extremes: those with professional or technical skills who may feel confident of their individual capacity to survive in the labour market; and those with no such resources but whose very vulnerability makes effective collective organization and action to achieve or perhaps even contemplate. (Hyman, 1999b: 3)

We are reminded that mechanical and organised forms of solidarity are imagined and constructed in ways that are historically particular (Hyman, 1999a; Thompson, 1963). As production is actively shifted into unprotected domains, programmes of restructuring have rendered past myths of solidarity more difficult to sustain, making it impossible to assume 'the existence of a "normal worker"', and raising the need for 'organic' solidarities based on 'direct experiences, immediate milieux and specific patterns of social relations' (Hyman, 1999b: 3; 1999a: 96). Challenges to existing workplace political institutions have broken open past patterns of solidarity and allegiance. There are clear dangers but also opportunities here. The dangers lie in assuming that the workplace, in being deunionised, has become depoliticised, thereby reinforcing emerging disparities in working practices. The opportunities lie in a recognition of the common experiences, feeling and challenges within these diverse practices. In contrast to the idea that labour must 'operate globally' in order to match the 'scale' of MNC activity (see Herod, 2001), workers everyday thoughts and actions defy a global/local opposition. The apparent 'global' activities of organisations such as the Clean Clothes Campaign, Women Working World Wide, HomeNet and the Self-Employed Women's Association, are informed by the everyday experiences of workers in precarious sectors. Likewise, the struggles that are labelled 'local', such as plant-level industrial action and campaigns, or the everyday acts of disruption in a stretched lean production system, are undertaken within frameworks of thought that blend the 'near' and 'far' in personal histories. Contrary to the assumption that the 'crisis of industrial relations' has removed the politics from work, the form and nature of change in work and its organisation remains politically open, contingent and contested.

Conclusion

The starting point of this chapter was a recognition that the dominant representations of global restructuring have rendered the voices, experiences and practices of workers unheard and invisible. Where in previous chapters I explored the contested nature of the restructuring of work through the lens of the policy programmes generated by state-societies, and the corporate agendas of MNCs, here I have mapped the political relationships of worker groups that transcend state-firm categorisations. In the wake of the Seattle-style visible and direct expression of disquiet with globalisation, IPE scholars are seeking to restore the 'P' to IPE (Hay and Marsh, 1999), and to uncover the agents who propagate or defy globalisation. Yet, where political struggle and agency has been uncovered in IPE inquiry, this has predominantly taken the form of individuals, groups and institutions who are perceived to 'wield' the power necessary to engage with the debate on global restructuring. National governments, corporate agencies, international economic institutions, and (much more rarely) trade unions, civil society associations and new social movements, feature in the contents pages of IPE texts and journals. Where workers do feature, they are assumed either to be contained within the parameters of the aforementioned collective agencies, or to be outside these boundaries as passive victims of change. Thus, in a very real sense, the capacity of ordinary people to comprehend, contest or give consent to global restructuring is seriously underestimated. This chapter has attempted to reopen some of this political terrain by asking which groups are visible in IPE analyses, and exploring the grounds on which others are considered insignificant and excluded.

A first order question to be raised in the consideration of the relationship between the GPE and ordinary working practices, is whether unprotected and precarious workers actually matter to IPE inquiry. Do they have a rightful place on our research agendas? I have argued that shedding light on the experiences and practices of a range of worker groups is not simply about highlighting what we might consider to be 'grassroots' or 'ground level' political activity. Indeed, I have shown that our conceptual categories of 'global' and 'local' are significantly problematised and transcended by the concrete thoughts and practices of people in their everyday lives. Not only does the neglect of unprotected workers further entrench them at the margins of globalised social relations, but their invisibility also obscures central aspects of transformation in the GPE. Even for those studying the activities of MNCs in mainstream IPE, an understanding of 'life in the supply chain' brings significant insights. The fractured firm moves production into unprotected sites, cutting across public/private boundaries along complex supply-chains so that it becomes difficult to trace lines of responsibility and relations of power and control. The failure to bring workers' experiences into the global restructuring debate actively allows the MNC to commit this sleight of hand without a trace of it in our analyses. While anodyne business management literature extols the virtues of 'successful outsourcing', IPE is slow to catch up with critical readings of the social power relations of outsourcing practices.

Raising the profile of unprotected workers not only exposes the 'new' sites in which work is done for the GPE, but it also makes visible the political contestation taking place over the reality and representation of the restructuring of work. Following the analysis of this chapter, workers do not simply passively respond to a global force that is somehow 'greater' than them and beyond their reach, rather they actually both constitute and contest the meanings of that force for their everyday lives. In their frameworks of thought and action, workers engage with the restructuring of their own practices: differentially, unevenly and contradictorily, and within the constraints of prevailing webs of power. The assumption that the perceived dictates of globalisation and flexibilisation are transmitted uncontroversially through the layers of organisations, states, firms and workers, is subjected to serious challenge. The insecurity that is evident in concrete working practices directly undermines the benign images of security, empowerment and choice that accompany doctrines of flexibility. It becomes clear that complex patterns of inclusion and exclusion emerge from transformations in the nature and form of work, with increased security for some resting upon and requiring intensified risk for others. For the insider 'portfolio person' the risks of flexibility can be reconciled comfortably with the opportunities offered by mobility. Meanwhile, for the most 'flexible' precarious worker at the end of the supply-chain risk and insecurity are intensified. An understanding of such relationships is vital to the mapping of potential political terrain that may connect formally and informally organised workers. Viewed in this way the restructuring of work is inherently political, contested and contingent. While we choose to depict or ignore particular 'realities' of global change, highlighting the sanitised spheres of technology and corporate strategy, we leave the 'messier' realms of work and labour in deep shadow. In doing so we risk obscuring the politics of restructuring that gives the character and form to contemporary change in the workplace and in a wider world order.

Notes

1 This focus on the relationship between epistemological bias and invisibility owes much to the work of Roger Tooze and Craig Murphy (1996). They suggest that poverty and the poor have been made invisible by an IR and IPE predilection for empiricist epistemology and positivist methodology. For further discussion of the positivist and empiricist underpinnings of international theory, see Smith (1996).

2 IMF Managing Director Horst Köhler outlined his view of the future of the IMF as 'an active part of the workforce to make globalisation work for the benefit of all' (2000a: 2). Similar themes are evident in the British Government's White Paper on 'Eliminating World Poverty: Making Globalisation Work for the Poor' (Department for International Development, 2000), and *The Economist's* 'The Case for Globalisation' (2000: 19).

3 The Outsourcing Institute (2000) estimate that outsourcing is growing in the US at around 15 per cent annually. While it is clear that this practice is growing across the OECD countries, its rate is difficult to estimate as the boundaries between 'inside' and 'outside' provision are increasingly fluid. For example, some German firms report the part-purchase of a supplier, making the production 'in house', yet maintaining the relationship of an external supplier. The supply of cleaning, maintenance and catering services is commonly outsourced in British companies, though is rarely recognised and reported as outsourcing, as it is not considered to be a production function. In terms of research on outsourcing, business journal articles on 'how to outsource' are burgeoning (see Elmuti and Kathwala, 2000), though there is little critical analysis of the nature and effects of outsourcing (see Bittman, Matheson and Meagher, 1999).

4 The ILO estimate that there are around 250 million children (5–14 years old) working in economic activity worldwide. For 120 million this work is full-time and excludes schooling. For the remainder this is combined with schooling (ILO Bureau of Statistics, 1998).

5 Harrod and O'Brien (2002) bring together the insights of labour studies, IPE, industrial relations, IRs and the sociology of work. The collection addresses the common problematics that global restructuring brings to these disciplines.

6 The ILO use the term 'homeworker' to define people working at home on tasks that are generally low paid, insecure and undertaken on a piecework basis, usually with no direct or formal contract. In contrast, a teleworker may be a manager, a senior professional or other employee who works flexibly between home and office via ICT links.

7 During 1999 the UK lost 12 days per 1000 employees due to industrial action. In Germany, where trade unions retain a central role despite declining density, 1 day was lost per 1000 employees (EIRO 1999).

8 The German Standortdebatte is the debate between the social partners surrounding the competitiveness of Germany as a location for production and investment.

9 The 1998 British Workplace Employee Relations Survey reveals that though two-thirds of workplaces report using teamworking, only 3 per cent of these actually devolve decision-making autonomy to the level of teams.

10 Confidential focus group interview, South Wales, 16 June 1998.

11 It is not uncommon for workers to be made directly aware of their individual performance vis-à-vis competitor plants and contractors. This can take the form of daily or weekly bulletins of benchmark performances, or visible screens on the factory floor displaying targets.

12 JIT production implies a reduction of slack or buffers in the system, requiring minimal materials and labour inventory, and an electronic data system, linking the customer to the firm and the supply chain. For large electronics MNCs this commonly manifests itself in weekly or bi-weekly estimates of production runs, necessitating instantaneous responses in working practices.

13 Soldatenko's (1999) study of Latina garment workers in Los Angeles reveals the complexities of feelings of shared experience and alienation. The intraworker and inter-ethnic conflict within sweat-shop conditions problematises the treatment of workers as a collective body of resistors. A central theme in the explosion of the subcontracting chain is what Soldatenko refers to as the difficulty in 'forging an effective culture of resistance' (1999: 319).

14 Confidential interview with contract workers of electronic component multinational, UK, 24 February 1998.

15 The Clean Clothes Campaign Network, for example, includes trade unions, women workers' groups and networks and worker education bodies. The purpose is to improve the working conditions of garment workers worldwide.

Conclusion:
~ international political economy of work

In the late twentieth and early twenty-first centuries, we are living in an era of social transformation that has been defined by the concept of globalisation, just as it has been shaped by programmes of restructuring carried out in the name of globalisation. Yet, our era is also one in which people's concrete experiences of transformation are diverse and contradictory. While for some, living in a GPE means holding and managing a portfolio of shares, business travel for a MNC, and increased prosperity and security, for others it means redundancy as a share price falls, contract work for a MNC, and increased risk and insecurity. Despite the rise of globalisation as a 'dominant discourse … which produces truth about individuals and their environment' (Penttinen, 2000: 203), multiple meanings and diverse concrete experiences persist that make this a debated and contested set of truths. The primary task of this book has been to offer a route into the revealing of these multiple meanings, experiences and contests.

A rethinking of our dominant mode of knowledge of social change is needed if everyday spheres such as work, family, consumption and leisure are to be understood as key realms of globalising social relations. Orthodox IPE perspectives – conceiving of opposed realms of state and market, domestic and international, and of power and knowledge as resources – have rendered invisible precisely those realms of social life where the meanings of globalisation are constituted. This book has engaged in some reflection on the dominant ways of thinking that have shaped IPE's research agenda. I have asked how particular readings of global social change have achieved 'common sense' status, and how they have been discursively employed to enable particular interventions to be made. This has primarily been an exercise in the politicisation of global restructuring, and the understanding of social change on which it is predicated. A first step in such an exercise involves the opening up of space for the discussion of alternative forms of political representation and, I have argued, this step can be taken via an exploration of the webs of power, tensions and contradictions that grip contemporary restructuring. In the spirit of this discussion, my concluding remarks should not be read as closing comments. Rather, I am seeking to open up some of the potential terrain for alternative modes of knowledge of social change, and a discussion of the utility of the social practice perspective on work and related spheres of life.

Problematising global social change

Global social transformation has predominantly been communicated to us in processual terms. That is to say, the common-sense accounts of 'what global-isation is' tend to make appeals to a *process* that is driven by technological and economic externalities. It is a short step from this inevitabilist image to the construction of 'imperatives', towards which all state-societies, firms and people must restructure. In such a reading, historical difference, political conflict and social contestation are extracted from a pure drive for global transformation. There is a hungry market for such representations of a process of global change, precisely because if one can simplify, codify and explain the dynamics of transformation in this way, it becomes possible to make prescribed neo-liberal interventions. When represented as an irrevocable and essential process, that can nonetheless be managed, globalisation becomes a powerful meaning-generating concept that accounts for 'what is happening' at the same time as it draws the parameters of 'what should be done about it'.

This book has explored one such representation of globalisation 'as process' – the widespread propagation of a discourse of labour flexibility, on which deregulatory interventions are founded. Representing globalisation in a deterministic and apolitical way, I have argued, decisively enables the restructuring of work to be ordered, disciplined, prescribed and depoliticised. It becomes possible for a range of international economic institutions, governments and corporate strategists to confine debate to an instrumental discussion of reforms, as seen in the World Bank's (1995; 2001) and the OECD's (1996; 1997) policy interventions. In many ways the sphere of flexibility in working practices does not serve simply as a 'case-study' of flexibilisation, but is pivotal in the transformation of social life. Work represents a governmental inroad to the restructuring of the spheres of home, welfare, family and household. In its broadest sense, flexibility defines the properties of a society that has embraced the imperatives of risk, self-responsibility and immediacy and is pervasive throughout the layers of social life, and across the presumed boundaries of global and local, public and private.

An alternative set of understandings of global social transformation has sought to restore the agency and power that is denied by process-centred readings. This book has depicted these accounts as grouped around a view of globalisation as a *project* that is shaped and directed by identifiable individual and collective agents. In one such representation, globalisation is 'put back in its box' by a restatement of the power of the state, and specifically the persistent role of 'national capitalisms' in shaping the parameters of global forces. In one sense, such accounts highlight difference and historical contingency within the globalisation debate. Yet, as I have argued in this book, the distinctive meanings ascribed to national 'models' within the construction of globalisation are rarely problematised. Indeed, there is an assumption that the pressures of globalisation have heralded an undisputed victory for Anglo-Saxon neo-liberalism, and a defeat for social market corporatism. As I have shown, however, the making of a 'global Britain' has served a particular set of functions in the framing of the need to 'harness' globalisation via labour flexibilisation. Such representations extend beyond the terms of a bounded national debate into an international discourse on global restructuring.

In a second conceptualisation, globalisation is represented as a trans-national project that is furthered through the actions of MNCs, financiers, or a global class or resisted through the actions of new social movements and trade unions. Despite a clear reinvestment of politics, the political tends to be viewed as organised, formalised and institutionalised activity. In an era when labour flexibilisation is making efforts to deunionise and depoliticise the workplace, there is a danger that indirect, informal and interstitial modes of political activity will be overlooked. In seeking to problematise the terms of the contemporary debate on global social change, this book has presented a challenge to those engaged in exploring the project of global restructuring, whether identified as national or transnational: that is to raise the question of how those who are governed or defined by the project are also implicated in its reproduction. The assumed project must be opened up to reveal the concrete practices that enable, confound or contest its dictates.

Politicising global social change

An IPE perspective that is attuned to the diverse social practices that together underpin or transform world order, I have argued, can unmask the tensions and contradictions of global social change. Research that sets out to explore the restructuring of social practices that is carried out under the banner of globalisation brings the abstract concept into the concrete realms of political bargaining, governmental intervention, social accommodation and contestation. A focus on restructuring can offer a countervailing pressure in an environment in which the mainstream media, political and academic commentaries construct an 'other worldly' globalisation – one that is unreachable, 'grander' than ourselves, and whose only link to everyday life is a top-down 'impact' on local practices. The multiple layers of the restructuring of work, when viewed from a practice perspective, are simultaneously undertaken in the name of global-isation, while they also interpret, contest and give meaning to that name. This book has sought to offer three preliminary steps towards an IPE of social practice.

Historicity, contingency, diversity

The critical potential of IPE, as Robert Cox has it, lies in its capacity to stand back from the prevailing world order, to ask how it came about (1981: 130), and to consider 'the ways reality is defined for different people in different eras' (1995: 35). Such a position assumes that social structures and social transformation are not predetermined, or externally driven, but are historically constituted through the actions and reflections of people. Viewed in this way, the restructuring of work does not simply 'happen to' people – either as a result of an unstoppable techno-economic process, or as a strategic and calculated project. Rather, it is always experienced, reflected upon, interpreted and lived in the context of historically-specific spaces. As I argued with reference to the restructuring debates in British and German state-societies, the making of a particular representation of globalisation, and a concomitant programme of restructuring interventions, is historically contingent, and generates its own distinctive tensions, problematics and divisions. The thoughts and actions of those living in the fractured world of contemporary global production are at least as central to the furthering or undermining of restructuring as the states, firms and technologies that constrain and limit them. Overall, a historical mode of thought reminds us that the material restructuring of MNCs that has so preoccupied IPE inquiry, is intimately bound up with the everyday histories of workplaces, and with our received understandings of what these workplaces constitute.

Webs of power

A central problematic in the analysis of the politics of global social change is the question of how power is exercised in the shaping of practices. On the one hand, an overly structural conception of power may overstate 'control' and leave no space for agency, while on the other, an overly individualistic conception may overstate the capacity for agent to resist (Clegg, 2000: 78). This problematic is exacerbated in some IPE inquiry which commonly identifies power with an elite group of 'global actors' and a set of institutions that act as 'bearers' of structure. As a result, the webs of power that circulate via social relationships, creating and constraining spaces and opportunities for trans- formation, are rendered invisible by conceptions of power 'as resource'. This book has positioned power-knowledge relationships centrally in the explor- ation of the restructuring of work. I have argued that in order to understand the knowledge and governmental techniques that have made the flexibility discourse possible, it is necessary also to reveal the webs of power relations that suffuse the restructuring of work. Such an approach transcends bounded 'global', 'national' and 'local' levels of analysis. In my analysis of the firm, for example, I focused on the relationships between social groups, demonstrating that these cut across the ascribed boundaries of MNCs. The transnational activities of bankers, corporate managers and management consultants are taken out of the realm of an ethereal global market, to consider their relationships to the practices of non-elite groups such as unprotected labour, contract workers and homeworkers. These relationships, I have argued, cannot be grasped by a simple opposition of the promotion of global restructuring versus the resistance to global restructuring.

The everyday

This book has argued that global social change is experienced, given meaning, reinforced and challenged through the everyday structured practices of individuals and social groups, such that the concept of globalisation should be understood through the contestation that takes place over its realities and representations. As Kaplan and Ross have it, 'the Political is hidden in the everyday, exactly where it is most obvious: in the contradictions of lived experience, in the most banal and repetitive gestures of everyday life' (1987: 3). Globalisation thus becomes one conceptual means of identifying and naming 'grand scale' social change, but is potentially also disguising the myriad of meanings and experiences that are translated in the networks of everyday life. As I have shown, the restructuring agendas of national governments, corporate actors or international institutions are never wholly predictable, linear and unproblematic. Interventions designed to transform working practices meet with ongoing social struggles and are translated in numerous ways. Out of the Anglo-Saxon drive for individualism in working practices has emerged a reforging of worker identities, with new patterns of alliance and division. Far from a benign and depoliticised workplace, the study of everyday working practices reveals a politics of direct experience that moves as fluidly as the MNC that moves to outsource and disperse production. To pronounce the 'death' of workplace politics is to neglect the ability of political life to transform itself.

Towards an international political economy of work

Having reconceptualised globalisation as an ongoing, non-linear and unpredictable transformation of social practices, this book opens up alternative routes into thinking about work within IPE.

First, I have challenged conceptions of work as merely a function of the global production process. The dynamics of the restructuring of work cannot be understood as an outcome of transformations in production, for this is to miss the diversity of experiences of working in a GPE. The restructuring of traditional paid production work, for example, is having significant implications for paid and unpaid domestic and care work. Indeed, an exploration of the roles and functions of unemployment in a GPE is also fundamental to thinking about work and the governmentality of work. As the ILO's 'Decent Work' agenda reminds us 'almost everyone works, but not everyone is employed' (1999b: 3). Societies face varied challenges and questions in their framing of future modes and forms of work. This will include necessary reflection on the function that unemployment or semi-employment may serve in their political economy, the consequences of the casualisation of work and the growth of a relatively unregulated service sector, and the rethinking of the concept of 'work' these questions require. In most cases this will also reveal complex patterns of inequality, inclusion and exclusion. The durability of the hyperflexibility discourse is dependent upon its ability to continually adapt and metamorphose in order to conceal its social consequences. The early twenty-first century linking of labour flexibility to concepts of corporate social responsibility is almost certainly just such an attempt to ameliorate the effects of corporate restructuring and silence the critics. A conception of work that extends beyond an understanding of productive or class relations is essential if we are to maintain a critical gaze on the slippery concept of flexibility, even as it adopts the mantle of corporate responsibility and risk management.

Second, this book has urged IPE to extend its understanding of workers and their agency beyond a conception of organised labour, to consider the complexity of patterns of solidarity, collaboration, fragmentation and dissent. There seems to be some comfort taken in IPE from the idea that organised labour may be a 'voice' for global civil society. But, in normative terms, is a single channel or formal voice what is being looked for? Following E. P. Thompson, a unified body of collective consciousness must always be wrought from something, and will necessarily draw boundaries and exclude practices. The practices of 'insider' workers, of whatever form, will have their 'outsider' counterparts whose working practices may be in tension. To speak of a single collective voice of a global civil society of workers is highly problematic. Alternative prospects for workers' agency must be found, and these alternatives must acknowledge that the potential for politics at work rests upon a competing and contradictory array of agencies. It is in the tensions and contradictions of diverse working practices that the politics of the transformation of work lie. An exploration of the competing practices reveals some common ground in unexpected places. The disruption of the boundaries between work and home (public and private lives), for example, is an experience felt by elite workers and contingent workers alike, opening up the possibility for a societal debate on the consequences of such transformation. Similarly, future research could fruitfully focus on the deepening of tensions and divisions in spaces where historically one looked for solidarities, such as on the manufacturing line and within the trade union movement itself.

Finally, this book has sought to reveal the political potentialities that may lie in the interstices of everyday working practices. There are predominantly two aspects that come out of my analysis: one is the sketching of a potential political terrain in spaces where work takes place, the other concerns the implications of an IPE of social practice for other spheres of social activity. Seizing the political ground in the contemporary globalisation debate has tended to imply a direct resistance, exemplified by the so-called anti-globalisation campaigns. Yet, it is interesting that these resistance groups tend to be depicted as united 'against' a single foe, despite the manifest diversity of their agendas.

There are other problems associated with 'contesting globalisation' as though it were a clearly defined single entity. Does resistance to globalisation need to be conscious and planned? Are the small and everyday acts of footdragging, or acts of 'getting by', also acts of resistance? How should we understand the negotiated engagement with global restructuring undertaken by some trade unions? Is this tactical resistance or have the unions been co-opted into a restructuring discourse?

In order to push the boundaries of our understanding of resistance (whether by unionised labour, social movements or people going about their daily lives), it is necessary for us to cast our gaze on the practices that enable and further neo-liberal discourses, as well as those that confound or resist. The individual and collective 'acts of survival' seen in the support networks of contract workers in Britain, for example, could be interpreted as acts of resistance in the sense that they defy attempts to individualise workers. Yet they could also be read as enabling greater functional flexibility, for example in the mutual provision of childcare. Similarly the growing number of German workers in the informal economy are, on the one hand excluded from formal representation in the 'flexi-corporatist' debate, yet their practices are also plugging a gap in state and private enterprise provision.

The identification of emergent contradictions and tensions in restructured working practices raises questions that may apply beyond work, to other related spheres of social life. With regard to the financial sphere, for example, the proliferation of credit unions, local currencies and local exchange trading schemes, reveals practices conceived as countering financial globalisation, while also representing spaces that are excluded from 'insider' financial practices. So, these could either be conceived as alternative practices and political gestures, or as the 'mopping up' of social groups who are excluded from elite practices, and thereby enabling global finance. The debate surrounding the contradictory 'furthering' and 'opposing' of global restructuring is one that will be significant in future analysis of the GPE. The growth of interest in ethical investments and consumer responsibility, for example, is simultaneously concerned with an engagement with global capital and a discussion of political-economic and social alternatives. I am not proposing that such questions can be resolved here, but that an IPE of social practice makes the raising of these questions possible, and that the power relations, contradictions and tensions visible in the restructuring of work may be present elsewhere.

The 'contestedness' that forms the title and subject matter of this book is present in many forms. I have founded my IPE of work on a critical questioning of the mode of knowledge that has been framed by the master concept of globalisation. The meanings ascribed to globalisation; the representations that dominate globalisation; and the experiences that make globalisation concrete and 'real': all are contested on a daily basis. Globalisation does not exist independently of the meanings, practices and discourses that are made in its name, nor is it confined to the elite global practices of states, multinationals and international institutions. In this book I have depicted an alternative image, and one that I argue reveals the power and politics of the making of globalisations. In my framing, globalisation stands alongside other master concepts used to render social transformation explainable, codifiable and manageable. We have seen industrialisation and modernisation function in similar ways. As mobile and empty concepts they become filled with meaning, and come to represent particular realities for individuals, states, societies and social groups.

Each chapter of this volume has addressed some aspect of the representations of globalisation that have given meaning to the flexibilisation of work. Once unpacked, the labour flexibility that is constructed as a panacea to globalisation, reveals a bundle of ideas and images that are appropriated and deployed to legitimate a range of interventions. There are other concepts worthy of exploration – risk, responsibility and mobility are also emerging within a lexicon of restructuring discourse. Ultimately, I have argued that the meanings of globalisation and flexibility directly engage with the everyday lives of people. They do so differentially, unevenly and contradictorily, as they simultaneously seek to remove the grounds for politics, while also redrawing the lines of shared experience, solidarity and identity. Bringing the rarefied restructuring practices of global corporate actors, financiers and governments into their concrete relationships with the everyday practices of work, renders the spaces of global restructuring reachable and open to debate. In this sense, our knowledge of global social change is itself subject to contestation, over how we have come to understand transformation, and who and what we have made visible and invisible.

Bibliography

Abraham, K. G., and Houseman, S. N. (1993) 'Job Security and Work Force Adjustment: How Different are US and Japanese Practices?', in Buechtemann, C. F. (ed.) *Employment Security and Labor Market Behaviour*, Ithaca: ILR Press.

Ackers, P., Smith, C., and Smith, P. (1996) *The New Workplace and Trade Unionism: Critical Perspectives on Work and Organisation*, London: Routledge.

Aglietta, M. (1979) *A Theory of Capitalist Regulation*, London: New Left Books.

Aglietta, M. (2000) 'Shareholder Value and Corporate Governance: A Comment and Some Tricky Questions', *Economy and Society*, 29: 1, pp. 146–159.

Agnew. J., and Corbridge, S. (1995) *Mastering Space: Hegemony, Territory, and International Political Economy*, London: Routledge.

Albert, M. (1993) *Capitalism Against Capitalism*, London: Whurr.

Allen, R. E. (1994) *Financial Crises and Recession in the Global Economy*, Aldershott: Edward Elgar.

Amin, A., and Palan, R. (1996) 'Editorial: The Need to Historicise IPE', *Review of International Political Economy*, 3: 2, pp. 209–215.

Amin, A., Gills, B. K., Palan, R., and Taylor, P. (1994) 'Editorial: Forum for Heterodox International Political Economy', *Review of International Political Economy*, 1: 1, pp. 1–12.

Amoore, L. (1998) 'Globalisation, the Industrial Society and Labour Flexibility', *Global Society*, 12: 1, pp. 49–74.

Amoore, L. (2000) 'International Political Economy and the Contested Firm, *New Political Economy* 5: 2, pp. 183–204.

Amoore, L., and Langley, P. (2000) 'Process, Project and Practice: The Politics of Globalisation', paper presented to the 25th Annual Conference of the British International Studies Association, 18–20 December.

Amoore, L., Dodgson, R., Gills, B. K., Langley, P., Marshall, D., and Watson, I. (1997) 'Overturning Globalisation: Resisting the Teleological, Reclaiming the Political', *New Political Economy*, 2: 1, pp. 179–195.

Amoore, L., Dodgson, R., Germain, R. D., Gills, B. K., Langley, P., and Watson, I. (2000) 'Paths to a Historicized International Political Economy', *Review of International Political Economy*, 7: 1, pp. 53–71.

Anderson, B. (1983) *Imagined Communities: Reflections on the Origin and Spread of Nationalism*, London: Verso.

Anderson, B. (2000) *Doing the Dirty Work: The Global Politics of Domestic Labour*, London: Zed.

Anderson, P. (1991) *English Questions*, London: Verso.

Aron, R. (1967) *The Industrial Society*, London: Weidenfield and Nicolson.

Arrighi, G. (1994) *The Long Twentieth Century: Money, Power, and the Origins of Our Times*, London: Verso.

Ashley, R. (2000) 'Sovereignty, Hauntology, and the Mirror of the World Political: Some Thoughts Too Long Re-tained', paper presented to the Annual Convention of the International Studies Association, Los Angeles, 14–18 March 2000.

Atkinson, J. (1985) 'Flexibility: Planning for an Uncertain Future', *The IMS Review*, 1, pp. 26–29.

Augelli, E., and Murphy, C. (1993) 'Gramsci and International Relations: A General Perspective With Examples from Recent US Policy Toward the Third World', in S. Gill (ed.) *Gramsci, Historical Materialism and International Relations*, Cambridge: Cambridge University Press.

Baglioni, G., and Crouch, C. (eds) (1990) *European Industrial Relations: The Challenge of Flexibility*, London: Sage.

Bales, K. (1999) *Disposable People: New Slavery in the Global Economy*, Berkeley: University of California Press.

Barry, A., Osborne, T., and Rose, N. (eds) (1996) *Foucault and Political Reason: Liberalism, Neo-liberalism and Rationalises of Government*, London: UCL Press.

Bassett, P. (1986) *Strike Free: New Industrial Relations in Britain*, London: Macmillan.

Bauman, Z. (1998) *Globalization: The Human Consequences*, Cambridge: Polity.

BBC, *News Online*, 'The Globalisation Debate', 15 April 2000, available at: http://news.bbc.co.uk/hi/english/business/newsid_714000/714972.stm.

BBC, *Panorama*, 'Gap and Nike: No Sweat', 15 October 2000.

Beatson, M. (1995) *Labour Market Flexibility*, London: HMSO.

Beck, U. (1992) *Risk Society*, London: Sage.

Beck, U. (2000a) *What is Globalization?*, Cambridge: Polity.

Beck, U. (2000b) *The Brave New World of Work*, Cambridge: Polity.

Becker, C., and Vitols, S. (1997) 'An Innovation Crisis in German Industry?: The German Innovation System in the 1990s', paper presented at the workshop on 'Modell Deutschland in the 1990s: Problems and Prospects', Wissenschaftszentrum Berlin, 27–28 June 1997.

Bell, D. (1961) *The End of Ideology*, New York: Collier.

Benders, J., and van Bijsterveld (2000) 'Leaning on Lean: The Reception of a Management Fashion in Germany', *New Technology, Work and Employment*, 15: 1, pp. 50–64.

Bercusson, B. (1997) 'Adapting Britain to the European Model', paper prepared for Conference on 'European Systems of Labour Market Regulation', University of Manchester Institute of Science and Technology, 31 January.

Berger, S., and Dore, R. (eds) (1996) *National Diversity and Global Capitalism*, Ithaca: Cornell University Press.

Bernard, M. (1997) 'Ecology, Political Economy and the Counter-Movement: Karl Polanyi and the Second Great Transformation', in Gill, S., and Mittelman, J. (eds) *Innovation and Transformation in International Studies*, Cambridge: Cambridge University Press.

Bienefeld, M. (1991) 'Karl Polanyi and the Contradictions of the 1980s', in

Mendell, M., and Salée, D. *The Legacy of Karl Polanyi: Market, State and Society at the End of the Twentieth Century*, Basingstoke: Macmillan.

Bingham, N., and Thrift, N. (2000) 'Some New Instructions for Travellers: The Geography of Bruno Latour and Michel Serres', in Crang, M., and Thrift, N. (eds) *Thinking Space*, London: Routledge.

Birchfield, V. (1999) 'Contesting the Hegemony of Market Ideology: Gramsci's "Good Sense" and Polanyi's "Double Movement"', *Review of International Political Economy*, 6: 1, pp. 27–54.

Bittman, M., Matheson, G., and Meagher, G. (1999) 'The Changing Boundary Between Home and Market: Australian Trends in Outsourcing Domestic Labour', *Work, Employment and Society*, 13: 2, pp. 249–273.

Blair, T. (1998) 'Speech at the Opening of AVCO Trust', 16 September, Sunderland, available at http://www.number–10.gov.uk.

Blair, T. (2000a) 'Speech at the World Economic Forum', Davos Switzerland, 28 January, available at http://www.fco.gov.uk/news/speechtext.asp?3260.

Blair, T. (2000b) 'Speech to the Global Borrowers and Investors Forum Conference', London, 22 June, available at http://www.fco.gov.uk/news/speechtext.asp?3843.

Blair, T., and Schröder, G. (1999) *Europe: The Third Way/Die Neue Mitte*, available from Montreal Economic Institute at http://www/iedm.org.

Blank, R. (1994) *Social Protection Versus Economic Flexibility: Is There a Trade-Off?*, Chicago: University of Chicago Press.

Bleiker, R. (2000) *Popular Dissent, Human Agency and Global Politics*, Cambridge: Cambridge University Press.

Block, F. (1990) *Postindustrial Possibilities: A Critique of Economic Discourse*, Oxford: Oxford University Press.

Block, F., and Somers, M. (1984) 'Beyond the Economistic Fallacy: The Holistic Social Science of Karl Polanyi', in Skocpol, T. (ed.) *Vision and Method in Historical Sociology*, Cambridge: Cambridge University Press.

Boyer, R. (1986) *La théorie de la régulation: une analyse critique*, Paris: La Decouverte.

Boyer, R. (1995) 'The Future of Unions: Is The Anglo-Saxon Model a Fatality, or Will Contrasting National Trajectories Persist?', *British Journal of Industrial Relations*, 33: 4, pp. 545–556.

Boyer, R. (1996) 'The Convergence Hypothesis Revisited: Globalisation but still the Century of Nations?', in Berger, S., and Dore, R. (eds) *National Diversity and Global Capitalism*, Ithaca: Cornell University Press.

Brodie, J. (1996) 'New State Forms, New Political Spaces', in Boyer, R., and Drache, D. (eds) *States Against Markets: The Limits of Globalization*, London: Routledge.

Brown, C. (1999) 'International Society and Agency Or Something Must be Done', paper presented to International Studies Association Convention, Washington DC, 16–20 February 1999.

Brown, W., Deakin, S., and Ryan, P. (1997) 'The Effects of British Industrial Relations Legislation 1979–97', *National Institute Economic Review*, 161, pp. 69–83.

Burch, K., and Denemark, R. (eds) (1997) *Constituting International Political Economy*, Boulder: Lynne Rienner.

Burnham, P. (1999) 'Historical Materialism, Getting it Right: The Politics of Economic Management in the 1990s', paper presented to the International Studies Association Convention, Washington DC, 16–20 February 1999.

Cammack, P. (2000) 'Making the Poor Work for Globalisation', unpublished paper.

Campbell, D. (1996) 'Political Prosaics, Transversal Politics, and the Anarchical World', in Shapiro, M. J., and Alker, H. R. (eds) *Challenging Boundaries: Global Flows, Territorial Identities*, Minneapolis: University of Minnesota Press.

Carr, E. H. (1961) *What is History?*, London: Macmillan.

Casper, S., and Vitols, S. (1997) 'The German Model in the 1990s: Problems and Prospects', *Industry and Innovation*, 4: 1, pp. 1–13.

Castells, M. (1989) *The Informational City*, Oxford: Blackwell.

Castells, M. (1996) *The Information Age: Economy, Society and Culture*, Oxford: Blackwell.

Cerny, P. G. (1990) *The Changing Architecture of Politics: Structure, Agency and the Future of the State*, London: Sage.

Cerny, P. G. (1994) 'The Dynamics of Financial Globalization: Technology, Market Structure and Policy Response', *Policy Sciences*, 27: 4, pp. 319–342.

Cerny, P. G. (1995) 'Globalization and the Changing Logic of Collective Action', *International Organization*, 49: 4, pp. 595–625.

Cerny, P. G. (1996) 'International Finance and the Erosion of State Policy', in Gummett, P. (ed.) *Globalization and Public Policy*, Cheltenham: Edward Elgar.

Chang, G. (2000) *Disposable Domestics: Immigrant Women Workers in the Global Economy*, Cambridge, MA: South End Press.

Chang, K. A., and Ling, L. H. M. (2000) 'Globalization and its Intimate Other: Filipina Domestic Workers in Hong Kong', in Marchand, M., and Runyan, A. S. (eds) *Gender and Global Restructuring: Sightings, Sites and Resistances*, London: Routledge.

Channel 4, 'Slavery', 28 September 2000.

Channel 4, 'Politics Isn't Working: The End of Politics', 13 May 2001.

Cheru, F. (1997) 'The Silent Revolution and the Weapons of the Weak: Transformation and Innovation from Below', in Gill, S., and Mittelman, J. (eds) *Innovation and Transformation in International Studies*, Cambridge: Cambridge University Press.

Clark, G. L. (1999), 'The Retreat of the State and the Rise of Pension Fund Capitalism', in Martin, R. (ed.) *Money and the Space Economy*, Chichester: John Wiley & Sons.

Clegg, S. (2000) 'Power and Authority, Resistance and Legitimacy', in Goverde, H., Cerny, P. G., Haugaard, M., and Lentner, H. (eds) *Power in Contemporary Politics: Theories, Practices, Globalizations*, London: Sage.

Coates, D. (1999) 'Labour Power and International Competitiveness: A Critique of Ruling Orthodoxies', *Socialist Register*, pp. 108–141.

Coates, D. (2000) *Models of Capitalism: Growth and Stagnation in the Modern Era*, Cambridge: Polity.

Coates, D., and Hay, C. (2000) 'Home and Away? The Political Economy of New Labour', paper presented to the 50th annual conference of the Political Studies Association, London, 10–13 April.

Collingwood, R.G. (1946) *The Idea of History*, Oxford: Oxford University Press.

Commission of the European Communities (CEC) (1993) *Growth, Competitiveness and Employment -- The Challenges and Ways Forward into the 21st Century*, White Paper, Brussels: CEC.

Commission of the European Communities (CEC) (1997) *Partnership for a New Organisation of Work*, Green Paper, Brussels: CEC.

Cook, R. (2001) 'Speech at the International Institute of Strategic Studies', London, 9 March, available at http: //www.fco.gov.uk/news/speechtext.asp?4784.

Corporate Watch (2000) 'The Brave New World of Work', Issue 9, Summer 2000.

Cox, A. (1986) *The State, Finance and Industry*, Brighton: Harvester Wheatsheaf.

Cox, A., Lee, S., and Sanderson, J. (eds) (1997) *The Political Economy of Modern Britain*, Cheltenham: Edward Elgar.

Cox, R. W. (1971) 'Labor and Transnational Relations', *International Organization*, 25: 3, pp. 554–584.

Cox, R. W. (1981/1996) 'Social Forces, States, and World Orders: Beyond International Relations Theory', *Millennium: Journal of International Studies*, 10: 2, pp. 127–155.

Cox, R. W. (1983) 'Gramsci, Hegemony, and International Relations: An Essay in Method', *Millennium: Journal of International Studies*, 12: 2, pp. 162–175.

Cox, R. W. (1987) *Production, Power and World Order: Social Forces in the Making of History*, New York: Columbia University Press.

Cox, R. W. (1991/1996) 'The Global Political Economy and Social Choice', in Cox, R. W., with Sinclair, T. J. (1996) *Approaches to World Order*, Cambridge: Cambridge University Press.

Cox, R. W. (1992a/1996) 'Take Six Eggs: Theory, Finance, and the Real Economy in the Work of Susan Strange', in Cox, R. W., with Sinclair, T. J. (1996) *Approaches to World Order*, Cambridge: Cambridge University Press.

Cox, R. W. (1992b/1996) 'Towards a Posthegemonic Conceptualization of World Order: Reflections on the Relevancy of Ibn Khaldun', in Cox, R. W., with Sinclair, T. J. (1996) *Approaches to World Order*, Cambridge: Cambridge University Press.

Cox, R. W. (1993) 'Structural Issues of Global Governance: Implications for Europe', in Gill, S. *Gramsci, Historical Materialism and International Relations*, Cambridge: Cambridge University Press.

Cox, R. W. (1995) 'Critical Political Economy', in Hettne, B. (ed.) *International Political Economy: Understanding Global Disorder*, London: Zed Books.

Cox, R. W. (1999) 'Civil Society at the Turn of the Millennium: Prospects for an Alternative World Order', *Review of International Studies*, 25: 1, pp. 3–28.

Cox, R. W., with Sinclair, T. J. (1996) *Approaches to World Order*, Cambridge: Cambridge University Press.

Coyle, D. (1997) *Weightless World*, Oxford: Capstone.

Crouch, C. (1993) *Industrial Relations and European State Traditions*, Oxford: Clarendon Press.

Crouch, C. (1997) 'Skills-based Full Employment: the Latest Philosopher's Stone', *British Journal of Industrial Relations*, 35: 3, pp. 367–391.

Crouch, C. (2001) 'Heterogeneities of Practice and Interest', *New Political Economy*, 6: 1, pp. 131–135.

Crouch, C., and Streeck, W. (eds) (1997) *Political Economy of Modern Capitalism*, London: Sage.

Cully, M. (1999) *Britain at Work: As Depicted by 1998 Workplace Employee Relations Survey*, NY: Routledge.

Cully, M., O'Reilly, A., Millward, N., Forth, J., Woodland, S., Dix, G., and Bryson, A. (1998) *The 1998 Workplace Employee Relations Survey*, London: HMSO.

Culpepper, P. D. (1999) 'Introduction: Still a Model for the Industrialized Countries?', in Culpepper, P. D., and Finegold, D. (eds) *The German Skills Machine: Sustaining Comparative Advantage in a Global Economy*, New York and Oxford: Berghahn Books.

Culpepper, P. D., and Finegold, D. (eds) (1999) *The German Skills Machine: Sustaining Comparative Advantage in a Global Economy*, New York and Oxford: Berghahn Books.

Curry, J. (1993) 'The Flexibility Fetish: A Review Essay on Flexible Specialisation', *Capital and Class*, 50, pp. 99–120.

Dahrendorf, R. (1959) *Class and Conflict in Industrial Society*, London: Routledge and Kegan Paul.

Danford, A. (1998) 'Work Organisation Inside Japanese Firms in South Wales', in Thompson, P., and Warhurst, C. (eds) *Workplaces of the Future*, Basingstoke: Macmillan.

Davies, M. and Niemann, M. (2000) 'Henri Lefebvre and Global Politics: Social Spaces and Everyday Struggles', paper presented to the Annual Convention of the International Studies Association, Los Angeles, 14–18 March.

Deakin, S., and Reed, H. (2000) 'River Crossing or Cold Bath? Deregulation and Employment in Britain in the 1980s and 1990s', in Esping-Andersen, G., and Regini, M. (eds) *Why Deregulate Labour Markets?*, Oxford: Oxford University Press.

Deeg, R. (1997) 'Banks and Industrial Finance in the 1990s', *Industry and Innovation*, 4: 1, pp. 65–92.

Denemark, R. A., and O'Brien, R. (1997) 'Contesting the Canon: International Political Economy at UK and US Universities', *Review of International Political Economy*, 4: 1, pp. 214–238.

Department for International Development (2000) *Eliminating World Poverty: Making Globalisation Work for the Poor*, White Paper on International Development, London: HMSO.

Department of Trade and Industry (1998) *Fairness at Work*, White Paper, London: HMSO.

Deutsche Bundesbank (1997) Die Aktie als Finanzierungs- und Anlageinstrument, *Monatsbericht*, 49: 1.

Douglas, I. R. (1996) 'The *Myth* of Globali[z]ation: A Poststructural Reading of Speed and Reflexivity in the Governance of Late Modernity', paper presented to the annual convention of the International Studies Association, San Diego, 16–20 April 1996.

Drainville, A. (1994) 'International Political Economy in the Age of Open Marxism', *Review of International Political Economy* 1(1), pp. 105 –132.

Dreyfus, H. L., and Rabinow, P. (1982) *Michel Foucault: Beyond Structuralism and Hermeneutics*, Chicago: University of Chicago Press.

Drucker, P. (1995) *Managing in a Time of Great Change*, Oxford: Heinemann.

du Gay, P. (1997) 'Organizing Identity: Making up People at Work', in du Gay, P. (ed.) *Production of Culture/Cultures of Production*, London: Sage.

du Gay, P. (1999) 'In the Name of "Globalization": Enterprising Up Nations, Organizations and Individuals', in Leisink, P. (ed.) *Globalization and Labour Relations*, Cheltenham: Edward Elgar.

Dunning, J. (1993) *The Globalization of Business: The Challenge of the 1990s*, London: Routledge.

Durkheim, E. (1964) *The Division of Labour in Society*, New York: Free Press.

Easton, D. (1965) *A Systems Analysis of Political Life*, New York: Wiley.

Economist, The (2000) 'Has Gerhard Got It?', 8–14 July, pp. 17–18.

Economist Intelligence Unit (1998) *UK: Country Report*, London: EIU.

Economist Intelligence Unit (2001) *Germany: Country Report*, London: EIU.

Eden, L. (1991) 'Bringing the Firm Back In: Multinationals in International Political Economy', *Millennium: Journal of International Studies*, 20: 2, pp. 197–224.

EIRR Various Issues, 1993–2001.

Elger, T., and Fairbrother, P. (1992) 'Inflexible Flexibility: A Case Study of Modularisation', in Gilbert, N., Burrows, R., and Pollert, A. (eds) *Fordism and Flexibility: Divisions and Change*, London: Macmillan.

Elliott, L. (1999) 'Unless WTO Cleans Up Its Act There Will be More Issues for the Protesters to Trade on', *The Guardian*, 6 December 1999.

Elmuti, D., and Kathwala, Y. (2000) 'The Effects of Outsourcing Strategies on Participants' Attitudes and Organizational Effectiveness', *International Journal of Manpower*, 21: 1–2, pp. 112–128.

Enloe, C. (1989) *Bananas, Beaches and Bases: Making Feminist Sense of International Politics*, Berkeley: University of California Press.

Enloe, C. (1996) 'Margins, Silences and Bottom Rungs: How to Overcome the Underestimation of Power in the Study of International Relations', in Smith, S., Booth, K., and Zalewski, M. (eds) *International Theory: Positivism and Beyond*, Cambridge: Cambridge University Press, pp. 186–202.

Esping-Andersen, G. (ed.) (1996) *Welfare States in Transition: National Adaptations in Global Economies*, London: Sage.

Eucken, W. (1949) 'Die Wettbewerbsordnung und ihre Verwirklichung', *ORDO – Jahrbuch für die Ordnung von Wirtscahft und Gesellschaft*, 2, pp. 381–398.

Eucken, W. (1951) *This Unsuccessful Age, or the Pains of Economic Progress*, London.

European Industrial Relations Observatory (EIRO) *Annual Review* (1999), EIRO: Luxembourg.

European Industrial Relations Observatory (EIRO) (2000) *Outsourcing and Industrial Relations in Motor Manufacturing*, EIRO: Luxembourg.

European Industrial Relations Review, various (1993–2001).

Falk, R. (1999) *Predatory Globalization: A Critique*, Cambridge and Malden, MA: Polity Press and Blackwell Publishers.

Feldman, S., and Buechler, S. (1998) 'Negotiating Difference: Constructing Selves and Others in a Transnational Apparel Manufacturing Firm', *Sociological Quarterly*, 39: 4, pp. 623–644.

Felhölter, G., and Noppe, R. (2000) 'Germany after the Millennium: Discourses and Strategies of Restructuring: Redefining the Role of the State', *Tijdschrift voor Economische en Social Geografie*, 91: 3, pp. 237–247.

Femia, J. (1981) Gramsci's Political Thought: Hegemony, Consciousness, and the Revolutionary Process, Oxford: Clarendon.

Foucault, M. (1980a) *The History of Sexuality Volume I: An Introduction*, New York: Vintage.

Foucault, M. (1980b) *Power/Knowledge: Selected Interviews and Other Writings*, London: Harvester Wheatsheaf.

Foucault, M. (1982) 'The Subject and Power', in Dreyfus, H. L., and Rabinow, P. *Michel Foucault: Beyond Structuralism and Hermeneutics*, Chicago: University of Chicago Press.

Freeman, C., and Perez, C. (1988) 'Structural Crisis of Adjustment, Business Cycles and Investment Behaviour', in Dosi, G., Freeman, C., Nelson, R., Silverberg, G., and Soete, L. (eds) *Technical Change and Economic Theory*, London: Frances Pinter.

Freeman, R. B. (1994) *Working Under Different Rules*, Russell Sage Foundation.

Fuchs, S., and Schettkat, R. (2000) 'Germany: A Regulated Flexibility', in Esping-Andersen, G., and Regini, M. (eds) *Why Deregulate Labour Markets?*, Oxford: Oxford University Press.

Fukuyama, F. (1992) *The End of History and the Last Man*, London: Heinemann.

Fulcher, J. (1991) *Labour Movements, Employers, and the State – Conflict and Cooperation in Britain and Sweden*, Oxford: Clarendon.

Gallin, D. (2001) 'Propositions on Trade Unions and Informal Employment in Times of Globalisation', *Antipode*, 33: 3, pp. 531–549.

Gallin, D. (2002) 'Labour as a Global Social Force: Past Divisions and New Tasks', in Harrod, J., and O'Brien, R. (eds) *Globalized Unions? Theory and Strategy of Organised Labour in the Global Political Economy*, London: Routledge.

Gamble, A. (1994) *Britain in Decline: Economic Policy, Political Strategy and the British State*, Basingstoke: Macmillan.

Gamble, A. (1995) 'The New Political Economy', *Political Studies*, 43: 3, pp. 516–530.

Garrahan, P., and Stewart, P. (1992) *The Nissan Enigma: Flexibility at Work in a Local Economy*, London: Mansell.

Germain, R. D. (2000) Globalization in Historical Perspective, in Germain, R. (ed.) *Globalization and its Critics: Perspectives from Political Economy*, London and New York: Macmillan and St. Martins Press.

Germain, R., and Kenny, M. (1998) 'Engaging Gramsci: International Relations Theory and the New Gramscians', *Review of International Studies*, 24, pp. 3–21.

Gerschenkron, A. (1962) *Economic Backwardness in Historical Perspective*, London: Praeger.

Gesamtmetall (1997) '*Bericht der Geschäftsführung des Gesamtverbandes der matallindustriellen Arbeitgeberverbände*', May 1995-April 1997, Köln: Gesamtmetall.

Giddens, A. (1982) *Sociology: A Brief but Critical Introduction*, London: Macmillan.

Giddens, A. (1990) *The Consequences of Modernity*, Cambridge: Polity Press.

Giddens, A. (1998) *The Third Way: The Renewal of Social Democracy*, Cambridge: Polity.

Giersch, A. (1985) 'Eurosclerosis', *Kiel Discussion paper*, 112, Kiel: Institut für Weltwirtschaft.

Giersch, H., Paqué, K. H., and Schmieding, H. (1992) *The Fading Miracle: Four Decades of Market Economy in Germany*, Cambridge: Cambridge University Press.

Gill, S. (1990) *American Hegemony and the Trilateral Commission*, Cambridge: Cambridge University Press.

Gill, S. (1991) 'Reflections on Global Order and Socio-historical Time', *Alternatives*, 16, pp. 275–314.

Gill, S. (ed.) (1993) *Gramsci, Historical Materialism, and International Relations*, Cambridge: Cambridge University Press.

Gill, S (1994), 'Structural Change and Global Political Economy: Globalizing Elites and the Emerging World Order', in Sakamoto, Y. (ed.) *Global Transformation: Challenges to the State System*, United Nations University Press, pp. 169–199.

Gill, S. (1995) 'Globalisation, Market Civilisation, and Disciplinary Neoliberalism', *Millennium, Journal of International Studies*, 24: 3, pp. 399–423.

Gill, S. (1997) 'Transformation and Innovation in the Study of World Order', in Gill, S., and Mittelman, J. H. (eds) *Innovation and Transformation in International Studies*, Cambridge: Cambridge University Press.

Gill, S. (1999) 'The Constitution of Global Capitalism', paper presented to the Annual Conference of the British International Studies Association, University of Manchester, 20–22 December 1999.

Gill, S., and Mittelman, J. (eds) (1997) *Innovation and Transformation in International Studies*, Cambridge: Cambridge University Press.

Gilpin, R. (1987) *The Political Economy of International Relations*, Princeton: Princeton University Press.

Gilpin, R. (2001) *Global Political Economy: Understanding the International Economic Order*, Princeton: Princeton University Press.

Glasman, M. (1996) *Unnecessary Suffering: Managing Market Utopia*, London: Verso.

Glasman, M. (1997) 'The Siege of the German Economy', *New Left Review*, 225, pp. 122–126.

Goldthorpe, J. H. (ed.) (1984) *Order and Conflict in Contemporary Capitalism*, Oxford: Clarendon.

Goldthorpe, J. H. (1996) 'The Uses of History in Sociology: Reflections on Some Recent Tendencies', in Bulmer, M., and Rees, A. (eds) *Citizenship Today*, London: UCL Press.

Gospel, H., and Palmer, G. (1983) *British Industrial Relations*, London: Routledge.

Grabher, G. (1993) *The Embedded Firm: On the Socio-economics of Industrial Networks*, London: Routledge.

Graham, A. (1997) 'The UK 1979–95: Myths and Realities of Conservative Capitalism', in Crouch, C., and Streeck, W. (eds) *Political Economy of Modern Capitalism*, London: Sage.

Gramsci, A. (1971) *Selections from the Prison Notebooks*, translated and edited by Q. Hoare and G. Nowell Smith, New York: International Publishers.

Gray, A. (1998) 'New Labour – New Labour Discipline', *Capital and Class*, 65, Summer, pp. 1–8.

Guzzini, S. (2000) 'Strange's Oscillating Realism: Opposing the Ideal – and the Apparent', in Lawton, T. C., Rosenau, J. N., and Verdun, A. (eds) *Strange Power: Shaping the Parameters of International Relations and International Political Economy*, Aldershot: Ashgate.

Hall, P. (1986) *Governing the Economy: The Politics of State Intervention in Britain and France*. Cambridge: Polity Press.

Hancké, B. (1997) 'Reconfiguring the German Production System: Crisis and Adjustment in the Automobile Industry', paper presented to workshop on 'Modell Deutschland in the 1990s', Wissenschaftszentrum Berlin, 27–28 June.

Handy, C. (1995) *The Future of Work*, London: Contemporary Papers.

Hannah, J., and Fischer, C. (2002) 'Trade Unions, Training and Globalisation: Initiatives in Britain and Brazil', in Harrod, J., and O'Brien, R. (eds) *Globalized Unions? Theory and Strategy of Organised Labour in the Global Political Economy*, London: Routledge.

Harding, R., and Paterson, W. (eds) (2000) *The Future of the German Economy: An End to the Miracle?*, Manchester: Manchester University Press.

Harding, R., and Soskice, D. (2000) 'The End of the Innovation Economy?', in Harding, R., and Paterson, W. (eds) *The Future of the German Economy: An End to the Miracle?*, Manchester: Manchester University Press.

Harrod, J. (1987) *Power, Production, and the Unprotected Worker*, New York: Columbia University Press.

Harrod, J. (1997a) 'Social Forces and International Political Economy: Joining the Two IRs', in Gill, S., and Mittelman, J. H. (eds) *Innovation and Transformation in International Studies*, Cambridge: Cambridge University Press.

Harrod, J (1997b) 'Globalisation and Social Policy', paper prepared for the 22nd Annual BISA Conference, University of Leeds, 15–17 December.

Harrod, J., and O'Brien, R. (eds) (2002) *Globalized Unions? Theory and Strategy of Organised Labour in the Global Political Economy*, London: Routledge.

Hart, J. (1992) *Rival Capitalists: International Competitiveness in the United States, Japan and Western Europe*, Ithaca: Cornell University Press.

Haufler, V. (1999) 'Self-Regulation and Business Norms: Political Risk, Political Activism', in Cutler, A. C., Haufler, V., and Porter, T. (eds) *Private Authority and International Affairs*, Albany: SUNY.

Hay, C. (1999) *The Political Economy of New Labour: Labouring Under False Pretences?*, Manchester: Manchester University Press.

Hay, C., and Marsh, D. (1999) 'Introduction: Towards a New (International) Political Economy?', *New Political Economy*, Vol. 4, No. 1, pp. 5–22.

Heise, A. (1997) 'The British and German Models of Labour Market Regulation Compared', unpublished paper presented to ICLS Conference on 'European Systems of Labour Market Regulation', University of Manchester Institute of Science and Technology, 31 January.

Held, D. (1998) 'Globalization: The Timid Tendency', *Marxism Today*, December, pp. 24–27.

Held, D., and McGrew, A. (2000) (eds) *The Global Transformation Reader*, Cambridge: Polity.

Held, D., McGrew, A., Goldblatt, D., and Perraton, J. (1999) *Global Transformations: Politics, Economics and Culture*, Cambridge: Polity Press.

Hepworth, M. E. (1989) *The Geography of the Information Economy*, London: Belhaven.

Herod, A. (2001) 'Labor Internationalism and the Contradictions of Globalization: Or, Why the Local is Sometimes Still Important in a Global Economy', *Antipode*, 33: 3, pp. 407–426.

Herrigel, G. (1994) 'A Surprise Crisis in German Decentralised Production: Unexpected Rigidity and the Challenge of an Alternative Form of Flexible

Organisation in the 1990s', draft paper, University of Chicago, 14 September.

Hettne, B. (ed.) (1995) *International Political Economy: Understanding Global Disorder*, London: Zed Books.

Hewitt, P. (1993) *About Time: The Revolution in Work and Family Life*, London: IPPR.

Hirst, P., and Thompson, G. (1996) *Globalization in Question*, Cambridge: Polity Press.

Hirst, P., and Thompson, G. (2000) 'Globalization in One Country? The Peculiarities of the British', *Economy and Society*, 29: 3, pp. 335–356.

Hirst, P., and Zeitlin, J. (1989) 'Flexible Specialisation and the Competitive Failure of UK Manufacturing', *Political Quarterly*, 60: 3, pp. 164–78.

Hobsbawm, E. J. (1962) *The Age of Revolution: 1789–1848*, New York: Free Press.

Hobsbawm, E. J. (1964) *Labouring Men: Studies in the History of Labour*, London: Weidenfeld and Nicolson.

Hobsbawm, E. J. (1975) *The Age of Capital, 1848–1875*, London: Weidenfeld and Nicolson.

Hobson, J. M. (1997) *The Wealth of States: A Comparative Sociology of International Economic and Political Change*, Cambridge: Cambridge University Press.

Hollingsworth, J. R. (1998) 'New Perspectives on the Spatial Dimensions of Economic Co-ordination: Tensions between Globalization and Social Systems of Production', *Review of International Political Economy*, 5: 3, pp. 482–507.

Hollingsworth, J. R., and Boyer, R. (eds) (1997) *Contemporary Capitalism: The Embeddedness of Institutions*, Cambridge: Cambridge University Press.

Hollis, M., and Smith, S. (1990) *Explaining and Understanding International Relations*, Oxford: Clarendon.

Hoogvelt, A. (1997) *Globalisation and the Postcolonial World: The New Political Economy of Development*, Basingstoke: Macmillan.

Hooper, C. (1999) 'Masculinities, IR and the "Gender Variable"', *Review of International Studies*, 25: 3, pp. 475–492.

Hooper, C. (2000) 'Masculinities in Transition: The Case of Globalization', in Marchand, M., and Runyan, A. S. (eds) *Gender and Global Restructuring: Sightings, Sites and Resistances*, London: Routledge, pp. 59–73.

Hooper, C. (2001) *Manly States: Masculinities, International Relations, and Gender Politics*, New York: Columbia University Press.

Hsiung, P. C. (1996) *Living Rooms as Factories: Class, Gender, and the Satellite Factory System in Taiwan*, Philadelphia: Temple University Press.

Hutton, W. (1994) *The State We're In*, London: Cape.

Hyman, R. (1997) 'The Future of Employee Representation', *British Journal of Industrial Relations*, 35: 3, pp. 309–336.

Hyman, R. (1999a) 'Imagined Solidarities: Can Trade Unions Resist Globalization?', in Leisink, P. (ed.) *Globalization and Labour Relations*, Cheltenham: Edward Elgar.

Hyman, R. (1999b) *An Emerging Agenda for Trade Unions?*, Labour and Society Programme, IILS: Geneva.

Ibarra, M. D. L. (2000) 'Mexican Immigrant Women and the New Domestic Labour', *Human Organization*, 59: 4, pp. 452–464.

Iggers, G. G. (1995) 'Historicism: The History and Meaning of the Term', *Journal of the History of Ideas*, 56: 1, pp. 129–152.

IILS (1999a) 'Labour and Society Programme', International Institute for Labour Studies: Geneva.

IILS (1999b) *Interactive Conference on Organized Labour*, available at http://www.ilo.org/public/english/

Ingham, G. (1984) *Capitalism Divided: The City and Industry in British Social Development*, London: Macmillan.

International Labour Organisation (ILO) (1995) 'Deregulation, Not a Cure All', *World Employment Report*, Geneva: ILO.

ILO (1997) *World Labour Report: Industrial Relations, Democracy and Social Stability*, Geneva: ILO.

ILO (1998) *Statistics on Working Children and Hazardous Labour*, Bureau of Statistics, Geneva: ILO.

ILO (1999a) *Negotiating Flexibility: The Role of the Social Partners and the State*, Geneva: ILO.

ILO (1999b) *Decent Work: Report of the Director General, International Labour Conference*, 87 session, Geneva: ILO.

ILO (2000) *Labour Practices in the Footwear, Leather, Textiles and Clothing Industries*, Geneva: ILO.

ILO (2001) 'Life at Work in the Information Economy', *World Employment Report*, Geneva: ILO.

Institut der Deutschen Wirtschaft (1999) *Trade Union Membership and Density in the 1990s*, Köln: IDW.

Institut der Deutschen Wirtschaft (2000) 'Industrielle Arbeitskosten im Internationalen Vergleich', *IW Trends*, 3/2000.

International Monetary Fund (IMF) (1999) 'Germany: Staff Report for the 1999 Article IV Consultation', *IMF Staff Country Report*, 99: 129, Washington: IMF.

IMF (2000a) 'Pressing Issues of Globalization and Poverty Reduction are Focus of 2000 IMF-World Bank Annual Meetings', *Finance and Development*, Washington DC: IMF.

IMF (2000b) Globalisation and Catching-Up: From Recession to Growth in Transition Economies. *International Monetary Fund Working Paper* (WP/00/100), Washington DC: IMF.

IRS (2000) 'Call Centres 2000', *IRS Survey*, London: Industrial Relations Services.

Jackson, G. (1997) 'Corporate Governance in Germany and Japan: Development within National and International Contexts', paper prepared for conference on 'Germany and Japan: Nationally Embedded Capitalism in a Global Economy', University of Washington-Seattle, 10–13 April.

Jessop, B. (1994) 'Post-Fordism and the State', in Amin, A. (ed.) *Post-Fordism: A Reader*, Oxford: Basil Blackwell.

Jones, R. J. B. (1995) *Globalisation and Interdependence in the International Political Economy*, London: Pinter.

Jones, R. J. B. (2000), 'Globalization in Perspective', in Germain, R. (ed.) *Globalization and its Critics: Perspectives from Political Economy*, London and New York: Macmillan and St. Martins Press.

Joseph Rowntree Foundation (1999) *Monitoring Poverty and Social Exclusion*, available at http://www.jrf.org.uk/knowledge/findings/socialpolicy/d29.asp.

Jürgens, U. (1991) 'Departures from Taylorism and Fordism: New Forms of Work in the Automobile Industry', in Jessop, B., Kastendiek, H., Nielsen, K., and

Pederson, O. K. (eds) *The Politics of Flexibility*, London: Routledge.

Kaplan, A., and Ross, K. (1987) 'Introduction to Everyday Life', *Yale French Studies*, 73, pp. 1–4.

Keenan, M. (1997) *Fables of Responsibility: Aberrations and Predicaments in Ethics and Politics*, Stanford: Stanford University Press.

Keohane, R. (1984) *After Hegemony: Cooperation and Discord in the World Political Economy*, Princeton: Princeton University Press.

Kerr, C., Dunlop, J. T., Harbison, and F. Myers. C. (1962) *Industrialism and Industrial Man*, Cambridge, MA: Harvard University Press.

Klein, N. (2000), *No Logo*, London: Flamingo.

Koch, K. (1992) *Coordinated Pay Bargaining - the German Experience*, London: Campaign for Work.

Krasner, S. (ed.) (1983) *International Regimes*, Ithaca: Cornell University Press.

Krasner, S. (1994) 'International Political Economy: Abiding Discord', *Review of International Political Economy*, 1: 1, pp. 13–20.

Krasner, S. (1996) 'The Accomplishments of International Political Economy', in Smith, S., Booth, K., and Zalewski, M. (eds) *International Theory: Positivism and Beyond*, Cambridge: Cambridge University Press.

Krieger, J. (1999) *British Politics in the Global Age: Can Social Democracy Survive?* Cambridge: Polity.

Lacher, H. (1999) 'The Politics of the Market: Re-reading Karl Polanyi', *Global Society*, 13: 3, pp. 313–326.

Lambert, R. (1999) 'International Relations and Industrial Relations: Exploring an Interface', paper presented to the Annual Convention of the International Studies Association, Washington DC, 20 February 1999.

Lambert, R., and Chan, A. (1999) 'Global Dance: Factory Regimes, Asian Labour Standards and Corporate Restructuring', in Waddington, J. (ed.) *Globalization and Patterns of Labour Resistance*, London: Mansell.

Lane, C. (1994) 'Industrial Order and the Transformation of Industrial Relations: Britain, Germany and France Compared', in Hyman, R., and Ferner, R. (eds) *New Frontiers in European Industrial Relations*, Oxford: Basil Blackwell.

Lane, C. (1996a) 'Industrial Reorganization in Europe: Patterns of Convergence and Divergence in Germany, France and Britain', in Warner, M. (ed.) *Comparative Management*, London: Routledge.

Lane, C. (1996b) 'The Social Constitution of Supplier Relations in Britain and Germany: An Institutionalist Analysis', in Whitley, R. and Hull Kristensen, P. (eds) *The Changing European Firm: Limits to Convergence*, London: Routledge, pp. 271–304.

Lane, C. (1997) 'The Social Regulation of Inter-Firm Relations in Britain and Germany: Market Rules, Legal Norms and Technical Standards', *Cambridge Journal of Economics*, 21: 2, pp. 197–215.

Langley, P. (2002) *World Financial Orders and World Financial Centres: An Historical IPE*, London: Routledge.

Lansbury, R., and Macdonald, D. (1994) 'Workplace Industrial Relations and Deregulation. Challenging the New Orthodoxy', *Employee Relations*, 16: 4, pp. 8–21.

Latour, B. (1988) *The Pasteurization of France*, Cambridge, MA: Harvard University Press.

Latour, B. (1991) 'Technology is Society made Durable', in Law, J. (ed.) *A Sociology of Monsters: Essays on Power, Technology and Domination*, London: Routledge.

Lawrence, P. (1980) *Managers and Management in West Germany*, London: Croom Helm.

Lazonick, W., O'Sullivan, M., (1996) 'Organization, Finance, and International Competition', *Industrial and Corporate Change*, 5: 1, 1996.

Leander, A. (2000) 'A Nebbish Presence: Undervalued Contributions of Sociological Institutionalism to IPE', in Palan, R. (ed.) *Global Political Economy: Contemporary Theories*, London: Routledge.

Lee, S. (1997) 'The City and British Decline', in Cox, A., Lee, S., and Sanderson, J. (eds) *The Political Economy of Modern Britain*, Cheltenham, Edward Elgar.

Lefebvre, H. (1984) *Everyday Life in the Modern World*, New Brunswick, NJ: Transaction.

Lefebvre, H. (1987) 'The Everyday and Everydayness', *Yale French Studies*, 73, pp. 7–11.

Lefebvre, H. (1991a) *Critique of Everyday Life*, New York: Verso.

Lefebvre, H. (1991b) *The Production of Space*, Oxford: Basil Blackwell.

Leisink, P. (1999) *Globalization and Labour Relations*, Cheltenham: Edward Elgar.

Lemke, T. (2001) 'The Birth of Bio-Politics: Michel Foucault's lecture at the College de France on Neo-Liberal Governmentality', *Economy and Society*, 30: 2, pp. 190–207.

Lipietz, A. (1987) *Mirages and Miracles: The Crisis of Global Fordism*, London: Verso.

Lipietz, A. (1997) 'The Post-Fordist World: Labour Relations, International Hierarchy and Global Ecology', *Review of International Political Economy*, 4: 1, pp. 1–41.

Lipset, M. (1960) *Political Man*, London: Heinemann.

Lipshutz, R. (1992) 'Reconstructing World Politics: The Emergence of a Global Civil Society', *Millennium: Journal of International Studies*, 21: 389–420.

Lui, T. L. and Chiu, T. M. (1999) 'Global Restructuring and Non-Standard Work in Newly Industrialised Economies: The Organisation of Flexible Production in Hong Kong and Taiwan', in Felstead, A. and Jewson, N (eds) *Global Trends in Flexible Labour*, Basingstoke: Macmillan.

MacLean, J. (2000) 'Philosophical Roots of Globalization and Philosophical Routes to Globalization', in Germain, R. (ed.) *Globalization and its Critics: Perspectives from Political Economy*, Basingstoke: Macmillan.

Mahnkopf, B. (1999) 'Between the Devil and the Deep Blue Sea: The German Model Under the Pressure of Globalisation', *Socialist Register*, pp. 142–177.

Marchand, M. (1996) 'Reconceptualising Gender and Development in an Era of Globalisation', *Millennium: Journal of International Studies*, 25: 3, pp. 577–604.

Marchand, M., and Runyan, A. S. (2000) *Gender and Global Restructuring: Sightings, Sites and Resistances*, London: Routledge.

Marsden, D. (1995) 'Deregulation or Cooperation? The Future of Europe's Labour Markets', paper prepared for *Labour: Review of Labour Economics and Industrial Relations*, Tenth World Congress of the International Industrial Relations Association, 31 May 31–4 June 1995.

Marsh, D. (2000) 'A Pattern of Light and Shade for the German Economy', in Harding, R., and Paterson, W. (eds) *The Future of the German Economy: An End to the Miracle?*, Manchester: Manchester University Press.

Maurice, M., Sorge, A., and Warner, M. (1980) 'Societal Differences in Organising

Manufacturing Units: A Comparison of France, West Germany, and Great Britain', *Organization Studies*, 1: 1, pp. 59–86. Reprinted in M. Warner (ed.) (1996) *Comparative Management: Critical Perspectives on Business and Management*, London: Routledge.

May, C. (1996) 'Strange Fruit: Susan Strange's Theory of Structural Power in the International Political Economy', *Global Society*, 10: 2, pp. 167–189.

May, C. (forthcoming) 'Proximity and Task Migration: The Information Society and Global Labour Markets', *New Political Economy*.

McCabe, D. (1996) 'The Best Laid Schemes O' TQM: Strategy, Politics and Power', *New Technology, Work and Employment*, 11: 1, pp. 28–38.

Mckenzie. R, and Lee, D. (1991) *Quicksilver Capital*, New York: Free Press.

McMichael, P. (2000) 'Globalization: Trend or Project?', in Palan, R. (ed.) *Global Political Economy: Contemporary Theories*, London: Routledge.

Middlemas, R. K. (1979) *Politics in Industrial Society*, London: Andre Deutsch.

Milkman, R. (1998) 'The New American Workplace: High Road or Low Road?', in Thompson and Warhurst (eds) *Workplaces of the Future*, Basingstoke: Macmillan, pp. 25–39.

Miller, P. , and Rose, N. (1990) 'Governing Economic Life', *Economy and Society*, 19: 1, pp. 1–31.

Millward, N. (1992), *Workplace Industrial Relations in Transition: The Report of the Employment Department, ESRC, Policy Studies Institute, and ACAS*, Aldershot: Dartmouth Publishing Co.

Millward, N. (1994) *The New Industrial Relations? Report of the 1990 WIRS*, London: Policy Studies Institute.

Millward, N., Bryson, A., and Forth, J. (2000) *All Change at Work? British Employment Relations 1980–1998, as portrayed by the Workplace Industrial Relations Survey Series*, London: Routledge.

Mittelman, J. (2000) *The Globalization Syndrome: Transformation and Resistance*, Princeton: Princeton University Press.

Mizruchi, M., and Schwartz, M. (eds) (1987) *Intercorporate Relations: Structural Analysis in the Social Sciences*, Cambridge: Cambridge University Press.

Moody, K. (1997) *Workers in a Lean World: Unions in the International Economy*, London: Verso.

Moran, M. (1992) 'Regulatory Change in German Financial Markets', in Dyson, K. (ed.) *The Politics of German Regulation*, Cornwall: Dartmouth Publishing.

Moran, M., and Wood, B. (1996) 'The Globalisation of Helath Care Policy?', in Gummett, P. (ed.) *Globalization and Public Policy*, Cheltenham: Elgar.

Murphy, C. (1994) *International Organisation and Industrial Change: Global Governance since 1850*, New York: Oxford University Press.

Murphy, C. (1996) 'Seeing Women, Recognising Gender, Recasting International Relations', *International Organization*, 50: 3, pp. 513–538.

Murphy, C., and Tooze, R. (eds) (1991) *The New International Political Economy*, London: Macmillan.

Nairn, T. (1993) 'The Sole Survivor', *New Left Review*, 200, pp. 40–47.

Negroponte, N. (1995) *Being Digital*, London: Hodder and Stoughton.

Nolan, P., and O' Donnell, K. (1991) 'Restructuring and the Politics of Industrial Renewal: The Limits of Flexible Specialisation', in Pollert, A. (ed.) *Farewell to Flexibility?*, Oxford: Blackwell.

O'Brien, R. (1997) 'Subterranean Hegemonic Struggles: International Labor and the Three Faces of Industrial Relations', paper presented to British International Studies Association, University Of Leeds, 13–16 December 1997.

O'Brien, R. (1999) 'Labour and the Study of IPE', discussion paper presented to IPEG Annual workshop, 21 February 1999.

O'Brien, R. (2000) 'Workers and World Order: The Tentative Transformation of the International Union Movement', *Review of International Studies*, 26: 4, pp. 533–556.

O'Brien, R. (2001) 'A Proposal for Evaluating the Emergence of a Global Labour Movement', paper presented at the ISA Annual Convention, Chicago, 22 February.

O'Brien, R., Goetz, A. M., Scholte, J-A., and Williams, M. (2000) *Contesting Global Governance: Multilateral Economic Institutions and Global Social Movements*, Cambridge: Cambridge University Press.

O'Connor, J. (1973) The Fiscal Crisis of the State, New York: St. Martins Press.

OECD (1991) 'Making Labour Markets Work', *OECD Observer 173*, Paris: OECD.

OECD (1994) *Jobs Study: Facts, Analyses, Strategies*, Paris: OECD.

OECD (1996) *The OECD Jobs Strategy: Pushing Ahead with the Strategy*, Paris: OECD.

OECD (1997) *Implementing the OECD Jobs Strategy: Lessons from Member Countries' Experience*, Paris: OECD.

OECD (2000) *Economic Survey of the UK*, Paris: OECD.

OECD (2001) *Economic Survey of Germany*, Paris: OECD.

OECD (2001) *Economic Outlook (2001)*, No. 69, June.

Ohmae, K. (1990) *The Borderless World: Power and Strategy in the Interlinked Economy*, London: Fontana.

Oliver, N., and Wilkinson, B. (1988) *The Japanisation of British Industry*, Oxford: Basil Blackwell.

Outsourcing Institute (2000) *Outsourcing Index 2000: Strategic Insights into US Outsourcing*, Outsourcing Institute and Dun and Bradstreet.

Overbeek, H. (1990) *Global Capitalism and National Decline: The Thatcher Decade in Perspective*, London: Unwin Hyman.

Palan, R. (1999) 'Susan Strange 1923–1998: A Great International Relations Theorist', *Review of International Political Economy*, 6: 2, pp. 121–132.

Palan, R. (2000) 'New Trends in Global Political Economy', in Palan, R. (ed.) (2000) *Global Political Economy: Contemporary Theories*, London: Routledge.

Panitch, L. (2001) 'Reflections on Strategy for Labour', in *Working Classes, Global Realities, Socialist Register*, London: Merlin Press.

Parsons, T. (1960) *Structure and Process in Modern Societies*, New York: Free Press.

Pauly, L., and Reich, S. (1997) 'National Structures and Multinational Corporate Behaviour: Enduring Differences in the Age of Globalisation', *International Organization*, 51: 1, pp. 1–30.

Payne, A. (2000) 'Foreword', in Germain, R. D. (ed.) *Globalization and its Critics: Perspectives from Political Economy*, London and New York: Macmillan and St. Martins Press.

Peck, J., and Tickell, A. (1994) 'Searching for a New Institutional Fix: The After Fordist Crisis and the Global-Local Disorder', in Amin, A. (ed.) *Post-Fordism: A Reader*, Oxford: Blackwell.

Pentinnen, E. (2000) 'Capitalism as a System of Global Power', in Goverde, H., Cerny, P. G., Haugaard, M., and Lentner, H. (eds) *Power in Contemporary Politics: Theories, Practices, Globalizations*, London: Sage.

Peters, T. J., and Waterman, R. H. (1995) *In Search of Excellence: Lessons from America's Best-Run Companies*, London: Harper Collins.

Pinch, S. (1994) 'Labour Flexibility and the Changing Welfare State: Is There a Post-Fordist model?', in Burrows, R., and Loader, B. (eds) *Towards a Post-Fordist Welfare State?*, London: Routledge.

Piore, M. (1990) 'Work, Labour and Action: Work Experience in a System of Flexible Production', in Pyke, F., Becattini, G., and Sengenberger, W. (eds) *Industrial Districts and Inter-firm Cooperation in Italy*, Geneva: ILO.

Piore, M., and Sabel, C. (1984) *The Second Industrial Divide*, New York: Basic Books.

Polanyi, K. (1957) *The Great Transformation: Political and Economic Origins of Our Time*, Boston: Beacon Press.

Pollert, A. (ed.) (1991) *Farewell to Flexibility?*, Oxford: Blackwell.

Pollert, A. (1999) *Transformation at Work: The New Market Economies of Central Eastern Europe*, London: Sage.

Porter, M. E. (1990) *The Competitive Advantage of Nations*, New York: Free Press.

Purcell, J. (1993) 'The End of Institutional Industrial Relations', *Political Quarterly*, 64: 1, pp. 6–23.

Radice, H. (2000) 'Responses to Globalisation: A Critique of Progressive Nationalism', *New Political Economy*, 5: 1, pp. 5–19.

Reich, R. (1991) *The Work of Nations: Preparing Ourselves for Twentieth Century Capitalism*, New York: Simon and Schuster.

Rhodes, M. (1997) 'Globalisation, Labour Markets and Welfare States: A Future Of "Competitive Corporatism"', paper presented at the Workshop on 'The State and the Globalization process', *ECPR Joint Sessions*, Bern, Switzerland, 27 February.

Rice, J., and Prince, M. (2000) 'A Double Movement: Implications of Globalization and Pluralization for the Canadian Welfare State', in McBride, S., and Wiseman, J. (eds) *Globalization and its Discontents*, Basingstoke: Macmillan.

Rifkin, J. (1995) *The End of Work: The Decline of the Global Labour Force and the Dawn of the Post-Market Era*, New York: Putnam's Sons.

Röpke, W. (1942) *The Social Crisis of Our Time*, London: George Allen and Unwin.

Rosenau, J. N. (1997) 'The Person, the Household, the Community, and the Globe: Notes for a Theory of Multilateralism in a Turbulent World', in Cox, R. W. (ed.) *The New Realism: Perspectives on Multilateralism and World Order*, London and New York: Macmillan and St. Martins Press.

Ross, A. (2001) 'No-Collar Labour in America's "New Economy"', *Socialist Register*, pp. 77–88.

Rubery, J. (1993) 'UK Production in Comparative Perspective', paper presented to the International Conference on 'Production Regimes in an Integrating Europe', University of Manchester Institute of Science and Technology.

Rubery, J. (1996) 'The Labour Market Outlook and the Outlook for Labour Market Analysis', in Crompton, R., Gallie, D., and Purcell, K. (eds) *Changing Forms of Employment*, London: Routledge.

Rubery, J. (1999) 'Fragmenting the Internal Labour Market', in Leisink, P. (ed.) *Globalization and Labour Relations*, Cheltenham: Edward Elgar.

Ruigrok, W. and van Tulder, R. (1995) *The Logic of International Restructuring: The Management of Dependencies in Rival Industrial Complexes*, London: Routledge.

Rupert, M. (1995) *Producing Hegemony: The Politics of Mass Production and American Global Power*, Cambridge: Cambridge University Press.

Rupert, M. (2000) *Ideologies of Globalization*, London: Routledge.

Ryner, M., and Schulten, T. (2002) 'The Political Economy of European Labour Market Restructuring and Trade Unions in the Social Democratic Heartland', in Overbeek, H. (ed.) *The Political Economy of European (Un)Employment*, London: Routledge.

Sabel, C. (1992) 'Studied trust: Building New Forms of Cooperation in a Volatile Economy', in Pyke, F., and Sengenberger, W. (eds) *Industrial Districts and Local Economic Regeneration*, Geneva: ILO.

Sadowski, D., Backes-Gellner, U., and Frick, B. (1995) 'Works Councils: Barriers or Boosts for the Competitiveness of German Firms?', *British Journal of Industrial Relations*, 33: 3, pp. 493–513.

Sally, R. (1994) 'Multinational Enterprises, Political Economy and Institutional Theory: Domestic Embeddedness in the Context of Internationalisation', *Review of International Political Economy*, 1: 1, pp. 163–192.

Sally, R. (1996) 'Public Policy and the Janus Face of the MNE: National Embeddedness and International Production', in Gummett, P. (ed.) *Globalization and Public Policy*, Cheltenham: Elgar.

Sassen, S. (1994) *Cities in a World Economy*, Thousand Oaks: Pine Forge Press.

Scharpf, F. (1998) 'The German Disease', *Prospect*, 26, January (there are issue numbers only).

Scholte, J-A (2000) *Globalization: A Critical Introduction*, Basingstoke: Macmillan.

Schröder, U. (1996) 'Corporate Governance in Germany: The Changing Role of the Banks', *German Politics*, 5: 3, pp. 356–370.

Scott, James C. (1990), *Domination and the Arts of Resistance: Hidden Transcripts*, Yale University Press.

Seccombe, W. (1999) 'Contradictions of Shareholder Capitalism: Downsizing Jobs, Enlisting Savings, Destabilizing Families', *Socialist Register*, pp. 76–107.

Sengenberger, W. (1993) 'Lean production - The Way of Working and Producing in the Future?' *Lean Production and Beyond - Labour Aspects of a New Production Concept*, Geneva: IILS.

Shonfield, A. (1965) *Modern Capitalism: The Changing Balance of Public and Private Power*, Oxford: Oxford University Press.

Silver, B. J., and Arrighi, G. (2001) 'Workers North and South', *Socialist Register*, pp. 53–76.

Silvia, S. J. (1997) 'German Unification and Emerging Divisions within German Employers' Associations', *Comparative Politics*, 29: 2, pp. 187–211.

Simons, J. (1995) *Foucault and the Political*, London: Routledge.

Sinclair, T. J. (1999) 'Synchronic Global Governance and the International Political Economy of the Commonplace', in Hewson, M., and Sinclair, T. J. (eds) *Approaches to Global Governance Theory*, New York: State University of New York Press.

Sklair, L. (1991) *Sociology of the Global System*, London: Harvester Wheatsheaf.

Sklair, L. (1998) 'TNCs as Political Actors', *New Political Economy*, 3: 2, pp. 288–291.

Sklair, L. (2001) *The Transnational Capitalist Class*, Oxford: Blackwell.

Skocpol, T. (ed.) (1984) *Vision and Method in Historical Sociology*, Cambridge: Cambridge University Press.

Smith, P., and Morton, G. (2001) 'New Labour's Reform of Britain's Employment Law: The Devil is not only in the Detail but in the Values and Policy Too', *British Journal of Industrial Relations*, 39: 1, pp. 119–138.

Smith, S. (1996) 'Positivism and Beyond', in Smith, S., Booth, K., and Zalewski, M. (eds) *International Theory: Positivism and Beyond*, Cambridge: Cambridge University Press, pp. 11–46.

Soldatenko, M. A. (1999) 'Made in the USA: Latinas/os? Garment Work and Ethnic Conflcit in Los Angeles' Sweat Shops', *Cultural Studies*, 13: 2, pp. 319–334.

Somavia, J. (1999) 'Trade Unions in the 21st Century', Keynote Speech, Geneva: ILO.

Soskice, D. (1996) 'German Technology Policy, Innovation, and National Institutional Frameworks', discussion paper, Wissenschaftszentrum, Berlin.

Stern (1997) 'Editorial', No. 8, January.

Stevis, D., and Boswell, T. (1997) 'Labour: From National Resistance to International Politics', *New Political Economy*, 2: 1, pp. 93–104.

Stopford, J. M., and Strange, S. (1991), *Rival States, Rival Firms: Competition for World Market Shares*, New York: Cambridge University Press.

Story, J. (1997) 'Globalisations, The EU, and German Financial Reform: The Political Economy of "Finanzplatz Deutschland"', in Underhill, G. R. D. (ed.) *The New World Order in International Finance*, Basingstoke: Macmillan.

Strange, S. (1983) 'Structures, Values and Risks in the Study of International Political Economy', in Jones, R. J. B. (ed.) *Perspectives on Political Economy*, London: Pinter.

Strange, S. (1984) *Paths to International Political Economy*, London: Allen and Unwin.

Strange, S. (1986) *Casino Capitalism*, Oxford: Blackwell.

Strange, S. (1988) *States and Markets: An Introduction to International Political Economy*, London: Pinter.

Strange, S. (1991) 'An Eclectic Approach', in Murphy, C., and Tooze, R. (eds) *The New International Political Economy*, London: Macmillan.

Strange, S. (1994) 'Wake up, Krasner, The World has Changed', *Review of International Political Economy*, 1: 2, pp. 209–219.

Strange, S. (1995) 'The Defective State', *Daedalus: Journal of the American Academy of Arts and Sciences*, 24: 2, pp. 53–74.

Strange, S. (1996) *The Retreat of the State: The Diffusion of Power in the World Economy*, Cambridge: Cambridge University Press.

Strange, S. (1997a) *Casino Capitalism*, Manchester: Manchester University Press.

Strange, S. (1997b) 'The Future of Global Capitalism; Or Will Divergence Persist Forever?', in Crouch, C., and Streeck, W. (eds) *Political Economy of Modern Capitalism*, London: Sage.

Strange, S. (1998a) *Mad Money*, Manchester: Manchester University Press.

Strange, S. (1998b) 'The New World of Debt', *New Left Review*, 230, pp. 91–114.

Streeck, W. (1984) *Industrial Relations in West Germany: A Case Study of the Car Industry*, London: Heinemann.

Streeck, W. (1992a) *Social Institutions and Economic Performance: Studies of Industrial Relations in Advanced Capitalist Economies*, London: Sage.

Streeck, W. (1992b) 'National Diversity, Regime Competition and Institutional Deadlock: Problems in Forming a European Industrial Relations System', *Journal of Public Policy*, 12: 4, pp. 301–330.

Streeck, W. (1996) 'Lean Production in the German Automobile Industry: A Test Case for Convergence Theory', in Berger, S., and Dore, R. (eds) *National Diversity and Global Capitalism*, Ithaca: Cornell University Press.

Streeck, W. (1997a) 'German Capitalism: Does it Exist? Can it Survive?', *New Political Economy*, 2: 2, pp. 237–256.

Streeck, W. (1997b) 'Citizenship under Regime Competition: The Case of the European Works Councils', *MPIfG Working paper*, Cologne.

Streeck, W. (1997c) 'Beneficial Constraints: On the Economic Limits of Rational Voluntarism', in Hollingsworth, J. R., and Boyer, R. (eds) *Contemporary Capitalism: the Embeddedness of Institutions*, Cambridge: Cambridge University Press.

Tétreault, M. (1999) 'Out of Body Experiences: Migrating Firms and Altered States', *Review of International Political Economy*, 6: 1.

Thelen, K. (1992) *Unions of Parts: Labor Politics in Post-war Germany*, Ithaca: Cornell University Press.

Thompson, E. P. (1963/1968) *The Making of the English Working Class*, Harmondsworth: Penguin.

Thompson, E. P. (1978) *The Poverty of Theory and Other Essays*, London: Merlin Press.

Thompson, E. P. (1976/1994) *Making History: Writings on History and Culture*, New York: The New Press.

Thrift, N. (1995) 'A Hyperactive World', in Johnston, R., Taylor, P. , and Watts, M. (eds) The *Geographies of Global Change*, Oxford: Blackwell.

Timmins, G. (2000) 'Alliance for Jobs: Labour Market Policy and Industrial Relations After the 1998 Elections', in Harding, R., and Paterson, W. (eds) *The Future of the German Economy: An End to the Miracle?*, Manchester: Manchester University Press.

Toffler, A. (1980) *The Third Wave*, London: Collins.

Tooze, R. (1984) 'Perspectives and Theory: A Consumers' Guide', in Strange, S. (ed.) *Paths to International Political Economy*, London: Allen and Unwin.

Tooze, R. (1997) 'International Political Economy in an Age of Globalization', in Baylis, J., and Smith, S. (eds) *The Globalization of World Politics*, Oxford: Oxford University Press.

Tooze, R. (2000a) 'Susan Strange: Academic International Relations and the Study of International Political Economy', *New Political Economy*, 5: 2, pp. 280–289.

Tooze, R. (2000b) 'Ideology, Knowledge and Power in International Relations and International Political Economy', in Lawton, T. C., Rosenau, J. N., and Verdun, A. (eds) *Strange Power: Shaping the Parameters of International Relations and International Political Economy*, Aldershot: Ashgate.

Tooze, R., and Murphy, C. (1996) 'Poverty of Epistemology in IPE: Mystery, Blindness, and Invisibility', *Millennium: Journal of International Studies*, 25: 3, pp. 681–707.

Towers, B. (1997) *The Representation Gap: Change and Reform in the British and American Workplace*, Oxford: Oxford University Press.

Treu, T. (1992) 'Labour Flexibility in Europe', *International Labour Review*, 131: 4, pp. 497–512.

TUC (2001) *TUC Produces New Enforcement Guide for the Minimum Wage*, Press release avilable at http: //www.tuc.org.uk/em_research/tuc–2595-fo-cfm.

Turner, L., and Auer, P. , (1994) 'A Diversity of New Work Organisation: Human-Centred, Lean, and In-Between', *Industrielle Beziehungen*, 1: 1, pp. 39–61.

Tüselman, H., and Heise, A. (2000) 'The German Model of Industrial Relations at the Crossroads: Past, Present and Future', *Industrial Relations Journal*, 31: 3, pp. 162–174.

United Nations Development Programme (1995) *Human Development Report*, New York: Oxford University Press.

United Nations Development Programme (2000) *Human Development Report: Human Rights and Human Development*, Oxford: Oxford University Press.

Upchurch, M. (2000) 'The Crisis of Labour Relations In Germany', *Capital and Class*, 70, pp. 65–93.

Van der Pijl, K. (1984) *The Making of an Atlantic Ruling Class*, London: Verso.

Vilrokx, J. (1999) 'Towards the Denaturing of Class Relations? The Political Economy of the Firm in Global Capitalism', in Leisink, P. (ed.) *Globalization and Labour Relations*, Cheltenham: Elgar.

Visser, J. (1995) 'Trade Unions from a Comparative Perspective', in Ruysseveldt, J. V., and Visser, J. (eds) *Comparative Industrial and Employment Relations*, London: Sage.

Visser, J., and Van Ruysseveldt, J. (1996) 'From Pluralism to … Where? Industrial relations in Great Britain', in Van Ruysseveldt, J., and Visser, J. (eds) *Industrial relations in Europe: Traditions and Transitions*, London: Sage.

Vitols, S., and Woolcock, S. (1997) 'Developments in the German and British Corporate Governance Systems', discussion paper prepared for Workshop on Corporate Governance in Britain and Germany, Wissenschaftszentrum, Berlin, June 1997.

Vogel, S. K. (1996) *Freer Markets, More Rules: Regulatory Reform in Advanced Industrial Countries*, Ithaca, New York: Cornell University Press.

VSME (2000) Firmentarifverträge der IGMetall in der Sächsischen Metall und Elektroindustrie: Eine Analyse, Dresden: Verband der Sachsischen Metall und Elektoindustrie.

Waddington, J. (ed.) (1999) *Globalization and Patterns of Labour Resistance*, London: Mansell.

Walker, R. B. J. (1993) *Inside/Outside: International Relations as Political Theory*, Cambridge: Cambridge University Press.

Walker, R. B. J. (1994) 'Social Movements/World Politics', *Millennium: Journal of International Studies*, 23: 3, pp. 669–700.

Walter, A. (1998) 'TNCs: Do they Really Rule the World?', *New Political Economy*, 3: 2, pp. 288–291.

Waterman, P., and Wills, J. (2001) 'Introduction: Space, Place and the New Labour Internationalisms: Beyond the Fragments', *Antipode*, 33: 3, pp. 305–311.

Waters, M. (1995) *Globalization*, London: Routledge.

Watson, M., and Hay, C. (1998) 'In the Dedicated Pursuit of Dedicated Capital: Restoring an Indigenous Investment Ethic to British Capitalism', *New Political Economy*, 3: 3, pp. 407–426.

Waxman, C. I. (ed.) (1968) *The End of Ideology Debate*, New York: Funk and Wagnells.

Weiss, L. (1998) *The Myth of the Powerless State: Governing the Economy in a Global Era*, Cambridge: Polity.

Wever, K. (1995) *Negotiating Competitiveness: Employment Relations and Organizational Innovation in Germany and the United States*, Boston, MA: Harvard Business School Press.

Whitley, R., and Kristensen, P. H. (eds) (1996) *The Changing European Firm: Limits to Convergence*. London: Routledge.

Wickens, P. (1987) *The Road to Nissan: Flexibility, Quality, Teamwork*, Basingstoke: Macmillan.

Williams, A. (1994) 'Enterprise Cultures in the Global Economy: Some Emerging and Theoretical Problems for Strategic Human Resource Management', *Employee Relations*, 16: 7, pp. 5–17.

Williams, S. (1997) 'The Nature of Some Recent Trade Union Modernization Policies in the UK', *British Journal of Industrial Relations*, 35: 4, pp. 495–514.

Womack, J. P. , Jones, D., and Roos, D. (1990) *The Machine that Changed the World*, New York: MIT Press.

Woolcock, S. (1996) 'Competition Among Rules in the Single European Market', in Bratton, W. (ed.) *International Regulatory Competition and Coordination: Perspectives on Economic Regulation in Europe and the US*, London: Wiley.

World Bank (1995) 'Workers in an Integrating World', *World Development Report*, New York: Oxford University Press.

World Bank (2001) 'Attacking Poverty', *World Development Report*, New York: Oxford University Press.

Wriston, W. (1988) 'Technology and Sovereignty', *Foreign Affairs*, 67: 1, pp. 63–75.

Young, B. (2001) 'The "Mistress" and the "Maid" in the Globalized Economy', *Socialist Register*, pp. 315–328.

Zumwinkle, M. (1995) 'Standort Deutschland: Can a Changing Germany Compete in the Changing World Market?', in Shingleton, A. *et al.* (eds) *Dimensions of German Unification: Economic, Social and Legal Analyses*, Oxford, Westview.

Zysman, J. (1983) *Governments, Markets and Growth: Finance and the Politics of Industrial Change*, Ithaca, New York: Cornell University Press.

Zysman, J. (1996) 'The Myth of a Global Economy: Enduring National Foundations and Emerging Regional Realities', *New Political Economy*, 1: 2, pp. 157–184.

Index

Alliance for Jobs 105, 108, 111
Australia 29, 101

Beck, Ulrich 1, 8, 28, 57, 147, 148, 153
Belgium 30
Bell, Daniel 17, 22
Bentley 96
best-practice 21, 70
Blair, Tony
    on foreign direct investment 12n.1,
      72
    on global change 67, 73
    on labour market policy 71, 73, 93
    Third Way 93, 95, 96
BMW 95, 128
Bretton Woods system 16, 24
Britain
    collective bargaining in 83–6, 107,
      130
    firms in 85–6, 126–8, 132–3
    foreign direct investment in 12n.1,
      72, 76, 81
    functional flexibility in 78–80, 102,
      164
    global Britain 11, 71–4, 76, 160
    and hyperflexibility 9, 11, 67, 68,
      70–4, 80, 85, 86–7, 89, 90, 137,
      139, 148
    industrial relations in 76–7, 83–4,
      86–9, 156n.7
    industrial revolution in 75–6
    and part-time work 12n.2, 80–3
    subcontracting in 12n.2
    unemployment in 82–3
    working time in 80–3

Canada 29, 101
capital flight 32
capitalism 22, 70
    Anglo-Saxon 11, 74–8, 83, 90, 160
    Rhineland 93, 100
City of London 76, 96
    Eurodollar market 76
civil society 21, 35, 49, 91n.2, 120, 144,
    147, 153, 163
class
    conflict 22
    consciousness 141, 147
Clean Clothes Campaign 154, 157n.15
competition state 1, 15, 18, 20, 31, 32
corporate social responsibility 89
Cox, Robert 5, 9, 15, 25, 37n.3, 38, 43,
    44, 53, 65n.7, 65n.9, 66n.13,
    91n.1, 91n.2, 122
    critical modes of knowledge 38, 56,
      57, 129, 160–1, 164
    ideal types 9, 128
    on precarious work 137, 152
    problem-solving modes of
      knowledge 5, 15, 21, 32, 39, 137
    on production 121, 123

Daimler Chrysler 96
Denmark 30
Department for International
    Development 20, 23, 26, 73
deregulation 23, 28, 29, 30–1, 72, 73,
    100, 104–6, 159
    see also flexibility; labour market
Deutsche Bank 96, 100
Deutsche Telekom 100

East Asian crisis 125
Economist, The 26, 31
education 80, 126
employee involvement 32, 37n.5, 103, 129, 130, 145
employers' organisations 129–30
employment agencies 149
Ernst and Young 149
European Commission 25, 27, 140, 145
everyday life 7–9, 15, 35, 55, 60–2, 64, 137, 139–40, 158, 162
    social practices of 7–9, 10, 36, 55–6, 60–2, 64, 134
    social space and 35, 60, 61
    theories of 60–2, 162
    see also Lefebvre, Henri
export processing zones 146

finance 17, 75–6, 164
    bank-based 125, 126
    equity 125–6
Finanzplatz Deutschland 100
firms 8, 11, 20, 21, 24, 59, 115–36, 161
    as agents 1, 11, 21, 41, 115, 116–18, 125, 133–4, 140
    the flexible firm 15, 16, 23, 24, 124
    and inter-firm relations 125, 126
    and relationship to governments 34, 116, 122, 125
    supplier and contractor 126, 129
    theories of in IPE 115–16, 118–133, 136n.15
    see also under Strange, Susan
flexibility
    disciplinary effects of 26–9, 36
    discourse of 14, 15, 23–4, 26, 29, 31, 34, 36, 71, 90, 159, 163
    functional 27, 78–80, 135n.3
    of labour markets 1, 5, 10, 20, 23, 26, 28, 29, 30, 34, 36, 74, 103, 165
    numerical 27–8, 135n.3
    pay 28, 83–6
    and policy agendas 20
    as responsiveness to global markets 23, 86–7
    and rigidity 28, 86, 123
    see also under firms
Ford 86

Fordism
    crisis of 16, 24–5
    and Taylorist management 146
foreign direct investment 12n.1, 19, 29
Foucault, Michel 33, 59, 66n.15
    on governmentality 70, 71, 91n.3, 94, 114n.2, 122
    on power-knowledge 33, 59, 122
France 31
Fujitsu 12n.1, 72

G7 see Group of Seven
gender 80, 142, 148, 151
Germany
    banks in 75, 99–100, 125–6
    co-determination 101, 105
    competitiveness of 24, 94, 96
    firms in 31, 95, 100, 105, 108, 125, 126, 132–3, 156n.3
    and flexi-corporatism 9, 11, 97, 113, 137, 148, 164
    functional flexibility in 102–4
    industrial relations in 100–1, 103–14, 156n.7
    industrialisation of 99
    part-time and temporary work in 12n.2, 104–6
    pensions in 129
    sick pay in 108–9
    tax reform in 96
    training in 103, 104
    unemployment in 95, 109, 111
    working time in 104–6, 114n.6
Gesamtmetall 104, 109, 130
Gill, Stephen 2, 3, 6, 19, 38, 44, 53, 54, 65n.4, 65n.7, 65n.10, 93, 120
Gilpin, Robert 40, 41
global restructuring 9, 11, 17, 20, 21, 23, 36
    contestation and disruption of 9, 11, 23, 31, 32, 34, 36, 74, 115, 120, 132–3, 154
    discourse of 24, 36, 138, 139
    historical contingency of 24, 36, 55, 118, 121
    of work 10, 23–5, 28, 70, 121, 137–57
    see also resistance

globalisation 14, 36, 68–71, 94–7
    contestation of 1–2, 11, 23, 36, 60,
        65n.8, 69, 100–1, 120, 133, 164–5
    as the death of conflict 10, 15, 22–3,
        34–5
    as disciplinary imperative 10, 15,
        17–19, 36
    forces of 10, 15, 16, 17, 18, 23, 72,
        115, 155
    harnessing of 26, 28, 34, 36, 73, 90,
        139, 160
    inequalities of 26
    and policy prescription 10, 15, 21,
        23, 32–4
    as practice 6–9
    as process 4–5, 7, 10, 15, 17, 18, 20,
        21, 23, 32, 35, 36, 69, 72, 116,
        159
    as project 5–6, 7, 12n.3, 51, 53, 58,
        60, 63, 69, 159
    of social relations 60–2
    typologies of   3–9
    see also global restructuring;
        production
global–local 54, 55, 58, 155, 159, 161
global political economy 3, 7, 153, 158
GPE *see* global political economy
Gramsci, Antonio 52–5
    and neo-Gramscian IPE 53–4, 55,
        63, 120
    on labour 53–5, 121
    on social structures 52–3, 120
Group of Seven 5

Harrod, Jeffrey 9, 37n.3, 65n.7, 121,
    122, 135n.5, 153
    on production and work 9, 53,
        135n.10, 156n.5
historicity
    E. H. Carr on 57
    R. G. Collingwood on 56, 57
    in IPE 10, 56–8, 63–4, 160–1
    E. P. Thompson on 56, 58, 133
Homenet 144
Honda 128
Hooper, Charlotte 33, 117
household and family 113, 114n.6, 139,
    142, 143, 146, 152–3, 158, 163

human resource management 32–4,
    37n.5, 130, 151
Hyman, Richard 128, 130, 153, 154

IG Metall 103, 104, 105, 109, 111, 114n.8
ILO *see* International Labour
        Organisation
IMF *see* International Monetary Fund
industrial relations 34, 37n.5, 154
    decollectivisation of 23, 145
    deregulation of 89
    studies of 128, 156n.7
    see also under Britain; Germany
industrial society 17, 18, 19, 22
    school of thought 10, 15, 18, 22
industrialisation 14, 19, 21, 165
    in Britain 75
    theories of 15, 17, 21, 35
International Labour Organisation 79,
    81, 143, 145, 153, 156n.4, 156n.6,
    162
International Monetary Fund 5, 12n.1,
    96, 156n.2
international political economy 8, 10,
    20, 36, 38–66
    and global restructuring 36, 116,
        118, 133
    and globalisation 1, 38, 118, 140–4,
        154
    and labour 100–1, 140–1
    new approaches to 7–8, 10, 38–9,
        42–4, 55, 62, 133, 143
    orthodox approaches to 10, 16, 39–
        42, 69, 118, 133, 143, 158
    of social practice 10–11, 55–62, 70,
        113, 121, 134, 138, 152–3, 160, 163
    of work 12, 138, 140, 143, 162–5
    see also Cox, Robert; power;
        Strange, Susan
international relations 22, 39, 143
    and globalisation 45
Ireland 29

Japan, competitiveness of 24
just-in-time 5, 23, 124, 130, 135n.3,
    151, 157n.12
    see also lean production

kaizen 5, 23, 130, 135n.3
kanban 130, 135n.3
Keynesian demand management 22, 24
Klein, Naomi 1, 150, 151

labour
    child 27, 89, 142, 156n.4
    contingent 135n.5, 148, 149, 151,
        163
    costs 32, 79, 86, 107–10, 108, 114n.3
    restructuring of 20, 24–5, 128, 149
    slave 146, 149
    see also trade unions; work; workers
labour market 23, 74, 95, 127, 131–2
    reforms 20, 29, 95, 96, 102, 103, 107,
        144
    see also under flexibility
Latour, Bruno 61, 66n.16, 78
lean production 23, 102, 117, 134,
        135n.3, 135n.4
    and vulnerability to disruption 35
    see also production
Lefebvre, Henri 60, 61
    on everyday life 60
    on institutions 70
    on social space 61
Lexus 95, 114n.4
Liberalism 22, 98
Lufthansa 111

management
    consultancies 32, 33, 37n.5, 149
    perceptions of restructuring 32
    strategies of 10, 32, 103
    see also human resource
        management; total quality
        management
Mannesman 96
maquila 146
Mercedes 95, 114n.4
Modell Deutschland 94–7, 107, 112,
        114n.1
modernisation 14, 18, 165
Motorola 31, 86
multinational corporations *see* firms
Murphy, Craig 7, 40, 42, 53, 65n.7, 121,
        142, 156n.1

national capitalisms 6, 11, 63, 67, 94
    convergence of 10, 15, 20, 30–2, 159
    perspectives on 68–71, 94
    see also capitalism
neo-liberalism 19, 27, 29, 58, 72, 87,
        90, 93, 95, 96, 97, 125, 145
neo-Marxism 18
neo-realism 135n.1
New Zealand 29, 101
Nike 55, 115
Nissan 33

O'Brien, Robert 3, 144, 153, 156n.5
OECD *see* Organisation for Economic
        Cooperation and Development
offshore 24, 76, 100
Ordo-liberalism 97–8, 114n.5
Organisation for Economic
        Cooperation and Development
        5, 23, 26, 30, 31, 34, 71, 73, 74,
        79, 83, 86, 91, 95, 96, 100, 106,
        145, 159
    Jobs Strategy 29, 30, 31, 73, 101,
        104
outsourcing 12n.2, 103, 109, 129, 132,
        135n.3, 137, 142, 150, 152, 155,
        156n.3

Panitch, Leo 147
Parsons, Talcott 17, 19
Pauly, Louis 119, 129
Polanyi, Karl 49–52, 65n.6, 118
    double movement 9, 44, 51–2, 63
    fictitious commodities 50, 97
    market society 50, 69, 75
    social embeddedness of economy
        51–2, 69, 119
Porter, Michael 17, 18, 114n.7, 117
post-Fordism 15, 16, 18
post-industrial society 15, 18
power 10, 14, 19, 20, 21, 23, 35, 59
    and agency 23, 41, 58–60, 64, 116,
        161
    in IPE 20, 36, 45–6, 49, 59, 161
    see also under Foucault, Michel;
        Strange, Susan
Pricewaterhouse-Coopers 149
production 17, 20, 53, 128

costs of 125
globalisation of 9, 16
see also flexibility; labour

quality circles 146, 151

resistance 11, 35, 36, 54, 65n.8, 73,
    100–1, 113, 115, 128, 141, 144,
    157n.13, 163–4
risk 15, 23, 31, 36, 80, 89, 125, 127, 132,
    146, 147, 158, 159, 165
Rolls Royce 96
Rover 96
Rupert, Mark 12n.3, 52, 135n.6

Sally, Razeen 119
Schröder, Gerhard 93, 95, 96, 106
    Neue Mitte 93, 96
self-responsibility 159
service industries 83, 149, 156n.3
shareholders 76, 100, 116, 125, 126
Siemens 72, 114n.3
small and medium size enterprises
    100, 106, 124, 150
SMEs *see* small and medium size
    enterprises
social market economy 98, 160
social movements 35, 153, 164
    new 160
sociology
    and globalisation 156n.5
Soviet Union 19
Standort Deutschland 95, 108, 113
state-market relations 15, 16, 18, 41,
    45–6, 74–5, 97–9, 116, 123, 133
state-societies 17, 36, 117
    convergence among 16, 20
    policy changes in 11, 15, 18
    see also national capitalisms
Stevis, Dimitris 141
Strange, Susan 11, 15, 16, 18, 20, 32,
    41, 43, 68, 114n.7
    and critique of IR 45
    on the firm 11, 15, 46, 62, 117, 139
    on IPE epistemology 20, 38, 42, 45–
    9, 65n.1, 65n.2
    on knowledge 47–8, 59
    on the state 15, 16, 18, 45–6, 69, 72

on structural power 45–6, 65n.3
on technology 16, 47
sub-contracting *see* outsourcing
supply chains 127, 135n.3, 150, 152,
    155
Sweden 30

teamworking 5, 23, 92n.7, 103–4,
    135n.3, 146, 157n.9
technology 16, 19, 22, 24–5, 47, 70,
    138–9
    as externality 15, 17, 24, 159
    and industrial society 16, 19
    information and communications
    technologies 16, 25, 139
Thompson, Edward Palmer 56, 58,
    133, 141, 153, 163
Tooze, Roger 7, 38, 39, 40, 42, 45,
    156n.1
total quality management 23, 32,
    37n.5, 130, 134, 135n.3
Toyotism 103, 118
trade 17
trade unions 34, 86, 128, 156n.7, 160
    bargaining 83–6, 107, 130, 131, 140
    declining membership of 12n.2, 34,
    111
    and deunionisation 12n.2, 34, 87–8,
    145, 151, 160
    and new social movements 35, 153
    new strategies of 104, 111, 131, 151,
    153
    see also Britain; Germany
Trades Union Congress 77, 89
training 127–8
    see also under Germany
transnational class 5–6, 143, 160
transversal struggles 59

unemployment 30, 145, 162
United States of America 19, 29, 101
    flexibilisation of labour in 29
    and hegemonic decline 16, 40

Vodafone Airtouch 96
Volkswagen 105, 114n.8

Womack, J. *et al.* 24, 32, 118

women 80, 152
  Self-Employed Women's
    Association 154
  Women Working Worldwide 154
  workers 83, 104, 106, 114n.6, 138,
    142, 157n.15
work
  everyday practices of 10, 11, 15, 25,
    60–2, 103, 134, 139–40, 146, 154
  feminisation of 83, 138
  homeworking 106, 113, 138, 143–4,
    150, 152, 152, 156n.6
  intensification of 150
  part-time 12n.2, 80–3, 101, 142, 151
  temporary 80–3, 142, 151
  see also flexibility; workers;
    workplace
workers
  contract 28, 131, 138, 142
  core 97, 104, 131, 148, 151–2
  empowerment of 28, 33, 34, 35, 146,
    155
  inequalities between 163
  and insecurity 15, 26, 86, 106, 127,
    132, 145, 155, 158

insider 109, 131, 148–9, 163
intermediary 149–50
invisibility of 113, 137, 138–40,
    141–4
migrant 27, 106, 114n.6, 143
outsider 106, 109, 150, 163
and skills 25, 27, 37n.2, 79, 127–8,
    148
tensions between 9, 11, 118,
    135n.13, 163
unprotected 12, 35, 113, 137, 142–4,
    150, 152, 153, 155, 161
workplace 34–5, 61–2, 122
  fragmentation of 130, 131, 142,
    147, 155
  and world order 9, 25, 37n.3
works councils 108, 129
World Bank 5, 20, 23, 24, 26, 27, 29, 72,
    74, 98, 139–40, 145, 159
World Trade Organisation 6
WTO World Trade Organisation

Young, Brigitte 152

Zwickel, Klaus 111